ATHLETES
WHO
ROCK!

Stories of Sacrifice, Setbacks and Success in
Sports, Music and Life

MOTEZ BISHARA

CRANTHORPE
—— MILLNER ——
PUBLISHERS

A CIP catalogue record for this title is available from the British Library.

ISBN 978-1-80378-029-0 (Hardback)

www.cranthorpemillner.com

First Published (2022)

Cranthorpe Millner Publishers

Contents

Prologue

In the summer before my freshman year of college, I watched Prince perform live on his Lovesexy Tour. The gig at London's Wembley Arena featured the pop star's biggest hits from the 1980's, including *Let's Go Crazy* and *Purple Rain*. What caught my attention, though, was that during instrumental breaks Prince would shoot baskets at a full-sized hoop placed on stage.

Prince, who was generously listed at five-foot two-inches tall, was skilled with the ball. He spun it on one finger, had a nice shooting touch and even threw a behind-the-back no-look pass to one of his dancers. But as a basketball player, his career peaked as a sixth man at Bryant Junior High School in Minneapolis. After that, his hoop dreams were confined to late night pickup games against the likes of Charlie Murphy and sinking undefended jump shots on stage.

There is no mistaking that Prince was one of the most gifted musicians in history, but he had a long way to go before he could hold his own as a professional on the hardwood too.

Months later in the fall of 1988, tucked away in my small Boston University dorm room, I watched an NBA game featuring Wayman Tisdale, who averaged nearly 20 points and 10 rebounds for the Sacramento Kings as a power forward that season. The announcer mentioned that Tisdale, a three-time All-American at Oklahoma, was also a professional bassist who played in jazz bands.

As someone who peaked as a trumpet player in 10th grade band class and a bench player on the varsity basketball team, I was astonished. Here was someone who was actually pulling off the elusive double dream – certainly my double dream – of being a pro in both sports and music.

Tisdale, as those who have listened to any of his eight albums can vouch for, was at least as talented a bassist as he was a basketball player. Before his untimely death from cancer in 2009, he was signed to Motown and climbed to the top of the Billboard Contemporary Jazz Album Chart with his 2001 release *Face to Face*.

Despite his cancer diagnosis, Tisdale was active up until his death, teaming with New York Yankees great and jazz guitarist Bernie Williams on the title track of Williams' album *Moving Forward*. Williams, who is my sixth interview for this book, gracefully picked up the baton from Tisdale in fusing the worlds of jazz and pro sports.

As a lifelong Yankees fan, I was excited to learn that Williams was performing as a classically-trained guitarist while prowling centerfield during the team's dynasty of the late 1990s and early 2000s. Shortly afterward, identifying those with the spirit and persistence to become professionals in both music and sports became a slight obsession of mine.

The road towards unearthing those elusive double-talents, however, was a bumpy one. There was, of course, Shaquille O'Neal releasing four rap albums during the height of his playing days. Shaq gained plaudits from fellow rappers for freestyling and writing his own verses. He went platinum with his debut album *Shaq Diesel* and gold on its follow-up *Shaq Fu: Da Return*, teaming with the likes of Warren G and Method Man. But even O'Neal admits that his success as a rapper had more to do with his fame than his talents, referring to them as "two terrible albums" to

Rolling Stone.

The seven-foot, four-time NBA champion now dedicates himself to spinning records at EDM festivals and releasing tracks as DJ Diesel. Seeing a crowd thumping to his beats is "the only feeling similar to a Game 7 monstrous dunk," he told edm.com. "Those moments bring people together and I am here for (them)."

Since O'Neal's foray into rap, several other NBA stars, including Allen Iverson, the player formerly known as Ron Artest, Chris Webber and even O'Neal's former Lakers teammate, the late Kobe Bryant, have released rap efforts to tepid reviews. So far, only Damian Lillard, aka Dame D.O.L.L.A., has what can legitimately be considered a dual career as an NBA star and hip-hop artist.

Lillard's three albums have garnered critical acclaim, and his flow has been talked up by some of the biggest names in the industry, including Common and regular collaborator Lil Wayne. In my final interview for this book, Lillard explains why he views rap through a different lens than other NBA players.

A groundbreaking precursor to Lillard's biting lyrics was the braggadocios poetry of Muhammad Ali. In 1963, the 21-year-old then known as Cassius Clay released *I Am The Greatest*, a collection of spoken word, comedy skits and a passable cover of the Ben E. King classic *Stand By Me*. Also included is the group singalong *The Gang's All Here* featuring Sam Cooke. Six months later, Clay fulfilled his promise on the album, winning his first heavyweight championship against Sonny Listen before changing his name and announcing his conversion to Islam. Sales took off and the album even earned a Grammy nomination, though for Best Comedy Performance and not his singing.

Muhammad Ali and Sam Cooke (right) recording 'The Gang's All Here' for Ali's 1963 album 'I Am The Greatest!'

Country music also has its share of sports crossovers, namely from the NFL. Former Cincinnati Bengals All-Pro defensive lineman Mike Reid, who is enshrined in the Nashville Songwriters Hall of Fame. Reid won a Grammy and has penned over a dozen No. 1 hits, including Bonnie Raitt's classic *I Can't Make You Love Me*.

Pittsburgh Steelers icon Terry Bradshaw charted with country songs at the height of his playing career and continues to release tracks today, including 2020's jokey *Quarantine Crazy*. The Shreveport, Louisiana-native, who has also featured in 22 movies, summed up his experience as an entertainer to the NFL Network: "If you win Super Bowls you get to do movies and you get to record. Whether you're good at either one, it doesn't matter."

Kyle Turley did not win a Super Bowl during his All-Pro NFL career, which, by Bradshaw's way of thinking, is a testament to his talent as a musician. The former New Orleans Saints offensive lineman moved to Nashville after his playing days and opened arena tours for some of the biggest acts in country music, including Lynyrd Skynyrd and George Jones. Turley, who also founded a record label and the metal band Delta Doom, describes how music helped ease the mental and physical anguish caused by his eight-year NFL career during our eye-opening conversation.

Across the Atlantic, European soccer players have been trying their hands at making music for years, again with mixed results. New Order's *World in Motion* – the band's only No. 1 hit – was created as England's theme song for the 1990 World Cup. The track features a memorable rap from Liverpool star John Barnes and is generally considered the best of the football-meets-pop experiments.

As the post-punk era of New Order and its peers was hitting a peak, Pat Nevin secretly moonlighted as an assistant at BBC Radio while leading Everton to the FA Cup final. Nevin, who also starred at Chelsea and four other clubs in his 20-year career, expands on his love for indie-music and his bustling role as a DJ and champion of the genre in the first interview on these pages.

John McEnroe is another athlete who often comes to mind when discussing the music and sports link. McEnroe is married to the rocker Patty Smyth, and together they formed The Johnny Smyth Band after his tennis retirement (perhaps reluctantly on her part). McEnroe was a competent guitarist who took vocal lessons and played small venues to mixed reviews. He was pelted with tennis balls in Italy, while a New York bar owner admitted that "he couldn't sing to save his life" to the New York Times.

Then, just as he was set to release an album, McEnroe abruptly pulled the plug on his music career. After a gig in Paris, Smyth admonished him for jumping into the crowd while she was singing. "The Lord doesn't let you be one of the greatest tennis players that ever lived and then be Keith Richards. It just doesn't work that way," she fumed.

"I looked in the mirror and knew she was right. My gigging days are over," McEnroe wrote in his book *Serious*. "The world is a safer place."

Since that episode, McEnroe's close friend and tennis rival Yannick Noah has essentially proved Smyth wrong. As a tennis Hall of Famer and Grand Slam singles and doubles winner, Noah is without a doubt one of the best to have played the game, but he is also one of France's most beloved pop stars and successful recording artists over the past 30 years. My fascinating talk with Noah is lined with stories spanning his three-pronged career as an athlete, performer, and triumphant national tennis coach.

In December 2020, the world lost a pioneering athlete-musician to Covid-19 with the passing of Charley Pride, known as the first Black country music star. Before cutting his first record in 1965, he made ends meet by playing baseball in the Negro Leagues, first with the Memphis Red Sox and then the Boise Yankees, the minor league affiliate of the New York Yankees.

It was an arm injury which ultimately derailed Pride's career as a pitcher. He found work in Montana at a smelter plant and played semi-pro ball for the local team whose manager gave him $10 to sing for 15 minutes before each game, doubling his pay. There, he caught the attention of country music singers Red Sovine and Red Foley, who persuaded Pride to take his talents to Nashville.

Meanwhile in Spain, star crooner Julio Iglesias started life as a goalkeeper for Real Madrid's reserve team in the second division of Spanish soccer. His sporting career ended abruptly in 1963, when a car accident wrecked his nervous system and left him unable to walk for nearly two years. While recovering, a nurse gave him a guitar to use as hand therapy, allowing the singer to unlock his musical talents.

Pride and Iglesias exemplify a classic trait of the athlete-musician that I have come to appreciate: the ability to turn a setback — often an injury — into an opportunity.

Olympian snowboarder Pat Burgener, sustained multiple injuries, including a ruptured ACL, early in his career and began making music as a needed release from the sport. Lillard broke his foot at the start of his junior year at Weber State, then developed a high-arching shot by launching 400 baskets a day from a chair.

A broken wrist suffered by teenage skateboarder Ray Barbee veered him away from daredevil vertical ramps and onto the sidewalks of Northern California, where he became an innovator of street skating. Swedish soccer star Kevin Walker picked up a guitar after he went down with a blood infection that derailed his athletic career. Walker got hooked on singing and songwriting, and won Sweden's *Pop Idol* competition just a few years after returning to the pitch.

Former New York Liberty guard Essence Carson tore her ACL early into the 2013 season, then hunkered down in her Harlem home studio to craft her second EP *No Subz*. Carson also personifies the time management balancing act of the athlete-musician.

All of the subjects in this book sacrificed thousands of hours of leisure to hone their skills in their chosen second careers. Carson graduated with degrees in psychology and music as an Academic All-American at Rutgers University and currently splits time as a WNBA veteran, an executive at Motown Records and a hip hop recording artist. "To me, this is how life functions," she explains. "To someone else, it might be too much, you know? But this is why they're them, and this is why I'm me."

A further commonality among those I interviewed is the persistent struggle to gain public acceptance in their second careers — mostly as established athletes looking to be taken seriously as musicians. Chris Jericho, the pro-wrestler-turned-singer for heavy metal band Fozzy, has said that he "had to work twice as hard to get people's respect" because he is in the band. He is not alone.

It's hard to believe that someone like Rony Seikaly, who has been DJing since he was a high schooler in Athens, felt the need to go incognito when he began working the club scene in South Beach. The former Miami Heat star would deny (to the best of his towering ability) that he was once an NBA player. Would Seikaly be subject to the same level of scrutiny if he began life as a schoolteacher, like Sting, or a hotel security guard, like Eddie Vedder?

Of course not.

Pro wrestler-turned-heavy metal singer Chris Jericho says he works twice as hard as other musicians for respect.

But that tide appears to be slowly shifting. Dual careers are suddenly proliferating at the highest levels of sports and music. Thanks to the show *The Masked Singer*, athletes like NBA All-Star Victor Oladipo are flaunting their singing chops in anonymity and holding their own against established acts like Seal and Patti LaBelle.

Justin Tucker of the Baltimore Ravens is not only the most accurate placekicker in NFL history, he is also a trained bass-baritone opera singer who studied music at the University of Texas. NBA veteran JaVale McGee is a skilled record producer whose beats made their way onto Justin Bieber's No. 1 album *Changes* in the same season that he won his third championship.

Lewis Hamilton is not content with just being the greatest F1 driver of all time. The seven-time racing champion spent the past decade making vocal appearances under aliases with the likes of Christina Aguilera before announcing in 2020 that he was set to release songs of his own.

I set out to meet with the 15 individuals profiled in this book for two reasons. First, I wanted to unlock the keys to their extraordinary accomplishments. I had a hunch that the backstories of how these overachievers established themselves in two incredibly competitive worlds would be worthy of sharing.

It turns out that their twin paths to success have far more complexity than I imagined. For every tale of playing the Royal Albert Hall or serving for the match in a Grand Slam final, there is another that involves overcoming one of life's big challenges – be it a catastrophic injury, a broken family, childhood trauma, depression or bigotry.

Second, I wanted to hear them describe the sensations that they've experienced at the tops of their games. How their athletic and musical thrills contrast with one another in their most memorable moments is something I've tried to capture on these pages.

For example, only Williams is able to compare hitting two World Series home runs with playing guitar to a packed house at Radio City Music Hall. The joy of hitting those home runs was fleeting, lasting no more than about a minute, he says, before thinking about his next at-bat or next game. His musical sensations, on the other hand, are "definitely a lot more vast and a lot more complex."

Damian Lillard keeps his cool on the way to a monster scoring performance so as not to "do something extra", unlike when he's coming up with new lyrics that he's excited to share with collaborators. Chelcee Grimes, the hit songwriter and English footballer, says writing a great song is the only thing that compares to the feeling of scoring goals – unless you count falling in love.

England cricketer Mark Butcher depicts every batting attempt as "a mini-death experience" with the potential for "an indescribable kind of shame," but never feels nervous on stage. World Series-winning pitcher Bronson Arroyo describes making eye contact with his band members in the same way he would with his catcher and infielders when setting up a pickoff play.

Finally, the more I examined these individuals, the more apparent it became that their achievements have not been limited to music and sports. They excel at just about everything they set their minds to.

Barbee is not only a world-class skateboarder and jazz guitarist, but also an accomplished photographer. Seikaly is not just a former basketball phenom and global house music DJ, but also an established Miami real estate developer. Daniela Hantuchova is not just a former world No. 5 tennis player and classical pianist, but also an in-demand broadcaster and podcaster. Lyndsay Perry is not just a former pro surfer and blues artist, but also a model, creative director, brand ambassador and techie geek. The list goes on.

NBA great and platinum-selling rapper Shaquille O'Neal has reinvented himself as DJ Diesel.

The interview process for this book took three years, beginning in December 2017 when I met with Pat Nevin in a room overlooking Chelsea FC's Stamford Bridge stadium. By March 2020, the coronavirus pandemic made traveling impossible, and my preferred method of conducting intimate sit-downs (and taking personal profile photos) was cast aside for extended video calls with interviewees. Fortunately, the answers to my questions were not compromised and the results have been just as revealing.

Social unrest also shifted the climate of my meetings over those three years. Although Black Lives Matter began in reaction to the Trayvon Martin trial in 2013, the historic protests that spread from the US to Europe after the killings of Ahmaud Arbery, Breonna Taylor and George Floyd in 2020 dominated news coverage for much of the year.

As such, questions about race and the impact of social justice entered a number of conversations. Discussing the careers of my interviewees without addressing how those events were affecting their work in music and sports did not seem right to me. After all, Noah is still one of only two Black men to win a tennis Grand Slam and remains a figurehead for racial equality in the sport. Lillard marched with protesters in Portland a few months before the NBA players' strike caused by the shooting of Jacob Blake in Wisconsin. Carson has been active in social justice since her days at Rutgers.

By now you may be sensing the breadth of these conversations, each of which is condensed and edited for the sake of clarity. I was speaking with extraordinary people who arrived at the interviews with a complex range of depth and emotion. There is good reason for this: They are all unicorns.

Most casual sports fans are aware that the chances of going pro as an athlete are incredibly low. According to the NCAA, only 32 out of every 10,000 American high school varsity athletes across the top five sports go on to play professionally at any level.[1] To put that into perspective, those odds of 0.32 percent are lower than the 0.41 percent chance that NASA assigned to an asteroid hitting the Earth in 2020.[2]

What is perhaps less understood is that becoming a working professional in the music industry is equally as difficult — and might be getting tougher in the age of digital streaming. Achieving both on merit, either at the same time or successively, should be unfathomable to any reasonable person.

Yet the individuals profiled in this book have collectively achieved incredible success in the sporting and entertainment spheres. They have played sold-out stadiums and arenas, written hit records for themselves and others, been nominated for awards and DJed at the most prestigious nightclubs. They have competed in multiple Olympics, played in numerous championship finals and won titles across the world's biggest sporting competitions.

The hurdles they have crossed to put themselves in those situations are at times hard to believe. Now their stories are ready to be told. This book celebrates achievement, but it is equally a testament to resilience.

---

1. Approximately one-third of one percent of high school varsity athletes in the United States competing in baseball, men's basketball, women's basketball, football and hockey go on to play professionally, according to 2019 NCAA data.
2. According to a NASA tweet dated August 23, 2020.

What Makes an Elite Performer?

Over the past three years, I've been on a mission to probe the minds of 15 humans who possess a special blend of musical and physical talents. During our conversations, several talking points related to peak performance and goal-oriented success in music, sports and many other fields stood out as being worthy of further analysis.

That drove me to study the works of a number of leading researchers in the fields of psychology, neurology, music education and sports science to shed light on brain functionality and personality traits of elite performers.

I have summarized four key findings to serve as a useful backdrop to the ensuing chapters. Although this book is not a work of scientific research, the material provided could be useful in establishing how consistent overachievers separate themselves from the masses.

The Flow State

During the interviews, I would often return to fundamental questions that explored the rarefied air these people occupy: How does it feel to be unstoppable on the basketball court, baseball field or tennis arena? And what is it like to be grooving on stage to a point where you and your audience are traveling together on an unpredictable journey?

When he is DJing in a club, Rony Seikaly refers to the perfect musical storm as "capturing the moment," whereas Yannick Noah describes his singing performance on stage as "transmitting" energy from himself to his fans. Pat Nevin labels the state of effortlessness that he sometimes experienced on the soccer pitch as being "in the zone," describing it as "a 360-degree understanding of everything that is going around you."

"Those moments are not that frequent," Nevin explains. "They require spatial awareness on a level that's almost beyond human. The great players have them all the time."

That spatial awareness that Nevin and many others commonly refer to as 'the zone' has been dissected over the past five decades by Mihaly Csikszentmihalyi, the groundbreaking psychologist credited for identifying the trance-like existence known as 'the flow state'.

Csikszentmihalyi (pronounced cheek-sent-me-hi), a professor at Claremont Graduate University who has written at least eight books on the topic, posits that humans are happiest when they achieve flow in whatever task they are working on.

Tellingly, he uses musicianship as a prime example. In an interview with *Wired*, the psychologist defines flow as "being completely involved in an activity for its own sake. The ego falls away. Time flies. Every action, movement, and thought follows inevitably from the previous one, like playing jazz. Your whole being is involved, and you're using your skills to the utmost."

In his research that involved thousands of participants, Csikszentmihalyi discovered that the flow state is described similarly among athletes, musicians and a range of specialists in other fields.

They experience the same sensations, he says, because the same eight "elements of enjoyment" are required to achieve flow in any activity.

They include: working on a task that has a defined completion, doing so with total concentration, feeling a sense of control over your actions, losing concern over yourself (dropping your ego), but gaining a stronger sense of yourself when the task is completed, and losing track of time – where the sense of duration becomes altered.

The final two conditions of flow – having clear goals and receiving immediate feedback for your effort – is where the road splits between athletes and musicians.

In sports such as tennis, the goal of winning the point is clearly defined, and the result is obvious. But artists must define their own set of goals and establish an "internalized criteria for 'good' or 'bad'," Csikszentmihalyi writes in his book *Flow*, noting that "without such internal guidelines, it is impossible to experience flow."

Finally, flow must be achieved with a level of immersion that suspends awareness of the problems and frustrations of daily life. This is because, as Csikszentmihalyi explains, there is no room for "irrelevant information" when someone is enjoying a task that requires full attention to detail.

That feeling is explained wonderfully by the English footballer Chelcee Grimes, who began writing songs professionally as a teenager. Putting together lyrics and chords that came to life was the only task aside from playing soccer that cleared her head.

"The closest thing I can say is it's like being in love," she tells me. "It's just that feeling inside you that is very content, like all your problems go away for a good few minutes. You know, when I'm focused on a game or on music, I'm enjoying it that much. It makes me forget about my problems.

"And I think that's when I know I'm enjoying something: when it takes me away from reality. And for that minute or two minutes or hour or whatever it is, I know I'm in love with it because I forget about everything else."

Creative Genius: The Benefits of Improvisation

New research has shown that musicians adept at improvisation, namely jazz musicians and freestyle rappers, have developed parts of the brain used for impulsive decision-making.

A 2019 study on brain connectivity by Georgia State University music professor Martin Norgaard and four colleagues examined 24 jazz musicians in an MRI machine. The musicians' brains were monitored as they sang and imagined pre-rehearsed melodies on top of 12-bar blues tracks. They then spontaneously improvised scatted melodies, either vocally or by imagining them, over the same progression.

The results showed that improvisation works parts of the brain associated with language, timing and motor movement sequences. At the same time, it disengages other parts of the brain associated with self-monitoring and planning that can be inhibitors to the flow state.

So a guitarist instinctively rattling off a solo is thinking a lot like an athlete who is reading and reacting on the go, says Norgaard. "Jazz improvisation is like the basketball player running down the court," he explains. "He has to bypass the defender and in real time pick particular moves. He doesn't have time to analyze it, so it's very much based on improvisational movements."

Skilled musical improvisers like Damian Lillard operate like athletes making decisions in real-time.

An equivalent test using freestyle rappers was previously conducted by the neuroscientist Dr. Charles Limb. Limb found that rappers creating lyrics in flow operate just like jazz musicians, activating and deactivating the same parts of the brain.

Both Essence Carson and Damian Lillard grew up learning to freestyle rap. Bernie Williams grew up learning to improvise on guitar. It is certainly possible that the improvisational skills they learned as young musicians have served them well playing in three of the world's most competitive sports leagues.

"When you're talking about battle rap, that's a sport," says Carson, who attended performing arts high school in Patterson, New Jersey, where she played multiple instruments and dueled with fellow rappers during lunch breaks.

When improvising, the athlete or musician is likely working in the flow state. That is because the brain has been able to silence the "little voice that tells you what to do" which sits in the dorsal prefrontal cortex, says Norgaard. "That is what we hypothesize. Because when you're in flow, you're just doing it. You're not evaluating at the same time."

That situation of being lost in improvisation is dependent on two factors: First, the improvisers must be at an advanced level, so that they are not encumbered by the learning process as they play. Second, the output must be created in real time, where revision is impossible and mistakes must be adapted to.

That eliminates the craft of songwriting, or perhaps working on a reverse layup move, which Norgaard classifies as "inventing" and does not stimulate the brain in the same way (though they may still be operating in flow).

In a previous study involving eighth grade music students, Norgaard also found that learning improvisation at a young age is associated with higher "cognitive flexibility," or the ability for the brain to adapt to new circumstances in real time.

Does this mean that learning musical improvisation as a teenager could be helpful to athletes? "It certainly seems logical that that is the case," says Norgaard, but he stresses that any extrapolation of that study is difficult to prove.

Williams certainly thinks so. The Yankee great says that both musicians and baseball players require "spatial awareness and the elasticity of mind to make adjustments – sometimes on the run, sometimes from at-bat to at-bat." His description of a batter making adjustments sounds a lot like Norgaard's explanation of cognitive flexibility.

"If you strike out on a blown inside pitch, then at the next at bat, you know for sure that (the pitcher is) going to try to throw it to you again," Williams explains. "Making the adjustment shows that you have this elastic mind, like a high performance computer that can refresh itself."

Given that Norgaard and Limb have both surmised that improvisation opens the language receptors in the brain, it is telling that Carson refers to language when comparing her flow experience in music and basketball.

"Being in a zone musically … It almost becomes your language. It becomes how you communicate with the world, with the listener," she explains. "It just feels like you're able to seamlessly communicate with the audience, and you don't have to speak one word. They don't have to question what you're playing or question what you've said in your lyrics. They just get it."

And how does that sensation translate on the hardwood?

"It's just like basketball when everything's clicking on the court," Carson adds. "It's like sweet music."

Mindfulness

Being mindful has become a catch-all phrase in meditation practice for being present in the moment. When meditating, this means avoiding thoughts about what's for dinner or paying the phone bill and focusing on the here and now instead.

In psychology, mindfulness takes on another dimension of "being intentionally in the present moment and accepting what's arising," says Amy Baltzell, a sports psychologist to pro athletes and musicians who served as an alternate on the United States 1992 Olympic rowing team.

"Mindfulness is the critical first step of being able to wisely choose how you want to be in the world, and this is essential for athletes and musicians," she says, adding that the practice is "super helpful" to those looking to improve their working processes. "They want to learn how to concentrate better, or deal with adversity better, or have more poise when a challenge is arising – then mindfulness is very helpful."

She gives an example of an elite runner who never lost a race in college having to accept failure on a professional level. "Suddenly that runner is bombarded by self-criticism," she says, stressing that the key is to focus on the positive. "It's just way harder to pay attention to the right thing when you're not feeling good."

Baltzell tells another story of a classical musician client who froze when auditioning for a seat in an orchestra. That fear of judgement caused her concentration to fall from 90 percent to 10 percent. "The more uncertainty, the more pressure, the more likely the mind is to be distracted by regret of mistakes and get lost in the past and the future," she says.

The pressure faced by musicians and athletes when the stakes are high can also lead to anxiety – another inhibitor to peak performance that can be contained by mindfulness, she says.

After a rash of injuries caused him to miss out on the 2014 Winter Olympics, Swiss halfpipe snowboarder Pat Burgener was overcome with negativity and thought about leaving the sport. Instead, he worked with a mental strength coach and focused on being mindful, learning to stay in the moment before launching into backflips 40 feet above solid ice.

"You get all kinds of thoughts, but then those thoughts are not part of you," he explains. "It's about turning off your thoughts – or if you have them, try and (frame) them in a positive way, not just turn them off – and then your life will change."

One method of practicing mindfulness is through visualization, or picturing critical moments before they arise in competition or on stage. Bernie Williams says he had "a whole movie" going on in his head before each baseball game, envisioning himself playing well in pivotal situations. He now uses the method to prepare for his jazz performances. Yannick Noah worked hard on his visualization process in the run up to his French Open win.

But not everyone I spoke to found the practice necessary. Despite pitching in several World Series and playoff games, Bronson Arroyo said he never felt the need to practice mindful meditation, nor did Rony Seikaly, who played in an NCAA championship game for Syracuse University (though he admits that he would struggle to face that pressure with millions watching now).

Damian Lillard says he thinks about situations that could arise in big games, "but I don't visualize it like, 'OK, tonight, you're going to score 50 points, and it's going to come true.' I'm not doing that kind of stuff."

That's OK, Baltzell says. "It's only essential if nothing else works. So if your things are working … and you're in your flow and you're loving it, you don't need to be mindful and aware of things that are unpleasant."

It should be noted that openly seeking out mindfulness is a relatively new concept in sports. The cricketer Mark Butcher, who retired in 2009, admits that his ego got in the way of getting counseling to improve mental performance during his playing days. He says the act would have been akin to "admitting to weaknesses," which could have been used against him by opponents or even teammates looking to take his spot.

The sporting world has evolved. In 2020, French Open winner Iga Swiatek thanked her mental health coach Daria Abramowicz after her finals victory. The 19-year-old did not lose a set in the tournament despite being ranked No. 54 going in.

Grit and Match Quality

All of these athlete-musicians have displayed two strong attributes in the build-up to their careers. One is the unshakable drive to pursue goals, and the other is the willingness to take on a variety of interests.

The first trait can be explained by the concept of 'grit', a measurement of "passion and perseverance for long-term goals" developed by the psychologist Angela Duckworth. Duckworth spent years demonstrating that a person's talent — which she defines as the rate of improvement in skill — is less important than a person's determination to get the job done.

She developed the Grit Scale questionnaire and used it as a predictor of success among everyone from Green Beret candidates to people selling vacation time shares. Components of grit include the ability to avoid distraction and brush aside failure and rejection — something nearly every successful athlete, musician or artist has learned to do.

It's no surprise, then, that several cases of overcoming rejection can be drawn from this book: Chelcee Grimes was dropped by her record label at 19 before becoming a megawatt songwriter. Pat Nevin was rejected by his boyhood team before turning into a Scottish national hero. Damian Lillard didn't play a minute of basketball as a high school sophomore before realizing his NBA dreams.

Two further indicators of grit are maintaining a desire to improve and feeling gratified by working towards a goal — not just by achieving the goal itself.

Those descriptors are ones that skateboarder, guitarist and photographer Ray Barbee emphasizes during our interview. He repeats Kobe Bryant's mantra of "loving the process" and looks back on his own approach towards chasing three pursuits with steep learning curves. "It's seeing that growth that is infectious," he says. "It just fuels itself."

Being gritty is certainly helpful for someone who knows exactly what they want to do early in life. But it is also possible that being too gritty can lead to missed opportunities in other pursuits that may provide a better fit — a concept known as match quality.

In his book *Range*, journalist David Epstein argues that Duckworth's Grit Scale is incomplete.[1] Sometimes, he says, it pays to be uncertain and drop one pursuit for another, even well into

---

1. After the publication of *Grit*, Duckworth researched other aspects of character, including curiosity. On the website of her NGO Character lab, she notes that "In general, people who are more curious are happier and better liked."

adulthood — decisions that her measuring system penalizes.

"Switchers are winners," he writes, pointing out that Vincent van Gogh bounced around odd jobs for a decade before enrolling in arts school at age 27. Van Gogh's career path, which included a failed attempt at becoming a pastor, would place him in the 40th percentile on Duckworth's grit test today, says Epstein, who had one of the artist's biographers complete the questionnaire.

Epstein warns that "persistence for the sake of persistence," can get in the way of finding a "high match quality." Put simply, it can be easy to miss out on your calling in life with blinders on.

Both Duckworth and Epstein's findings relate to the stories of the athlete-musicians who you will come to know in the following chapters. Although neither concept applies wholly to their journeys, nearly all of the interviewees have displayed a combination of grit and range to find multiple high match qualities in their lives.

Case in point: Bernie Williams. As a teenager attending performing arts school in Puerto Rico, Williams immersed himself in music theory and guitar. Outside of school, he was a stellar baseball and track athlete.

On his 17th birthday, he signed for the New York Yankees and months later began life in the minor leagues. Williams had the grit to stick it out in the minors for five years before he was called up to play for the Yankees. In the interim, he suspended his pursuit to play guitar professionally. Remarkably, he also dropped out of medical school, where he qualified and attended for three semesters during baseball off seasons.

After his historic 16-year career with the Yankees ended, Williams enrolled in the Manhattan School of Music and graduated at age 47 with a Bachelor of Music in jazz guitar. At this stage of his life, Williams is not planning to re-enter medical school, but I wouldn't bet against him if he did. Williams found two, and possibly three, high match qualities in life, but he never would have hit the mark on his legendary baseball career without taking a singular approach before his 20th birthday.

Pat Nevin

London, December 2017

One of the most outrageous clauses in the history of sports deals was written into Pat Nevin's second contract with Chelsea FC, and it explains everything about the man.

The club's two-time player of the year was set to sign an offer to keep him in west London, but there was one problem. A pending preseason match clashed with his plans to watch the seminal indie-pop trio Cocteau Twins perform at the Royal Festival Hall.

So the Scotsman had an idea. Holding the upper hand, he insisted on a stipulation that would allow him to leave at halftime to watch the show.

"I obviously couldn't go see the gig if I played for Chelsea," Nevin recalls, only slightly more aware of the absurdity of it all. "You could see the exasperation on their faces, as if I were going to ask for an extra £200 a week or whatever. The manager was furious."

"I walked off at halftime and I thought that was perfectly reasonable. I just put my clothes on above my kit. I didn't have a shower because I was late. I zoomed in at the start of the gig and never missed a moment."

Throughout Nevin's life, music has always taken precedence over soccer. When he was signed by Scottish football giants Celtic as a schoolboy, he saw no reason to tell his classmates, preferring to obsess over the vinyl records his brothers left around the house.

"I (was) more interested in people who liked music, absolutely," he says. One passion, it turned out, ignited a career in the other.

At age 16, Celtic dropped Nevin for being undersized, so he turned to a local boys' club instead. That's where a teammate bet him on who could score the more dramatic goal – with the loser buying the winner the album of his choice. Pat scored with flair and collected.

"I'll be honest, it was a Genesis double album," Nevin admits sheepishly. "It was just at that crossover period between punk and prog, so that's what he had to buy me." He also won a contract from the manager of the opposing team that day, Scottish League club Clyde. Despite that, Nevin continued to separate his sporting life from his personal life.

Although he went on to star for Scotland's under-18s, scoring a goal in the 1982 European Championships final and being named player of the tournament, he didn't tell his girlfriend he was going to Finland for the event. She simply thought he needed time apart to study for his exams (which was also true, as Nevin took his books with him).

Coming home a hero, Nevin's photo was plastered all over Scotland's newspapers – and his girlfriend was owed an explanation. "We won the final, and I came back to take the exams," he says. "I took her out the next night, so I made up for it."

Why would a teenager hide his growing football stardom from his own girlfriend? It turned out Pat had his reasons.

"I've worked in this industry a long time, (both) on the outside and within it, and I do see that once a lot of people retire, they're divorced within a year or two," he explains. "They married a footballer; they didn't marry a person. I wanted to have someone who liked me because of the person I was. And football was what I did, not who I was."

It was a remarkably mature way for a teenager to think. But that was Nevin: always the intellectual, and never one to be pigeonholed. His take on relationships has served him well as a family man to wife Annabel, son Simon and daughter Lucy – a former Scottish badminton champion who is now a medical doctor.

'Suddenly the world opens up'

1970's Glasgow had a bustling music scene and Nevin was in the thick of it. He grew his hair out to look like one of his friends, Jim Kerr, the lead singer of local punk band Johnny and the Self-Abusers (known famously now as Simple Minds).

"This all happened really quickly," Nevin says of the cultural transformation of his Glasgow youth. "You could be listening to Thin Lizzy in '76, The (Sex) Pistols in '77, Joy Division in '78, and suddenly the world opens up to many young people, as it did to me."

Over the years, Nevin saw thousands of concerts, some of them now considered classics – though he narrowly missed out on perhaps the biggest one. He had tickets in hand to see Bob Marley at the Glasgow Apollo when the reggae star canceled due to illness and sadly never recovered.

Usually, Nevin dashed in and out of concert venues without incident, but once in a while he would be reminded that the worlds of football – followed mostly by the working class in those days – and music did not always mesh.

The first time he saw The Clash perform was in Brixton, still a rough part of south London in 1984. An opposing fan recognized the Chelsea star and lunged at him with a knife.

"I caught him with one (punch) and sprinted out, dragging the girl I was with behind me," he recalls. "The gig was good; it was right at the end, thankfully, so I didn't miss much."

There was some benefit to the lack of mixing between musos and footballers. It allowed Nevin to keep his apprenticeship with legendary BBC DJ John Peel quiet from his Chelsea team-mates, and his fame on the pitch away from BBC staffers. "Nobody knew (that I was a footballer). Why should they?" he asks. "I was doing it for the love of it."

A similar level of anonymity for Nevin the DJ exists today, with many of the revelers at his *Scared to Dance* indie nights in London's East End born well after he scored the FA Cup semifinal winner for Everton in 1989, one of the highlights of his storied career.

'There's got to be some beauty there'

In his heyday, Nevin took creativity on the pitch to another level. Much like DJing his current set lists, it was entertaining that gave him joy on the field — culminating in one special move in every match that was a nod to his father in the stands.

"Pretty early on in my Chelsea career against Newcastle, I remember Kevin Keegan tried to tackle me. He was European Player of the Year; I beat him twice and he landed on his backside," he recalls. "And I dribbled the entire length of the pitch, probably took on seven or eight players. It didn't end up in a goal, but in a way it didn't matter.

"If I walked off a game and it was dull and it was brutal, I had no happiness in that game, none at all," he adds. "Even if I scored the goal that won the game, forget that. There's got to be some beauty in there, there's got to be some artistry in there, there's got to be creativity."

It all makes sense; creativity, after all, is what spurred Nevin's second career as a DJ, along with his third career as an off-the-grid football analyst and columnist.

"Sportsmen sometimes forget that. That's why you're doing it. It's entertainment — it really is. It doesn't matter if you're doing it in front of 50,000 or 20 people. It's the joy of creation."

What was it like growing in Glasgow in the '60s and '70s?

It was a very rough city. I lived in a place called Easterhouse, which was known as the roughest area in Western Europe. It's basically what would now be considered the slums. I was very fortunate, as one of six kids. Our parents wanted all of us to be educated. All six of us went on to get university degrees, which was very unusual. I also learned how to fight a little bit. Coming out of a hard area, the ability to fight made you stronger as a person, but a little bit deeper as a person too. You knew what was important.

Did that come in handy on the pitch?

No, because intellectually I wouldn't let that happen. Maybe back in those days you would hear the odd player who was racist, and I would tell them exactly what I thought. And he might not like that. Tough luck. What's he going to do, punch me? I doubt it. When I went to Chelsea I was quite into the arts and theatre, which was unusual for soccer players. So I would get abuse. But I came from the east end of Glasgow, so I could give it back as good as I could get it.

Nevin celebrates with Chelsea teammates in the stands of Stamford Bridge after winning promotion to England's First Division in 1984. He secretly worked as a BBC radio assistant at the time.

How did you get started in football?

My dad coached football, so he just started taking me out every day from the age of about 4. Day after day, month after month, year after year, he showed me how to use the ball. He went down to see Celtic train with one of the greatest coaches in history at the time, Jock Stein.[1] He was miles ahead, so my dad came back and we would use their techniques. He left the house at 5 a.m. and got back at 5 p.m., sometimes later, from his job at British Rail. I had to be standing there with my boots on to go out and do these dribbling and shooting skills. It's extraordinary to think that he was doing that and working 12-hour days. He was a great guy. Losing him a couple of years ago (was tough).

I'm sorry. And he kept his job the whole way through your career?

Absolutely. Well, why wouldn't he? We didn't earn enough … different times. Out of the 850 games I played, my dad missed 30 or 40 of them. Good going, considering it's an 800-mile round trip by train, and there's away games that are even (further). He just couldn't miss it. He'd go to every game. And of course he worked in the railway, so he got free tickets. But the time, the effort, the trouble getting here… stunning.

---

1. Stein won 10 Scottish League titles and one European Cup in his 16 seasons at Celtic.

That bond must have translated onto the pitch. How did you show your appreciation to him?

Very early in my career with Chelsea, I had an agreement with my dad: During the game there would always be a moment where I would do a mad creative dribble, just for the pure joy of it. Every game would have one. There was not even any attempt to make or score a goal. That was me saying, 'Hi Dad!' because he taught me that. Very early I learned why I loved (football): creativity, pure creativity.

In a way music gave you your first big break in football, didn't it?

I played in boys' clubs with good friends, a couple who were big musos as well. One day my friend and I had a bet that whoever scores the best goal and beats the most players has to buy the other person an album. And in that exact moment my entire life changed because I beat about five players and scored a goal. I won the bet and got the album.

As I'm walking off, the manager of the other team says, 'Come here.' I didn't know I was playing against a professional team. I basically trashed their first team. So he said to me, 'Do you want to play for Clyde?'

And I said, 'Well, I'm studying, mate. Maybe not.' And he said, 'But we'll pay you, and you only need to do two nights a week and a Saturday.' And I said, 'You pay me? Where do I sign?' I was a student, you know, so I kept on being a student and was a pro.

And how old were you?

I was 17. So, within 18 months, I'd signed up for Clyde, and less than 12 months later Chelsea tried to buy me and I said no. I wanted to finish my degree, which they found quite strange. I was also very happy in Glasgow.

What were you studying?

I was doing economics and accounting, business studies kind of things, very dull. I wanted a job. I come from that background where you kind of need to have a job. It was sensible to do that at the time.

After a 20-year career in which you played about 850 games, what memories stand out the most for you?

Twenty years! Who does that now? The highlights were actually moments. Sometimes they were goals, but more often they were creations. When you create something, and maybe nobody else on the ground has seen it, maybe only I did.

Again, it's kind of like music … you go to hundreds of gigs, but there will be a moment when you close your eyes and think, 'Remember when?' It may be a guitar solo or a vocal, and the moment was just there. Now, it might not be the best moment or the best song they ever played, but it's a moment where everything fitted. And the football field is like that.

There are moments when you play certain games and there is no effort – none at all. You can call it a zone, which is dumb as dishwater, but it is a 360-degree understanding of everything that is going around you. The best example came many years later in the film *Inception*. Those moments when everything comes at you in slow motion and you can move them away? That's what it feels like.

Nevin evades Liverpool's John Barnes in the 1989 FA Cup Final.

So the ball is coming in here, there's a guy running there trying to clump you, a guy running over there trying to thump you, and there is somebody over there who just made a run behind another defender. And you see him without trying. You know before that ball is going to come to you that you're going to chest it, turn the ball away and head it back over to that person making the run – and you know it's going to get there. Those moments are not that frequent. They require spatial awareness on a level that's almost beyond human. The great players have them all the time.

How did you handle the low moments of your career?

I had a career high and a low point that worked together. I scored the winning goal of the FA Cup semifinal for Everton against Norwich City. This is one of the biggest games in world football to reach. It's historic, it's like getting to the Super Bowl. Everton had spent £1 million on me (about $1.6 million at the time), which was a lot of money in those days. We hammered Norwich that day. It was only 1-0, but we played brilliantly and I floated off the field.

And as I walked off, the BBC reporter was ready to interview me. But just before it he said, 'Pat, I just wanted to tell you that in the other semifinal (Liverpool vs. Nottingham Forest), there are a lot of people who died in a crush at Hillsborough.'[2]

---

2. Ninety-six fans died from overcrowding at Hillsborough Stadium in Sheffield in April 1989, in what remains the worst sporting disaster in British history.

I've never had a gear shift from fifth to first, and everything just goes (flat). He started talking and I said, 'You know, I don't want to do this anymore.' And he said, 'Neither do I,' and we stopped. It was live, and we handed back. And that's the level of how it should have been dealt with on the day. Forget football, sod football. So the highs and lows ... there it was, within a minute. Same day, same moment, same everything.

The game was far more brutal when you played. As a five-foot six-inch winger, how did you cope with it?

Yeah, when you look back at it now, it was vicious. To be honest, I didn't complain about that. My mind is slightly different from most people's. When (the rules) started to change late in my career I was really unhappy about it. Because the first thing a lot of my opponents wanted to do was run towards me and hammer me. The great thing about it is if a guy tries to come and hammer you at full speed, you dummy him one way, go past him, and he goes flying by. They realized much later that if they slowed down and tried to jockey you to the side slowly, it's actually better. It made it harder for me (after rules changed), so I had to readapt. You adapt throughout.

Did that make the decision to retire that much easier?

The kicking is not a thing, I never had a pain problem. I've now got two metal hips because of all the injuries, yeah (true), but I've been out this morning for an hour and a half run. It's not affected me at all.

There was an incident right at the end that I remember really well. At that point I was playing in Scotland, still at the top level. And I'm also chief executive of the club – Motherwell – so that's a tough one to pull off. You have to be one of the guys, but you're also chief exec. We were training one day and I heard two of the guys sniping at me saying, 'Oh he only gets a game 'cause he's chief exec.' Now, the reason they were trying to get at me is because they weren't playing. Anyway, 100 strides later in the warmup I went (*grimaces with a fake injury*), 'Ah, I've done my hamstring.' I hadn't. I walked off and I never went back. Purely because if you can't exist within the group then you shouldn't be on the field.

At what point did you think you could pull off DJing as a second act to your football career?

I've been DJing for years. The first time I ever DJed I was probably 16 in Scotland with a couple of friends. We had decks and we were trying to get stuff we could dance to like disco, or school dances or whatever. And it didn't go very far, but we learned how to do it. I started doing it late in my career for little indie clubs around the country. Now, nobody knew (that I was a footballer). Why should they? I was doing it for the love of it. And it was all going quite well. And then I made a mistake. I didn't realize how big a turnout there would be at this festival I played at in 2010.

Your secret life as a DJ was finally revealed to the public!

Yes, the festival was called Bowlie 2 in a place called Minehead (a small town on the west coast of England). They were all bands that I loved, so it was going to be a great night. Belle and Sebastian, Camera Obscura, Edwyn Collins, Julian Cope and Franz Ferdinand were all playing, and then there's me DJing on the last night. And all the bands came and danced during my session; it was a magical, fabulous, brilliant night.

I played for three and a half hours. By the end of the night, with lights up I thought, 'I'm going to start playing rotten records that you couldn't dance to just to get rid of you,' but I couldn't do it! They kept on dancing, and everyone was howling and laughing, and I'm yelling, 'I'm trying to get rid of you!'

I was up till three or four in the morning. And, of course, the next day I had to get up and travel 250 miles to cover the Manchester United vs. Arsenal match on the radio. What I hadn't realized is Twitter had hit in the meantime. So all these people tweeted what a great night it had been, and suddenly the secret was out.

Afterwards, I thought, 'I won't have a better session than that.' In actual fact, I was very close to never DJing again. I just thought, 'Why keep on doing it to try and find that moment again? It's not going to come back.'

Can you come close to recreating the thrill you had on the football pitch when you're DJing to thousands of people?

No, not quite. Nothing gets close. It's a shame because, you know, (as a DJ) it's not all you. Recently at an event a girl asked for a song, and she said, 'Look at that, you've got them all going mad on stage and dancing. You've done that.' And I'm going, 'No it was the bands that did it. I'm just playing their music.'

It's a bit of both.

Well, yes and no, but it's mostly the musicians. So I'm never stealing the musicians' possessions because it is their creative position. But it's an interesting question you ask because you're right. Forever the fact that I wanted a life away from football; that adrenaline rush is totally addictive — even for me, who refused to be (stereotyped). I played football for 20 years and I was known for it, but that's not who I was. There are more important things than being a footballer, like being a father. Still, that adrenaline kick is a hard one to ignore.

But you must get adrenaline from DJing too?

Yeah, you say that, but then my other current job is broadcasting. I'll sometimes be broadcasting to two or three million people, and there actually is no kick in that at all. None, not a thing. It's just fun. Not a buzz.

Which came more naturally to you? Entertaining football spectators or revelers on the dance-floor?

They're both great. If I were a musician playing gigs, then maybe I would think differently. In fact the joy of creation (in music) — that's not the DJ really, that's the musicians. The other side of it is, even if a musician had some great songs and toured, (he or she would end up playing) the same songs every night for a year, and then the next year the same. But in football, it's never the same. It's always totally different, new and creative — every single game. I recently saw a fabulous play, and then I thought, 'If I go back tomorrow night it will be more or less the same. And the next day.' That doesn't happen in sports, and that's where the advantage is.

Did you have one passion greater than the other?

Music was over football, always. Oh yeah, that didn't take a breath or a beat to say that, because it was my joy, my passion, my love. My friends were musicians. If I had any downtime, I was buying music or buying the music papers and reading about it. Or listening to the next band or listening to (ground-breaking DJs) John Peel or Kid Jensen's show. Taping the shows, going out to find the next gig … it was a passion.

It's easier now for people; you just go online. But back then it was a fight to find your music. And if someone was coming over, let's say Suicide was coming over from the States to play in London, you'd (have) to be there. They might not get to Glasgow!

Can you score an own goal DJing?

Yeah! I never saw it coming as well. It was the latest gig I did. It was in Shoreditch (east London). It was kind of easy, I knew where I was going, the Pixies were on then and (I played) another easy record by The Pains of Being Pure at Heart. It's a real good song, real danceable. And I thought, 'This is a piece of cake.' Then I put on this New Order track which you don't often hear. Lots of New Order songs are very danceable, but this one – *Ceremony* – it's my favorite. The crowd went dead. And I thought that was their best song! That was their best ever single! So yes, you can absolutely blow it.

What bridges the two worlds for you, football and music?

Entertaining is one (aspect) of it, but it's not the biggest thing. It's the creativity. Creativity beats entertainment any day. If I do something spectacularly special – a goal or creating a chance for someone else – whether there are three people watching it, or three million people watching it on TV, it doesn't matter. It's exactly the same feeling. It's creation. It's bringing something from nothing. And delivering it and thinking, 'Oh you like that?' You may call it entertainment, but it's more than that. It's not even a self-gratification thing, it's almost a giving thing.

People ask me, 'Don't you want to be dead famous?' And I say, 'No, fame is horrifying,' so it's not very clever of me to then find myself doing TV and radio. But I hate the idea of fame. I cannot stand celebrity. And anytime someone treats me that way I'm mildly offended. Like, 'You think I want a limousine to pick me up? I'll get the tube.'

[ED: Nevin and I exit the hotel at Stamford Bridge. I ask him to pose for some photos by Chelsea FC's historic Shed End, and we end up taking the District Line on the London Tube together.]

Pat Burgener

Manhattan Beach, California, August 2018

Before he set off on the most important snowboarding run of his life, Pat Burgener playfully strummed an air guitar to the sounds blaring from his headphones.

The Swiss 24-year-old then nailed a near-perfect halfpipe routine, full of flips, twists and turns that briefly placed him in bronze medal contention at the 2018 PyeongChang Olympics.

Burgener, who is also a singer-songwriter, credited music by Australian artist Kim Churchill for allowing him to focus during the competition.

"It was so intense; his album kind of saved my Olympics," Burgener tells me of Churchill's release *Weight Falls*. "I was so into the music that at some point I was not even thinking about what I was doing anymore. I was just feeling it, you know?"

Using melodic sounds to clear his headspace is how Burgener enters the flow state — commonly known as 'the zone' — a mixture of intense concentration and surrender to muscle memory that nearly all competitors and creative minds aspire to.

"At the Olympics I was not in the zone until I got to the first round and stomped it," he says, using snowboarding jargon for landing an entire run cleanly.

"That's the whole fight, it's about being in the zone all the time. It's not easy, and that's what I have been fighting for since I started competing in snowboarding — just trying to find the zone and trying to be in the zone even before I wake up."

Staying focused throughout the day of the Olympic finals would prove tricky. On the second of his three runs, Burgener stumbled on his bugaboo, the 'double Chuck', a double backflip meant to end his routine with a flourish.

Pat had just one more shot to stay in contention.

His brother and business manager Marc-Antoine waited nervously at the bottom of the pipe. "Dude, I can't…" he said among the crowd. "I'm going to faint."

After stomping his final run in PyeongChang — a mesmerizing performance complete with a perfectly planted double Chuck — Burgener threw off his helmet in jubilation and kissed the TV camera.

Marc-Antoine cried. "It's the craziest and most intense thing I have ever seen," he said, shaking his head in disbelief and finally cracking a smile. "There are no words to describe this."

Though Pat would finish fifth, his performance was worthy of celebration. The Burgener family had been through an emotional rollercoaster that began way before the Olympics.

"Four years ago I was not even riding halfpipe anymore," Burgener says. "No one would have thought that this year at the Olympics I'd get fifth place. I was far from that."

'Expectation is what kills you'

Burgener's mental process that brought him within arm's reach of Olympic glory was honed over years of injuries and setbacks.

At 14, he made the Swiss national team and was considered a snowboarding prodigy. At 16, he landed the world's first switch backside triple cork 1440 in big air, the extreme competition where snowboarders launch off a giant ramp.

By that point, however, Burgener was already racking up a niggling injury each season. At 18, he damaged his ankle and collarbone, and required ACL surgery on his knee which nearly forced him out of the sport.

"When you have an injury, you get too into thinking, 'What's going to happen? I have to get back,'" he explains. "(It was) maybe too much pressure, too much expectation. Expectation is what kills you in sports."

The teenager failed to qualify for the 2014 Sochi Olympics, the event set to be his coming-out party. Instead, it was his low point.

"I was like, 'This is too much, I don't want to do this anymore,'" he reflects. "I was just in a bad mood and I couldn't get out of it. And sometimes you need something really strong in your life to just tell you to stop."

"That's when the music came," he says, crediting the practice for saving his snowboarding career. "Music was just a (way to) step away."

A native of the Swiss resort town Crans-Montana, Burgener played various instruments as a kid. While nursing his injuries, he picked up the guitar again and began writing songs, forming a band with his younger brother Max on lead guitar.

The snowboarder developed into a performer who has gigged in front of thousands at some of Switzerland's biggest music festivals. He even signed a deal with Universal Music, where he released the 2018 EP *The Route* and 2019 EP *Icar* featuring acoustic hit *Staring at the Sun* (2.5 million Spotify streams). His third effort *Better Man*, independently released in 2020, solidified his position as a prolific, evolving musician willing to take risks.

As a songwriter, Burgener became much more aware of his senses, making note of every heightened emotion as potential material for the studio. The same process would later provide an unexpected calming influence before a run.

"That's what I didn't have when I wasn't a musician," he says. "That's why I say today, I wouldn't be playing music without snowboarding and I wouldn't be snowboarding without playing music."

The process of recording music and the frustrations he faced in the studio — sometimes taking days to perfect a song — also lent perspective to his job as a pro athlete.

"It is crazy how much work it takes to get a song done," he says. "The cool thing is, the more you struggle, the more you are going to love it afterwards. Because when you get it, oh my God, it's awesome."

Burgener soon realized that being in the zone in a music studio — where he has a hand in production, along with playing guitar, keyboards and drums — shares a quality to being up in the air on a snowboard.

"Music is the same," he says. "I've written songs in 10 minutes, and that's when you're in the zone, because you just start and everything flows. The lyrics come, the melody comes, and you just feel it."

The real challenge, however, is to operate even when things go astray. After multiple setbacks in snowboarding, no one understands this better than Burgener.

"When you're in the zone everything is easy," he notes. "When you're not, that's when you really learn how to be better."

'It's about never freaking out'

As his music career took hold, Burgener — who had previously competed in big air and slopestyle events — turned his focus back to his first riding passion: the halfpipe. The competition, where snowboarders push their limitations by performing multiple flips off a 22-foot high super-pipe, is known as one of the most exhilarating sports in the world.

He marked his comeback in 2016, winning the FIS World Cup event at Copper Mountain, Colorado as he nailed the first-ever switch backside double cork in halfpipe competition.

"It was a trick that I needed to get that taught me so much about my mental (state)," he says.

One lesson was to avoid thinking about a challenging trick until the final day of competition. "You get your head tired," he says. "Sports is a mental game; it's about never freaking out and staying calm all the time."

That is especially true in halfpipe snowboarding, where the risks of losing control can be lethal.

"It's icy and it's big and it's got a sharp edge — so if you touch the edge you're fucked," he says. "I think I control it pretty well, but anything can happen."

Hours after his successful showing at the 2018 Olympics, Burgener celebrated at a Korean nightclub, downing his first few beers in four months before being summoned to appear live on French TV.

Then he went straight back to work. After wrapping up production on his second EP in California, Burgener trained rigorously for the next snowboarding season.

He took bronze in the World Championships in Salt Lake City in February 2019 — showing steady improvement on the world's biggest stages. Ultimately, Burgener is aiming for another

Olympic moment, with an eye towards the Beijing 2022 games.

"A lot of people ask me, 'Isn't it too much?'" he says. "And I'm like, 'Too much of what?' I'm not doing anything. To me, I'm just living."

What was it like growing up in Switzerland?

Switzerland is a beautiful country to grow up in – but it's just so tough when you're trying to make it in an artistic way, because not many people trust that way of living, you know? They're really into university and studying, and that kind of stuff. I was not into that, and I really had to fight hard to finally live my own way through sports. And once you make it, people are like, 'Ah he's one of them that makes it.' There aren't many.

Did you get encouragement from your parents to practice snowboarding or music?

I started both together. Our parents pushed us to do one instrument and one sport as we were kids. We did many sports, tennis, football, all of them, but I started snowboarding first, that was my first way out of that whole system.

Our parents are really hard workers. [ED: Pat's father is a pharmacist, and his mother is the founder of a luxury cosmetics brand.] I think parents are really a big part of your success as a kid, because you look up to your parents. If they made it, I could make it. If your parents never did anything, it's hard to relate to something stable. But they didn't say, 'You have to go to school because that is the only way.' That's what makes us hard workers, not doing things halfway.

How old were you when you started snowboarding?

I was 5, and then when I was 9, I found out about freestyle snowboarding and just got so into it. That's what I wanted to do with my life. I think what got me this far is that I wasn't doing it for money or success or the Olympics, it was just because I love snowboarding. And no matter what, I would do it every day on the snowboard. There is no limit when you love something.

At what point did you think you could become one of the best snowboarders in the world?

One day, in your head, it flips and you think, 'OK I can make it.' I think the big problem in our society is that people believe it's a huge step between wanting to do something and then just doing it – but there is not a big step, it's just about doing it. You want something, and the next day you wake up and you start doing it. It's really that simple.

How many hours a day did you put into snowboarding?

So many. Just all day every day.

It just took over?

Yeah, even though at some point when I was 17 or 18, I had a moment where I was wondering whether I should keep doing it. I had so many injuries. That's when the music came. And I think the music sparked me.

Tell me about the injuries.

I had many. The first at 13, second at 15, then third I was 16, 17 … pretty much every season I had a little something. And then when I was 18, I had three injuries in a year, and that was messed up. That's the time when I was like, maybe it's not made for me.

What were the injuries?

Ankle, collarbone, hands … my knee. The ACL was my last big one actually. I had the surgery to take off the screws for my collarbone, and just a couple of days later I tore the ACL in my knee. That to me was like: I'm not meant to do this. I was just in a bad mood and I couldn't get out of it, you know? And sometimes you need something really strong in your life to just tell you to stop, and injuries are the best lesson you can get.

So you jumped into music while rehabilitating from your injuries, but already had some musical training?

Yes, I was already playing, from age 5. I started with the guitar and played till I was 10 or 11 and then stopped; I didn't want to take lessons anymore. Then when I was traveling (for snowboarding competitions), I saw a couple of friends had guitars and I picked it up again. I just enjoyed it so much, and it came from (inside) me. And then I bought my guitar. The thing is, when I was a kid, it was my parents pushing me, and now it was me wanting to do music.

Could you say in a way that music saved your snowboarding career?

Yeah totally. The problem is when you have an injury you get too much into thinking, 'What's going to happen? I have to get back.' That's not too healthy. I had to get away from all of that pressure at some point. I didn't qualify for the (Sochi 2014) Olympics because of injuries, and I was like, 'Am I going to make it?' And music was just a (way to) step away.

Four years ago I was not even riding halfpipe anymore. I was just doing slopestyle. No one would have thought that this year at the Olympics I'd get fifth place. I was far from that. I was fifth on the Swiss team. And now with Iouri (Podladtchikov – the 2014 Olympic halfpipe gold medalist from Switzerland), I'm the first in the team.

You talked about how the music basically saved your snowboarding career, is this why so many snowboarders play music and jam? Is it for the release?

I don't think so. I think it's just to be cool honestly.

Really?

Yeah, it is, it's just because we have a lot of time in between competitions, and who doesn't want to play guitar? It's fucking cool.

So at first, it's about looking cool, it's something good and everyone enjoys it. But it's a lot of work to really know how to play and sing and record an album. It's insane how much work is involved. You know, I've written a hundred songs. I've recorded so many songs that I've never released, and it's such a brain fuck to get to the point where you have an EP like the one we recorded last week in San Diego. It sounds friggin' good when you listen to it. But it's a long, long friggin' road to get there. It's so much work and requires so much energy and time and money invested. But to me it's worth it.

Are you friends with some of the other guys in the circuit who play?

Yeah totally, all of them. We're kind of family you know. [ED: Burgener had recently stayed in the home of musician Luke Mitrani, whose snowboarding career ended after breaking his neck in 2013.]

Do you take a guitar with you on the road when you're snowboarding?

Always. A proper Gibson Hummingbird, not a mini guitar.

How did it feel to get signed by Universal Music?

For sure it was exciting because it means they have trust in my project. But I'm never satisfied, man. If things like that happen and you're like, 'Oh I made it,' and you just wait for things to develop, then nothing's going to *really* happen. So that's cool, but it's not going to change anything in my life at this point. I'm just going to keep snowboarding now. Go back and do a second album.

Describe the feeling of getting that contract with Universal relative to the feeling of making the Swiss Olympic team.

(*Breathes hard.*) It's hard to describe. I was not so impressed with the contract; it was more about getting the first vinyl and CD released. When it's in your hands and you see something has happened … You've worked so hard to get this and it's finally done; it's crazy.

It's thrilling!

It is thrilling, totally, this is what keeps you going. You have that one in your hands and you're like, right let's do the second one. We released the first one in March and the week after I was already booking the producer to do the second EP. A lot of people said, 'You're crazy, how can you go this fast?' And I'm like, 'Why would you wait?' Life is short enough.

What is your songwriting process?

It's me. I just sit down and write, pretty much.

Do you write the chords sequence first or lyrics?

I usually start with the music, and then I put the lyrics on. I play something on the guitar and I know what it has to be about. As soon as I get the vibe, I know. It's weird to say – maybe you think I'm crazy – but when you have a melody, you just know what the song is about. And some songs, I don't have to even understand the lyrics, I can just know what the song's about.

It just comes to you.

Yeah. The vibe, it tells you so much.

Do you play keyboards too?

Yeah.

And you write songs on keyboards too?

Yeah, a lot, but I try not to have too many keyboard songs. It's really easy to write on the keyboard, it's a really good instrument to write music because you can do anything. With the MIDI (keyboard) tools, you can put on more instruments and synth and everything.

I've gotten into production for the last EP. I just have a small MIDI keyboard, my guitar, my flute and my harmonicas. I get the songs to a certain level, and hand them to my producer who pushes them to the next level.

Do you consider yourself as more of a singer, or a guitarist, or multi-instrumentalist?

I never thought about it (*laughs*). I almost have to laugh when I hear people say I'm a multi-instrumentalist. I just play whatever I get. I don't think I'm a singer. I don't have this crazy Ray Charles voice or whatever. I just sing with emotion more than having a great voice.

Does music give you control that is maybe missing when you're snowboarding and about to go on a run?

Yeah, I mean, you're more sensible when you play music. When you make music, you are so much more sensible about life. First of all, when you're a writer I think you're able to remember important things about life, because you write them down and try to capture all this stuff about life which is really interesting. That's what I didn't have before I was a musician – because things happened and they just passed by.

What do you mean you're more sensible as a musician?

You're more sensible about your feelings, because when something happens, I try and capture it. When I'm sad because of a girl, because of whatever in life, I'll try and capture its emotion because I know it's really important in writing.

So maybe more in touch with your feelings?

Yeah, way more in touch with the feelings because I know I need that to make music.

You started out competing in slopestyle and big air, where you were seen as a future star when you were just a teenager. What made you decide to switch to halfpipe?

Because after all those injuries, I didn't have fun riding slopestyle anymore. I was always really competitive and halfpipe was the thing I learned to do for contests. Big air and slopestyle were more the fun parts of snowboarding.

That's how it used to be. The first Olympics where they had slopestyle was in Sochi (2014) … Everyone was like, 'Oh Pat can be the medalist in the Sochi Olympics,' and, I mean, I just freaked out I guess.

Too much pressure?

Yeah maybe too much pressure. Too much expectation. Expectation is what kills you in sports.

Did you have sponsors at that point?

Yeah.

And did that add to the pressure?

Not really. The sponsors themselves, they never pushed me. They just helped me by inviting me to events and allowing me to snowboard. It's not even my coach's fault, it's the pressure I put on myself due to all these people that were around me …

How I feel today is so settled. I know where I am going; somebody can try and push me, and I don't even listen to it. I know (my coach is) pushing me, but I understand his point too. If he pushes me, he wants the best for me, but again you choose if you put big pressure on yourself or not.

It sounds like you have reached a level of confidence in yourself.

Totally, and music is the same. My producer told me he worked with a guy who freaked out and couldn't sing for two weeks because he lost his voice. I don't think you just lose your voice like that. That happens because you freak out. And sports is a mental game. It's about never freaking out and staying calm all the time.

How do you battle anxiety when you're up on the deck before a run? Is it common to think, 'What the fuck am I doing up here? This is not natural.'

Yeah, but then it's too late. You get all kind of thoughts, but then thoughts are not part of you. That's something you should know, and if you don't know you should read some books about it.

I read *The Untethered Soul*, by Michael A Singer. It's a book about that: that you're not your thoughts. So many people get lost in their lives because they believe they are their thoughts. It's about turning off your thoughts – or if you have them, try and (frame) them in a positive way, not just turn them off – and then your life will change.

Do you have a mental coach that you work with?

Yeah. I met this guy when I was 18 when I got all those injuries, and I think he's a big part of why I kept on snowboarding. He taught me all this stuff as I was injured and it stayed with me.

You know, a lot of people went away when I was injured. It's insane how when you're on top, everyone is here to help you. Everyone is so happy to be with you. And as soon as you get injured and you're out, a lot of people (are gone). It's not because they don't like you or it's not because they don't' trust in you anymore, it's because they don't know how to handle it.

But in a way maybe that's a positive? As you said, expectations can be a killer in sports. So it brought the expectations down and maybe released some of the pressure?

Yeah but, you know that you create your own problems. Like, I talk to kids sometimes and they complain about the team, 'Oh, this coach is not pushing me enough.' They actually put their failure on others, but you are the one who makes it, you know? When you are 30 feet up in the sky, you are by yourself and there is no one holding your hand,

So you don't really consider the dangers and the risks of your sport?

I do for sure, and I know that anything can happen. That's why when people ask me if I'm going to the next Olympics (Beijing 2022), I say I want to. It's my goal, for sure, but you don't know what happens. I hope nothing negative – I know nothing negative is going to happen, because every negative thing is just a way of seeing (something) in a bad way. But good things are going to happen, and as long as I love doing it I'm going to keep doing it.

What gives you the bigger rush, the music or the halfpipe?

The halfpipe, totally.

Really?

Yeah, because it's dangerous, you know?

And which made you more nervous, performing the Gurtenfestival in Bern, Switzerland to thousands or snowboarding at the Olympics?

It's not the same, because to me music is so easy. You go up and you say, 'Whatever happens, I'm not going to break my neck.' That's the difference. Snowboarding is way harder because you put your life in danger, and that's why it teaches you a lot.

You were the first to release as switch backside double cork in halfpipe competition. What was that feeling like when you nailed that?

That's crazy, I won the (2016 FIS) World Cup due to that. It was a trick that I needed to get, that made me learn so much about my mental state. Without those kinds of tricks, I would have just done contests and got to fifth place and been happy with it. But I learned that you shouldn't think too much about a trick before the finals of a contest, because you know what you're doing. The time to think about it is before the final day – otherwise you get your head tired.

Was nailing that your highest point in snowboarding so far?

Probably, yeah. That and the switch triple cork when I was 16 (using a big air ramp) was also insane. There are so many big steps in my career. I can't even believe I did all of them – but it's crazy, it happens.

Was finishing fifth in the Olympics a high or low? How did that feel?[1]

I felt good, because I knew that I did well, and everyone was really impressed about my performance. But I should have got fourth … it's stupid to think about it, you know? I shouldn't even think about it, it's like, whatever.

---

1. Burgener was in contention for a medal, then dropped two spots due to judges' scores.

It just kind of breaks your heart whatever happens because you work hard for it. But at the same time it's a judging sport and that's why we do it. So you just have to take it. That's also something big you really learn about life.

Does it grate on you, not getting fourth place at the Olympics? After all, there is no medal for fourth.

Yeah (it does), but it teaches me. And I think that's why you should take every step in life as an opportunity to learn about things.

It's funny, I can feel you're competitive, and you're annoyed that you didn't finish one spot higher. That's what makes champions.

Why would you even do this if you were not trying to win? It doesn't even make sense. If you want something you have to be competitive. And all these guys out there like (two-time X Games winner) Danny Davis are super cool and everyone says they are so chilled and not like the others. They are – but when you see them backstage, they're freaking out if they don't stomp their run. And they wouldn't be here without that attitude.

So we talked about your highs in snowboarding, what about your highs in music?

It's coming; it's like asking me about my highlight in snowboarding when I was 14. I didn't have that moment yet.

What links the two fields for you, music and snowboarding? Is there a link?

Yeah totally, they are both creative. I wouldn't do music the way I do it if I wasn't snowboarding the way I snowboard. I grew up wanting to experiment, trying to find a new trick, trying to find a style. That is the link with music, it's creative. And you get adrenaline too, you have anxiety before going on stage, there are so many things in common. It's really deep, you have to love both so much.

I can see that's why I want to keep playing music throughout my life, because I realize that I can't really live without this feeling I (also) get through snowboarding – the adrenaline and creativity and just being free to do whatever I want to. This is the best life ever.

What about the discipline that it took to go pro in both?

I think it's about just standing back up. My coach told me once, don't count how many times you fall, but how many times you stand up. If you fall 10 times and you stand up 11 times, then you're still making it.

It's just about doing it. If not for the snowboarding, I would have started on my second EP the week after I did the first one. Some people only work on music and they wait four years to write a second album. That makes no sense to me.

Why wait? People think you have to wait, but for no reason. Ask them, 'Why are you waiting?' They don't know. They just say, 'Well because it's life.' Life doesn't mean anything, just fucking do it.

Do you get restless being idle?

Tomorrow we record the last song on voice, and then we have four days off. The thought of that is so boring to me.

But I'm learning that I need to take these days sometimes. That's also a big part of success: to be able to do nothing for a couple of days. But to me that's the hardest part: to do nothing.

You like the challenges.

Yeah I love it … These are the moments you remember, (ones) when you have a mission. Life without a mission is not worth living. That's the way I see it.

Ray Barbee

Redondo Beach, California, August 2018

There aren't many things that Ray Barbee doesn't do extremely well.

Credited as one of the early pioneers of street skateboarding, Barbee is also a highly respected jazz guitarist who walks into our interview with a classic Leica Rangefinder strapped around his neck.

Photography is another obsession of his that's turned into a profession, with a prestigious 2018 exhibit for Leica cameras cementing his talents in the field.

Barbee has just returned from his 15th tour of Japan, promoting *Tiara for Computer*, a free-flowing album of futuristic jazz. It's his third solo record, accompanying 10 others as part of bands and other collaborative efforts where he plays guitar, bass and drums. His solo instrumental work, abetted by his recent discovery of a Korg synthesizer, has also been featured in several film scores.

Suffice to say, he's a creative force of nature.

Barbee first emerged as the skinny kid from San Jose, California swerving through sidewalks and gliding down handrails in the 1988 cult video *Public Domain*. That cameo, which popularized tricks like 'no complys' and kick flips, catapulted him into a career of skateboarding which has extended into its fourth decade.

As a 17-year-old high schooler, Barbee was signed to leading skateboard brand Powell Peralta, with a signature model sold under his name. The cartoon graphic created in his likeness remains adorned on his sponsored boards and inked on the bodies of hardcore fans.

He also became a member of the renowned Bones Brigade team, led by icons Tony Hawk, Steve Caballero and Rodney Mullen. These were his first pinch yourself moments in a career that has been full of them.

"You talk about a sense of, 'I've arrived'." he reflects. "To me, that was it. I grew up dreaming of that. I used to draw the Tony Hawk graphic in class but put my name on there."

Around that time, Barbee began playing guitar in Bay Area punk bands, but was forced to give up his music aspirations to the demands of the Bones Brigade tour. Although he didn't release his first EP until he turned 29, Barbee gives full credit to skating for exposing him to different genres of music in an era where punk rockers, metalheads and rap fans did not always mix.

"We don't have that now, but in the '80s, there were hard lines. There were really hard lines," he explains. "But when you're open to a person of another nationality or ethnic background because of skateboarding, you're more open to what they bring to the table. You might get turned on to something you wouldn't have listened to before."

While the newly formed street skating style was chipping away at racial barriers, Barbee was confronting stereotypes within his own community as one of the first Black skateboarders to turn pro.

"In the '80s, if you were interested in skateboarding, it was perceived as being a white thing. It was perceived as: you're trying to be white," he explained.

In brushing aside that line of thinking, Barbee fulfilled a career full of accolades, including the 2017 TransWorld Skateboarding Legend Award. "People form relationships based on interests," he says. "They don't form relationships based on the color of skin, you know what I mean?"

'You can't just hop in and be great.'

For Barbee, taking an interest in something has always meant putting in as much time as possible into perfecting his craft — a process he refers to as "woodshedding" throughout our interview.

In a recent example, he selected 20 of his most alluring black and white shots for his photography exhibit at Leica's headquarters in Wetzlar, Germany from a catalogue of more than 300 rolls of film that he manually developed.

"A huge part of the enjoyment is getting in the darkroom and being able to print the images," he says. "I have so much respect for things that you have to work hard at. It's craftsmanship. You can't just hop in and be great. You gotta put your time in."

That process of totally immersing himself in an art form also serves as a means of truly appreciating it, he explains. "In music, unless you play that instrument, you can appreciate it from afar, but you've got no way to really have an emotional connection with what they're doing.

"I've got no way to have a deep emotional connection to what Coltrane was doing on the sax because I'm not trying to do it on a sax. I can appreciate it, but it stops at a certain point. Skateboarding functions like that."

Today, Barbee shuffles his time between his family life with his wife and two teenage sons, his dedication to photography, and his commitments as a pro skateboarder and musician. Among his continued sponsors are Fender Guitars, Krooked Skateboards and Vans, where his signature shoes are worn by a new generation of skaters.

"I'm very thankful that these interests I have – that I was going to do no matter what – have allowed me to still be in the industry and be a part of what I love," says the easy-going Californian.

"Because the brands can utilize these other interests that I have along with my history in skateboarding, I just kind of function in a way where they call us legends. And I'm thankful that they want to keep me around."

On your recent tour of Japan, did the people in the audience generally know about your legacy in skateboarding?

Yeah, in some of the shows for sure. At the smaller venues, we actually function like you would in a skateboard demo, in that after we play the gig, we hang out and sign albums or branded products. So I get to hear feedback from some of them, like 'I got your skateboard,' or 'I dug you in this video.' In the last tour, we raffled off one of my boards for each gig and somebody in the crowd would get my skateboard.

So there's definitely a blending of the cultures, because the skateboarding scene is pretty big in Japan, right?

Oh yeah, it's all one thing.

Your latest album *Tiara for Computer* took me on an emotional roller coaster. Like your other albums, it was all instrumental. Do you sing at all?

No I don't. Early on I tried to, but ideas and melodies and things I would hear – I couldn't go there with my voice. And I grew up with a lot of jazz, because my dad was a saxophone player. So there was always an affection and appreciation for jazz music, and a lot of those records were instrumentals.

Was he a professional musician?

No, he never really recorded. He played with friends and early on he was in a band. He was a marine and then became an auto mechanic. But while in the service he played with the band at their base. Then when he got out, he kept with it. I remember when I was really young, like 4 or 5, seeing him practicing with his band at our house. This was in the '70s. I would hear stories of him always bringing in his sax when my parents would go out to eat at certain places. He'd get called up by the band, and they would say 'Come on up and blow over certain songs.'

What is it about jazz music that appeals to you?

There's something in it that I have also noticed about my photography – because I love to shoot in black and white, and one of the things I love about it is that it's abstract by the very nature of it. Because we don't see in black and white, it's not a very literal representation of what you're seeing. It's another take on what you're seeing. So I feel like there's way more room for people to see what they want to see in it and let it speak to them. I don't use color because we see in color. It's very hard to experiment or to push (the boundaries of it). Like, if I wanted to push out a photo of you and I felt like I wanted you to be lighter, I'd probably get called out. Like, 'That's not the right skin tone!' There is less freedom to explore and express yourself.

I feel like instrumental music has that same kind of thing that black and white has, where people can go on their own journey with it. I feel like vocals and lyrics will scare you to feel a certain thing. So with instrumentals, you get what you get out of it. There's something about that I like.

You've dabbled with many instruments, including a synthesizer on this album. How easy is it for you to pick up a new instrument?

What's funny is that I used to play in punk bands growing up because of skateboarding. That's how I got into playing music. I always had the desire to play music, but it wasn't until I got with skateboarders that I was around instruments. Skateboarding basically made playing music accessible for me. So getting into skateboarding in the '80s, it was punk rock that we were listening to. And the coolest thing about punk was that the person in the crowd could very easily be the person on the stage.

How so?

Because it was all about the desire to do it, not so much the technique or ability. It was a lot of passion and you just kind of stumbled over the technique part. People in that movement who followed that approach weren't afraid because of their lack of technique to chase what they wanted. So it wasn't intimidating for the person in the crowd.

In the '80s, a lot of the bands that were happening on MTV, say, Ozzy, AC/DC, Def Leppard and even The Police – I name those bands because as skateboarders, we were listening to things that were gonna drive us and put energy into it – they're playing stadiums. They're playing long solos. The level of their musicianship is functioning pretty high, especially if you're talking about Rush and Yes and these bands. So as someone in the crowd, you're looking at that being like, 'I'm so far from that. I love it. But that's a whole other world.'

What punk did is it demolished that barrier of us being up here and you guys being way down there, because we've got all of this talent and we've woodshedded for years and years to be here. Punk leveled that out. It just said, 'We have the guitars and we're just excited about sound and we're developing our technique, but it's not developed to the point where you can't hop in right away.'

What I appreciate about getting into skateboarding is the accessibility. Because of skateboarding, I loved punk rock. And the way punk rockers approached their music had a lot of parallels with how skateboarders went about their skating. So that dream to play guitar and play music became manageable, because it was functioning in a community that I wasn't intimidated to hop into.

I've watched your skating videos and there's stuff you do like sliding down a handrail and jumping down a flight of stairs that are very dangerous. There's no other way to put it.

For sure.

It's not very natural for people to want to do that, so there's clearly a 'fuck it' attitude going on. Like, 'I'm just going to do this and see where I land.' Is that what you mean when you say that skateboarding functions like punk rock for you, where there's a feeling of, 'If I bomb, so what?'

Yeah, skateboarding has a very steep learning curve, right? So most skateboarders have a tenacity that's not very common. Well, I shouldn't say that because athletes have it (in general). And so the personality that gets drawn to that challenge, and enjoys the process – even though it can be grueling, even though there's a lot of rejection and pain – is needed to ride a skateboard. There's that thrill-seeking kind of thing.

What turned you on to skating?

I was hanging out with my friend Danny the summer before seventh grade, and for his birthday he got a skateboard. I had seen skateboards before and didn't think anything of them, because they were always these little banana boards. But this skateboard was not a banana board. It's one that the pros were riding. It was like 10 inches wide and 30 inches long, as opposed to 3 or 4 inches to 7 inches long with that banana board. And so I see that, and I was just like 'Whoa! How can I get one of those?' Luckily, his dad had an old skateboard from when he was skating in the early '70s and gave it to me.

So the first day of school in the seventh grade we see these other guys hanging out. And we're like (whispering), 'I bet they're skaters.' And that brotherhood of dudes embraced us that day. They played in punk bands and they had a ramp. So now they're opening me up to this whole world of skateboarding and everything that comes along with that culture of it, which is punk rock and being creative and into the arts, all of it. I would always hang out with them while they were playing and practicing. Then after practice, I would pick up a guitar and bug them to show me some songs. Before long, I was in the band.

What kind of stuff were you playing?

Just straight punk. You had the whole punk scene that was happening in England in the late '70s, like the Sex Pistols and Buzzcocks, and we were listening to the generation that came after them in the States, like Bad Brains and Minor Threat and The Vandals and Circle Jerks and Black Flag.

Do you remember the first gig you saw?

Not the first, but I remember there were a lot of small punk bands in Northern California, around San Francisco, Sacramento and San Jose that we would see. One of the bands in San Jose was (groundbreaking vertical skateboarder) Steve Caballero's band called The Faction. And that was an influence on us.

What is it about board sports that draws many of its top performers to play in bands?

You know, I don't snowboard and I don't surf. But that being said, I do see a lot of parallels between surfing and snowboarding and skateboarding. And I think the main parallel is its creativity. There are a lot of things that I've noticed over the years with the arts, if you will. You know, it's funny because I have a hard time seeing them as sports. Because the way that skaters function in all of their disciplines calls for them to be so creative. Like, there's no cruise control or autopilot. And so much of it is left to you on how you want to develop and express yourself in it, like your trick selection and what way you want to skate.

There's a lot of room for improvisation, like in jazz.

Yeah, for sure. Improvisation and creativity to me are the same thing. So you are building that muscle to create, because whether you're conscious of it or not, that's what's happening – especially in street skating. You're taking whatever's in front of you and you're constantly trying to get ideas. Like, 'What can I do there? Can I hop on that? Oh that would be cool.' When you're functioning like that, you're building that ability. And so what happens is that it doesn't just stop with that. It gets applied to whatever other interest you might have.

How does that creativity jibe with the business end of skateboarding?

I see it like a big quilt, right? I'm talking about the culture around skateboarding. All the ingredients that make skateboarding what it is. Because it's not just the activity. You've got to present it too, right? So you've got fashion and you've got this world where now there's a canvas for some more creativity. So what happens? You do your own art, right? You have skateboard companies and brands that are like, 'OK, we've got a market.'

If you want to sell things then you have to market them — no different than you would for a band. So there becomes the need for art direction. And then if you want to show the world what these guys are doing, you have to film it or put it in magazines. So there becomes a need to shoot. So all these things are different patches of this quilt, but they all need to happen for it to function the way that it does. For guys like me to make a living, we've got to sell product. For people to want to buy the product, there's got to be some kind of draw to the product, through videos, photos, artwork and everything else. And what I love about skateboarding is that it always wants to function in-house.

It doesn't outsource anything?

It has to, but it doesn't want to. So the creative part is where they least need to outsource. The business part yes, you have to outsource.

Like the manufacturing?

Just all of that. Especially when it gets to a point where it's like nobody went to business school. But the creative aspect, like the music, photography, videography, design and graphics — any of the stuff that can stay in-house. Because there's enough interest and talent within to where that's going to convey and represent and speak the language of skateboarding more than anybody else probably can.

At what age did you start to get really good at skating?

I would say about two years into it at 14. It was after I broke my wrist skating ramps, and I couldn't skate ramps with my cast and I still wanted to be on my skateboard. At that time, people were making little jump ramps on the streets and I really got excited about that approach because it was so new. So by the time I got into skateboarding, there were a list of tricks that were already developed (on large ramps) and there was a sense of playing catch-up to learn those tricks. In street (skating), that list was very minimal.

So breaking your hand steered you towards street skating, which was still in its infancy. Were there people doing those tricks that you began to make famous?

Yes there were, but it was this new generation, this new thing bubbling under me. Skateboarding at the time was about vert, and that was the bulk of what was being covered in the magazines.[1]

But there were lots of kids like me that were getting excited about street skating and exploring that. And that hadn't really surface yet. So what was really cool for us was that we wanted to be with other like-minded skaters who were getting excited about the same things. There were these contest series being held, and we would travel to them and meet people from other cities that were super into street skating. That was our world.

At what point did you start competing in skateboarding?

Pretty early. Once we started hearing about these contests, we're like let's go for it. That was our way to be a part of what we did. Because everybody in our town was getting ramps, and we wanted to be with what's happening, you know? First, we would just go and check them out. But what was so cool about it was whether you entered or not, you could still go out there and skate. Just hang out after the contest.

But here's what's interesting: Because skateboarding doesn't function like a sport, the contests served their thing early on and then street skating really moved past it.

Into the videos?

It became way more about videos. To this day that's almost its own thing, people who skate contests. Many of skateboarders' heroes are dudes who don't skate contests at all. They're just dudes who go out and express themselves. Because skateboarding isn't a sport, it doesn't really function in those parameters.

But certainly, it's athletic.

Skateboarding is very athletic. But the competing thing is the one element that can be there or it cannot be there. And skateboarding functions at its highest when it's not competing.

In what sense?

In videos nobody's competing, they're just expressing themselves. Just trying tricks that they want to work on, and then they show them and you're like, 'Whoa!' And then somebody can look at that and try and learn how to do it. But they're doing it to express themselves. They're not competing. They're not getting any money out of it.

Was there no money at all in those videos?

There was no money in the videos; videos were an advertisement. Videos are what you do for people to get turned on to you.

And then you get sponsorship deals?

Typically, if you're sponsored then part of your paycheck is to do a video. You're getting a salary, you're getting royalties to be a part of this program. Part of that is you go out and get in the magazines, you go out to film video parts and you do demos.

---

1. Vert, also known as vertical skateboarding, involves airborne tricks performed in curved ramps. The style began in empty California swimming pools in the 1970s.

What age did you achieve that level?

I turned pro at 17.

What did turning pro mean exactly back then?

Turning pro entailed, at that time, getting paid. It meant getting a paycheck and putting my name on a skateboard where I would get royalties from it. I'd get a certain percentage of everything sold with my name.

So I came up in a time where it was on the tail end of the contest thing. I think being in contests kind of helped with me getting sponsored. But to be honest with you, it was more through skating with other guys that were already on the team telling the owners of the team, 'We need to get this guy.' It was a word of mouth thing from skating together.

How did joining the Bones Brigade and getting that first contract with Powell Peralta change your life?

It's why you even want to interview me now, because of that video (*Public Domain*). Here's the thing, me and my friends stumbled across tricks that people hadn't seen. And that was put on display with the top skateboard brand of the day with probably the biggest distribution at the time of any of the skate companies. On the back of that video, to travel and go everywhere showing these new ideas, that's what changed everything for me. That's what allowed me to turn pro, because I was an amateur when the first one came out. From there, because of the response from the video, that's when Stacy (Peralta) was like, 'OK, you're ready to turn pro.' So, again, it goes back to the videos. I was ready to go pro because of the videos, not the contests.

And how much preparation would it take to learn these tricks to go into the videos?

Oh, I was skating all day.

Hours and hours?

Yeah. It's funny because I saw an interview with Kobe Bryant where he said, 'You have to love the process.' For him, he was talking about all those nights in the gym, just working on the shot. The woodshedding. You really have to love it, right?

When I think about the time that I was functioning in that, I just loved it so much. And I had the ability to just do it as much as I could, so that's what I was doing. So when it came to filming, I wasn't doing anything different than what I always did. It was just that the cameras were on. So I wasn't prepping for the filming.

You get so lost in the preparation that you don't even consider it preparation?

Don't get me wrong, you're definitely aware that you're developing and you're working on stuff, because that's the way skateboarding is. And that's what keeps it fun. You're constantly trying to learn new tricks, and very rarely does it just come easy. You've got to work at it. It's seeing that growth that is infectious. It just fuels itself. Like, OK, I want to get back out and do it.

Right: Barbee performs a trick at a photo shoot in Orange County, California in 1989.

Does that happen in your experience as a photographer too?

Especially with photography, because that requires a lot of time in the darkroom. It's just like, all these things I'm interested in have a steep learning curve. You can't just go in the darkroom and print, and you're not even going to be in there for a month and be good at printing. And I knew that going into it.

Can you describe the thrill of nailing a big trick for the first time?

It's funny, the reason why I can't surf is because I don't have the patience for it – because the pace of skateboarding with intervals is quick. If you're working on a trick, as soon as you can get that board back upright and hop back on it, you can try again. With surfing, it was like I'd try to stand up, fall over, and it wasn't for like another hour that I could try again.

So skateboarding has got that dynamic of a lot of short-lived victories, if you will. So you get that rush, but you quickly move on. Don't get me wrong, there are certain tricks where you might be able to ride on the high of them for a couple days – especially if you're trying to film for a video part, and you've been dreaming about getting this trick happening – but for the most part, they're a bunch of small victories. I don't want to say small victories. They're just victories that you keep moving on from. You don't ever rest. So the feeling is quick, but it makes you keep chasing it. Like, 'That was cool, let's get another one.'

Do you also experience that by playing guitar, where you're learning little licks and putting them together to form a solo?

Yeah. Or it could be you jamming with dudes and there's like, a moment that you're in it and you're like, 'That was cool.' But you don't just stop and admire it, you're still moving on.

Which flowed more naturally for you, learning these tricks as a skateboarder, or learning how to really express yourself on guitar?

With all the stuff that I do, there has never been a moment where I've been really excited about something and felt like, 'You know what? I can't do this.' Thankfully, what I choose to endeavor in, whether it's photography or skateboarding or music, it goes through the same process of pushing through its learning curve.

None of it just flowed to where I didn't have to put work in. It will flow to a point where you can start to get there, but you have to put the time in. All of it is the same in that sense. When I put the time in, it starts to meld into the same thing across the board. Like, it feels comfortable to where I can put my signature on it now.

A part of the learning curve is trying to figure out what direction you want to take your skill to take ownership of what you're doing. Because everybody's working on their skills. There are a lot of people doing whatever it is you're trying to do right now.

That's one of the things I had to determine when I got excited about using synthesizers for my new album. At the same time I was learning it all, I quickly had to try to figure out: where's my fingerprint in this? What is my voice in this?

So I'm seeing parallels there. That's what brings it all together to a common flow. What is awesome about skateboarding is it operates much like music. For example, how many songs are there with three chords?

'All these things I'm interested in have a steep learning curve,' says Barbee.

Probably more than a million.

That's what I'm saying. You have loads of different songs, but it's still the same three chords, right? So it has way more to do with your fingerprint and your idea. Skate tricks are like that too. You might not be creating a new trick, but you might be doing it in a way that makes it look different or it's specific to your style. Like, this dude catches his kick flips up here. This dude doesn't catch his kick flip – so there's enough variation within all of it to still have an aspect of originality. It really functions in a highly creative space. So it's not safe to just say, 'Oh, it's already been created so there's nothing there.' This is also true because so much of what informs our creativity changes geographically. The person in Barcelona or Sao Paulo, he's got a way different environment to skateboard in than we do here.

How does it feel to be known as a pioneer in street skating culture? Do you feel like you've cemented yourself in skateboarding history?

I don't know. I feel like time will tell. But what's really interesting about social media and Instagram is that I didn't have any idea of the emotional connection that people had towards my parts in those early videos. To be able to see people expressing that on Instagram has been amazing. So I'm just thankful.

But I just want to clear this up: I was a part of a bunch of dudes that were pushing innovation at that time. And so I'm not sitting here trying to take credit for it all. I was a part of a movement.

I'm very thankful that the movement is still appreciated to this day, and very thankful to have opportunities to still generate an income and provide for my family because of being a part of that movement.

What's the biggest thing that has changed in the skateboarding world over the past 30 years?

The longer things are around, the tougher it becomes to come up with something new to do. Now with social media, that window (to be original) is smaller and smaller, because everybody gets to it real time and everybody can see that it can be done, so they just hop straight to it. So much of the process before was spending a lot of time knowing whether it could be done, because you had never seen anybody do it. It was battling doubt. You would have to push over, and that consumed a lot of my time.

I'll never forget going on those early tours when *Public Domain* first came out in Europe, and all the street skaters were doing tricks that were happening about a year earlier in California. It's like when you go overseas, the movies that were out here in Blockbuster rentals were just coming out in the theaters. That's how it was in skating. We'd go there and they were so behind. There's none of that anymore. Now everybody's in real time, and that's why all over the world everyone is just ripping.

In popular culture, skating has often had an association with smoking weed and sometimes indulging other drugs. The Bones Brigade had the reputation of avoiding that scene, while other skaters were famously less in control. Is there something about skating that lends itself to that kind of destructive behavior?

Because of what it takes to ride a skateboard, you get a lot of intense personalities. And it doesn't stop at skateboarding, so it's gonna rage full on with whatever it's doing. So if you're ragin' full on with a skateboard, it's not going to stop with the skateboard. It's going to rage full on with drugs or with anything that it wants to do. I put that rage towards these other interests I had, because that was my desire.

Can you describe some of the challenges you faced for being a skateboarder when the scene was less diverse than it is today?

I got into skateboarding in the '80s. At the time, people were building backyard ramps because of the closure of the skate parks that were built in the late '70s. Now, to have a backyard ramp your parents either had to own the home or had to have finances to build a ramp. That excludes a lot of people, because that means you've got to be friends with either the person that has the ramp or friends with a friend that knows the person. It's a social economics thing.

And you have to remember that skateboarding came from surfing. Surfing functions in that same way. Geographically, you have to live by the water to surf, right? That's not cheap. A surfboard isn't cheap. So what I'm trying to say is that it was a white thing, basically.

And what comes with that is a style of music (for skaters). Rock music started to turn into punk because that wasn't aggressive enough once skateboarding developed. So when you fast forward to punk, well that's more of a white thing. And that being super tied to skateboarding, that whole package is sitting in one kind of ethnic group.

So in the '80s if you were interested in skateboarding, it was perceived as being a white thing.

It's perceived as you're trying to be white. And that's what I heard from others in the Black community. They're just like, 'Surfing and skateboarding is a white thing.' Blacks don't surf, Blacks don't skateboard. And so that was the grief I got. Like, 'Why are you trying to be white? Why are you wearing that?'

How did you react to that?

I could care less.

You know, I grew up with all that Motown and Stax music. These are record labels that have studios with in-house musicians that play on all of the releases from those labels, right? They would just plug in the artists, just like The Funk Brothers with James Jamerson basically being the band for Smokey, The Supremes, Marvin and Stevie. Just like The Swamp Brothers in Muscle Shoals (Alabama), or the Hi Rhythm Section with Al Green, or the Wrecking Crew in LA, and the list goes on. But what you will see in all of those bands is integration.

Because of the music, they could care less about the color of each other's skin. And when they were in that studio, that was the last thing they were thinking about. They were thinking: You're either bringing it or you're not. And that's skateboarding. Skateboarding could care less about the color of your skin. It's more concerned with whether you're bringing it or you're not. You're either stylish and not a (fraud), or you are. So when I was in my version of the studios, dude it was easy to be like, 'I hope you have something you dig, because you don't even get what I'm a part of.'

When did you notice things becoming more integrated in skateboarding?

Things were moving so fast in the '80s, because when street skating happened, it did away with the gatekeeper. You didn't have to know the dude that had the ramp anymore. All you had to do is get a board, and now your ramp was your neighborhood. You walk outside and you can make it happen. So more people were getting turned on to skateboarding because it was accessible.

And when you're open to a person of another nationality or ethnic background because of skateboarding, you're more open to what they bring to the table. You might get turned on to something you wouldn't have listened to before. If your buddy is Hispanic and you're going to link up with him to go skate, you may hear his parents playing mariachi music and you become open to it and (think), 'That's kind of cool.' It just made it to where everybody could be open to each other's cultures.

I know you faced a horrifying racial incident when you were 20 years old and got chased by a group of skinheads after a punk concert was shut down in Huntington Beach. Can you take me through how that changed your life?

Well, dude, it put me off into this idea of just how heavy hate is. I was dealing with hate that I hadn't had to deal with before and I didn't know how to manage it. I knew I was mastered by it, because of that experience.

Like, I believe there is justified hate. I believe in hating that which is evil and clinging to what is good. But the hate that I had for these dudes was spiteful, a revengeful type of hate. And I knew that what I was dealing with was no different from the hate that they had towards me. It just came from a different place. And that was huge for me. That really made me look at life in general, people in general, our hearts in general, the human condition in general.

I realized there was something going on that I'm mastered by that I have no control of. I understand it and I don't want to be here, but I'm in this now and I don't like this. And it made me seek truth. It made me realize that the good that I want to do, I can't do. There are things that I want to stop doing that I keep doing. And how it changed my life is it led me to Jesus. It led me to calling on the name of Jesus and being saved. You talk about a game changer.

How long were you in that funk before you felt enlightened?

I was searching a year and a half before that (incident). And then another year after that. So three years. But for that year and a half prior, I was just kind of done. I was done with being confused and I was getting really annoyed with it. And that (added to the confusion). It was heavy. I saw the look on those dudes' eyes; it was so crazy.

Do you remember how it started?

What happened was this punk band got broken up. And this punk band, Guttermouth, they're not a skinhead punk band, but skinheads loved them — which I always thought was such a bummer for a band, you know? That would be the worst thing.

What started the chase was just this massive dude coming up to me and being like, 'What are you doing here? Aryan race, white power! Shouldn't you be in Compton or something? You better run nigger, you better run.' And then I saw a dude in a flannel shirt and a ball cap who looked like a skater start coming after me. And I was like, 'I'm out,' and I'm running and I'm hitting corners and I'm trying to think, 'OK, how do I get back with my ride?' And then I see this truck pull up with all these skinheads in the back. So they had it all set up. I saw the look in their eyes. I saw that hatred. It's just like a hundred percent pure and I can never forget it. And what was so crazy is that I had never seen these dudes before my life.

Thankfully, I ran and I found a community center, or it might have been a church, I'm not sure. It was open … and I ran in and thought that they're going to come in and get me.

This was late at night, around 10 o'clock and (inside) they were having a birthday party. No one spoke English, except for the janitor, who was like, 'They're gone. We can call the cops.' I think the skinheads at that point were worried about witnesses, so they bounced.

The cops come, there's one white cop and there was one Black cop. The Black cop comes up to me and he takes my report. He's like, 'Don't worry. We're going to look into this.' And at that moment, I was like, my mom's from Alabama. My dad's from Arkansas. My grandmother was my hero. My dad's mom is from Arkansas. And I just think about what they went through. Like, I experienced maybe that much of it (puts thumb and index finger together). They weren't going to have those cops (help) them. First of all, cops were doing it (themselves).

Did skateboarding help give you something to focus on after the incident?

Skateboarding functions how it always functions for me. It's just what I love to do. I get a joy from it that I can't explain. But a part of that is this sense of accomplishment, like I'm doing something. Especially if I have a good day out to escape. I can come home and just feel like, 'Yeah!'

More so than guitar?

Yeah, playing guitar doesn't have that. Music doesn't.

Why not?

Because what I'm talking about is a very physical thing. There's a sense of my body being fatigued after a long day of skating and I just feel like I laid it out. There's a sense of releasing something.

When you're playing a good set, you do get these moments. What music has, that I've been noticing a lot lately, is I'll hit ceilings and there's this feeling of wanting to push it a little further. Especially with soloing, there are moments when you're in with the crowd and you just want to push that little bit more and you're reaching. Sometimes you can tap into a little something, and other times it falls apart. But when you do get there, there's a sense after it where you're just like, 'Wow, that was cool.' So maybe that is the same thing. Maybe that is a similar kind of satisfaction. I'm definitely exhausted after a set, much like skateboarding, I'm drenched in sweat and I'm drained mentally. Like, I'm in it.

What is the link between skateboarding and music for you?

I always tell people the link is me: I'm the source. That's the link.

Bronson Arroyo

Covington, Kentucky, September 2018

Bronson Arroyo is responsible for a lot of firsts.

As a starting pitcher for the mythical 2004 Boston Red Sox, Arroyo is remembered as the cornrow-wearing member of the self-titled 'Idiots' who stayed loose in the clubhouse and played fast and free on the field. That attitude helped the Red Sox slay the 86-year 'Curse of the Bambino' with an unprecedented comeback from a 3-0 hole to the archrival New York Yankees in the American League Championship Series. Eight days later they went on to win the World Series.

As a guitarist, Arroyo was the first baseball player ordered by a doctor to put down his beloved instrument, when continuous practicing caused carpal tunnel syndrome in 2010. As a vocalist, he was the first World Series winner to rock out in front of a sold-out Fenway Park, accompanying Pearl Jam in 2016.

The former All-Star and Gold Glove winner was also very likely the first power-lifting adolescent in the Florida Keys. Arroyo showed me videos of himself as a tiny 8-year-old lifting weights with his father Gus, who incredibly trained his child to squat and deadlift more than 200 pounds. Cuban-born Gus, who co-owned a sheet metal company when Arroyo was growing up, remains an outsized presence in his son's life.

"I'd watch this guy come home from being up on a metal roof in the Keys. It's a hundred degrees out there and he's putting down hot tar every day. It's just brutal work," Bronson recalls.

"Then I'd see him pound the weight room like a maniac."

Arroyo credits his dependability as a pitcher – starting at least 32 Major League games 10 seasons in a row – on observing his father's work ethic. "You can't help but respect that and say, 'Man, if it gets tough, I can still push through.' That's what made me who I was in the game."

He also had a steeliness that could test opponents. One of his antagonists during the 2004 season was the Yankees' divisive superstar Alex Rodriguez, who was hit by an Arroyo pitch during the regular season – a play that ignited an infamous brawl – and underhandedly tried to swat a ground ball out of Arroyo's glove in a pivotal playoff game.

"In Red Sox mythology, those were two of the biggest plays that year. It just happened that I was in the middle of both of them," Arroyo recalls. Rodriguez, who faced Arroyo when both were high schoolers in Florida, was less interested in discussing those moments when I interviewed him for a CNN story in 2018. "Can we not talk about Arroyo?" he steamed. (In subsequent interviews, Rodriguez has called Arroyo "a good guy" and "a very good athlete.")

'He was loved by all'

About two minutes into meeting Bronson Arroyo in person, I knew I was in for a fun day. A year removed from completing a 20-year career in baseball, he maintained the straggly hair and carefree demeanor of an overgrown teenager.

We spoke in his basement studio in Covington, Kentucky for about two hours before he played some tunes on a custom-made guitar gifted to him by the Cincinnati Reds, his team for 10 of his last 11 seasons.

Arroyo is a competent guitar player, but his true talent lies in singing. Honed over years of practice, his voice is classic grunge rock in the mold of his close friend Eddie Vedder. It's no wonder that after his final game in 2017, he treated Cincinnati fans with a 40-minute set filled with Pearl Jam songs.

In 2005, on the heels of his World Series win, Arroyo launched his music career with a fun covers album. It was backed by experienced session musicians and featured celebrity appearances from the likes of author and Red Sox fanatic Stephen King, who cameoed on *Everlong* with a spoken word sequence.

"Being in New England allowed me to sit with an acoustic guitar and play shows in front of people that I probably had no business playing shows for at that time," he recalls. "It was very, very rough. I was totally unseasoned as a musician. There are so many levels to playing music that people don't realize."

His musicianship has come a long way since then. Apart from appearing with Pearl Jam, Arroyo has graced the stage with Counting Crows and the Goo Goo Dolls and has played to thousands as a solo artist. He is now ready to take on his own mantle by working on his debut album of original material.

When we arrived at a large warehouse for his band practice, his buddies were already in full groove, blasting the backing lines to REM's *The One I Love*. I stuck around for six or seven songs – all loud covers that sounded terrific – then took some photos and said my goodbyes. Before I left, Bronson handed me a couple of customized picks made for Pearl Jam's 2018 world tour that Vedder had given him. It was a touching gesture.

It's no wonder that his house is adorned with plaques that include a 'Good Guy Award' from the Cincinnati Chapter of the Baseball Writers' Association of America. As teammate Jonny Gomes told the Cincinnati Enquirer: "He was like a chameleon. This dude would get down with the country guys, this dude would get down with the hip hop guys. He'd play the bongos with the Latins. He was loved by all."

Although his passion for different genres of music opened doors with teammates, Arroyo's connections with them went deeper than jam sessions in the locker room.

"What Jonny's talking about is not so much just about music," he explains, "but the fact that I can come and go anywhere, anytime, anyplace. If you came into my room at night in the hotel, you might catch three guys that don't speak English and you might catch the whitest richest guys on the team. You didn't know what you would get. I just really enjoyed giving love to everybody."

What did baseball mean to you as a kid?

From the age of 6 onwards, baseball was definitely the most significant thing in my life. I'd be in the weight room as a young kid with my father and he'd be talking strategy, talking about carbs and proteins and supplements we were taking. I was living a life of a professional baseball player at a very young age.

That obviously dominated most of my world. I don't know what an average kid did when he came home from school. I would come home and have a little snack and take some vitamins, and then go to the weight room and do the baseball thing for a couple of hours. And then I would come inside for dinner and homework and wake up and do it again.

I was living like a college athlete in a way where I was having to manage both (academics and sports). I was always managing the structure and the preparation that was going to be needed in order to play in the big leagues. By the time I was 7 or 8 years old, I was damn sure I would be a professional ballplayer. I was having these conversations with my father, like, 'If we just stay the course and don't get in a car accident, we're going to play in the big leagues.'

So from age 6, your dad thought you had the power to be a professional athlete?

Well, he saw the athleticism. He didn't necessarily see the power. I was always a very thin guy like I am now. But what people don't generally realize is that if you dedicate yourself to the weight room, you can become really strong and not look huge. We always think of power as Schwarzenegger, but I was a really skinny kid who was building these small muscles and getting stronger. Meanwhile other people were skinny like me, but not as strong. So I was taking my athleticism to a whole other level. My father saw the marriage of those two things as a way to at least get a free college education.

When did music first become a thing for you?

Everyone in my family plays the piano or at least sings. My grandmother was a music teacher down in the Keys and I spent a lot of time in her house after school. She taught people anywhere from the age of 65 down to 6. At least three or four people were coming to the house every day getting lessons on the cello, the piano and violin.

I heard Stone Temple Pilots when I was 15 and thought, 'Oh, there's something a little darker there.' I don't know what it is, but it seems like it's coming from a place that's a little bit more true and real to whatever's going on the world at this time. And that's what really unlocked my brain.

By 22, I was playing for the Pirates' Double-A club and the general manager of the Altoona Curve gave me an old Yamaha guitar of his. Then it started becoming a thing, because once I could create the music with the guitar, it gave me the ability to sing along with it. It was the only thing that I had ever come across other than baseball that felt like it was calling my name every day. It was like the guitar was sitting over there saying, 'Come on man, you got to pick me up.'

Did singing come naturally to you? Have you taken lessons?

I've never had a lesson. It was one of those things where I got the guitar and started playing a Creed song. And I thought, 'No one else is going to sing this for me except me.' Over time, I realized that what I really love is the singing. Playing the guitar was just a foundation to be able to do that. I don't love playing the guitar.

I really love singing, because it feels like a workout. Like you're getting something off your chest. You know when you go to the gym, have a good sweat, get those endorphins going and then come home and go, 'Wow, that feels fantastic'? That to me feels much more creative and natural than the guitar part.

What was a bigger dream as a kid, being a rocker or a ballplayer?

Definitely a ballplayer. And a lot of times people ask me what's the difference? I've been to enough Pearl Jam shows to honestly say their gigs never get old. But if you go to enough of them, and you go to two or three in a row, you realize that — even though they have a giant catalogue and have flexibility in the keys they play in — the guys have to perform a few of the same songs again and again. It's still a performance.

But baseball-wise it's completely different every single night. There is no replicating anything. So in a lot of ways I could never get tired of the game. But I could see myself getting a little tired of music if it was my fulltime profession and I had to tour constantly. I would need to put it down for a bit of time.

What is your creative process when writing lyrics and music?

All the music that I love comes from this dark place. But my life has just always had that optimism, because of my father who made the glass half full under all circumstances.

But because of that, it's been hard to write the songs that I've loved: the really heartbreaking stuff, the tragedy. That seems to bring a lot of the great music out, and I haven't had a lot of that. So now I always try to write with someone else. It's very difficult to finish a song myself, but I'll bring the music and I'll bring an idea. Here in Cincinnati I meet up with a guy named Eliot Sloan, who's a member of Blessid Union of Souls, and we knock it out in four hours. I don't try to over-think the lyrics or anything, we just go there.

We'll put like a demo down with some drums and the track and then we just start writing. Sometimes I'm just thinking of a feeling, man, like you're riding in a car with a top down and it's a gorgeous night and you're with your girl and you feel like you're 17 years old and on top of the world. What does that feel like?

I'm trying to do that, because it's almost an exercise in something that I'm not used to. And the more I finish them, the better it feels. It's getting a little addictive to finish songs, because I haven't been able to do it in the past.

How does that compare to the process of perfecting your pitches, like working on the slider or working on the change-up? Is there a creativity in music that you didn't quite have as a pitcher?

It feels totally different. But the part that's similar is that in both areas I don't think you can be so hyper-critical. You can't kill yourself over every lyric thinking that it has to be absolutely perfect. I mean, it's subjective, right? So it's not perfect regardless. And pitches are kind of the same way. Because I can throw my nastiest curve on and get hit out of the park. And I can throw a terrible one and it can get popped up to shortstop. So what do you value here? Are you valuing how sharp it is, or do you value the result?

Some guys can be too critical of themselves, and aren't able to brush things off. And I always could do that. That's what made me who I was in the game: I can stay cool, calm and collected and have a bad first inning, and still pull out six innings. So that part feels very similar.

Pitching in a game is a mental challenge. You're trying to pick apart your opponent like a chess match. But the preparation for pitching is mostly physical. It's about what my body is feeling. As far as trying to craft a song, the process is totally mental. You're trying to create a mood. How does that feel? You don't really get that in sports, or you can only get that when you're walking off the mound. After you've thrown seven good innings and the crowd is cheering, then it can feel like a mood. But not when you're in the battle.

How did you combat nerves as a pitcher in big game situations?

All of us get nervous when we're doing anything at a high level. You've got those butterflies, but once the game starts, it makes it a little bit easier. I felt like I had been in those situations so many times prior to being a professional because of what we were doing the weight room. My father was talking to me about strategy, and he's treating me as this professional athlete when I'm 8 years old. While I'm listening to the national anthem on the mound to pitch this Little League game, I probably was more nervous than everybody else in the field.

So by the time I got to Boston and I'm playing in those Yankees - Red Sox games and pitching against the Anaheim Angels in game three of the ALDS, the media is asking me, "How do you stay so cool and calm?" I said I was probably more nervous playing in games as a kid.

I also had to break down my reasoning and think, 'What am I trying to accomplish here?' Starting pitchers have got to get deep in the ballgame. If I allow my adrenaline to take over just to get out of the first inning, then I know I'm going to run out of gas. So I'm trying to temper that back all the time.

OK, so taking that mentality, how do you apply it to performing music in front of a crowd? Do you remember your first time on stage?

At first, I was so worried about making sure it was right that I couldn't sit there and enjoy singing the music. It all felt rushed. Years later, I almost feel like I can just pause and there's all this space in between the verses. You can just go, 'Oh man, that's no problem. I've got all the time in the world to get to that.' I'm just now getting to the point on a stage where I can relax and think, 'I'm going to enjoy this. We're going to rip right now, and this is going to be fun and I'm not going to be so sped up that it's going to ruin the moment.'

Baseball-wise I can get to that place much quicker. Although from the minor leagues to the big leagues, that took some years to do that too. To stand on the mound and be in Yankee Stadium and have Derek Jeter at the plate and enjoy it, and go, 'I'm here right now, but I'm relaxed. I know we're in an intense situation. But you know what? Come on, let's go,' and it doesn't feel rushed. That took some time too, but musically it's taken longer. Because I'm not as comfortable with the guitar in my hand.

Is what you're describing being in the zone?

I would say so, yes. It's where you're so comfortable in a situation that would normally bother someone else but isn't bothering you at all. You're just having pleasant time inside of what seems like it could be a very nerve-racking environment. But for you, it slows down and you can enjoy it.

And how does being in that zone musically compare to being on the mound?

Oh, they are very similar. I'm just now getting around playing enough shows where I can pick up things with my guitarist and make eye contact with the guys in the band and do the same things that you would do on the mound with your catcher or your middle infielders in a pickoff play.

But musically I still have a lot more room for growth, to where it feels like I was super comfortable on the mound. I could have the bases loaded in the World Series with nobody out and I wouldn't give a shit. I'm not there musically. But I hope to get there sometime.

Is there a certain rush you get from performing music on stage that you maybe did not get from playing baseball?

You definitely get an adrenaline rush from both which feels about even to me. The music for some reason feels a little more satisfying as you're doing it. For one, with music you've prepared yourself and there's not anyone combating you. So when you go on stage, as long as your voice is there and you feel like the band is rehearsed up, you might have one or two little blemishes in the night that only you would probably hear. But you're not going to have a train wreck second inning and give up seven runs. It shouldn't happen if you're prepared. But in baseball you can be prepared as you want to be and the shit can hit the fan really early. (Disaster) is always in the back of your mind. You can pitch four scoreless innings, and then blink and you're out of the game. You're losing 4-1 and go, 'What just happened?' That doesn't really happen on the stage.

As a pitcher you were actually a pretty good batter. You had 16 doubles in your career and even hit six home runs. What does it feel like as a pitcher to hit a major league home run?

That was a rush. In one quick moment in time, you can't compare anything in pitching to that.

Really?

You can't, because for one, I think there's just something built into a kid's mind that a home run is just really special. So it's hard to do, and it doesn't happen that often. You strike people out more often; you do a lot of things more often. But to hit a home run, it's like whoa. Even if you hit 30 in a year, it's only 30 and you might have gone to the plate 500 to 600 times. As a pitcher, you know how hard it is for us to hit. We rarely get the chance to even swing the bat sometimes, and we're bunting a lot. So when you're floating around those bases man, it's pretty hard to beat that feeling.

'My experiences with the Red Sox … are at the pinnacle of sports history,' says Arroyo.

When you hit those home runs, was there a sense of not wanting to celebrate too much because you knew what that other pitcher just went through?

Absolutely. I've given up homers to pictures, and I hit two off the same guy within five days.[1] I can definitely empathize with the fact that it's the beginning of the season, you're trying to get off to a good start and it's already tough enough to deal with everybody else. And then the pitcher gets a couple home runs off you. It's not a good feeling.

What was it about your personality that made you connect with guys from all different backgrounds?

I don't know if it's because I grew up in a household with a Cuban father and everybody else at school was pretty much American, but I just enjoyed having everybody feel comfortable around each other. When I got to the rookie league with the Pirates, I saw white guys, American Black guys and Latin dudes. It was like this weird segregation in the cafeteria. It wasn't because they didn't like each other, it was just because they weren't comfortable with each other. Latin guys are talking different language, they're using their hands, they're really loud. And other dudes are like, 'I don't know what's going on here.' Everybody's like, 'They're talking about us.'

But I was one of the few guys who could float through all circles. Some of the Latin guys, like (future All-Star) Aramis Ramirez, I would take them to the mall to get their food, to get their lights turned on, everything. They were coming from a place where they had nothing. And to this day, when those guys see me, it's like mad respect. Nobody at 18 was doing that because they

---

1. The opposing pitcher was Glendon Rusch of the Chicago Cubs.

were too scared to come out of their own (shell). And I just didn't feel that way. When people know that you won't embarrass them, and you're taking their information and giving back love all the time, and really care about their wellbeing without being selfish, that really helped me out in the game.

Take me back to what was going through your mind when your team rallied to beat the Yankees in the 2004 ALCS.

Earlier in that series against the Yankees, I got my butt kicked in Game 3. We got smoked 19-8 in Fenway Park.[2] We were down three games to none, it looked like the series was over and we came back to win four in a row.

But in that comeback two days later, I pitch out of the bullpen in the 10th inning (the score was tied 4-4). And I'm facing Jeter, A-Rod, and Sheffield. If I give up a run here, the season's over. I was on death's door. I got a pop-up, strikeout and strikeout. One of my favorite pictures I have is me jogging off the field that day in Fenway and seeing the whole crowd standing on its feet.

One year after that magical World Series run with Boston, you were traded to the Cincinnati. What did that feel like?

The Pirates took me off their 40-man roster in 2002 and offered me up to every other team. The Red Sox claiming me is really what propelled me into being a frontline Major League starter, a guy who unquestionably wouldn't go back down the minor leagues. So that was kind of a blessing.

But being traded from the Red Sox hurt after I signed an undervalued three-year deal. Both my agents did not want me to sign it. They said, 'You're going to be the most tradable guy on the planet if you sign this deal.' I said, 'I know, but 12 million bucks to a young kid from Brooksville Florida (is a lot). It's my first deal, I've got to take it just in case I get hit by a bus.'

They told me they wouldn't trade me, and five weeks later — I haven't even played a real game yet, we're in spring training — they traded me to the Reds. That was a bummer because I had just bought a house that I'd only walked into twice. I was really bummed for about two or three months that year until I could find my way into making Cincinnati feel like home. People don't realize how much your life is uprooted by the way they move you around.

You were able to come back and play for the fans in Boston in 2016 — not as a Red Sox player, but on stage with Pearl Jam. How did it feel to play *Black* in front of 40,000 people in Fenway Park?

It's my favorite song of all time. I'm standing on stage playing the acoustic guitar next to (guitarist) Stone Gossard and looking over at Eddie (Vedder), and Stone's not going up to the microphone because he doesn't feel like singing the backup vocals on it anymore. I look over at Eddie and he doesn't even speak, but I can tell by the body language, like, 'You're going to sing the backup vocal, right?'

Eddie's just genius enough to sing the low harmony on the 'duh dah dah dah do da dah' and I could do the high one, and it's just me and him going back and forth after (lead guitarist Mike) McCready just ripped a two-minute solo.

That night I really got to take it all in. I could see the tarp on the mound — because they don't

---

2. Arroyo lasted two innings and gave up six runs.

put people on the infield to keep the grass nice – and the moonlight was shining off this green target and there were 40,000 people with their cell phone lights on. That was absolutely fantastic. And there was nothing nervous about it at all. It was just pure joy to be able to stand in a place where I won a World Series, where I was being recognized by the people in that stadium for what I brought to the table baseball-wise. And I'm also standing with my favorite band since I was a 15-year-old kid and playing my favorite song of all time. It doesn't get any better than that at all.

How did you become friends with Vedder?

I first met him backstage at show in 2010. There is something about Eddie; when you walk into a room with the guy, it feels like he is just different. For some reason, Eddie just has that air about him that it almost seems like he has a little bit more insight to the answers to the universe, in a weird way. And that hasn't left, even though I've been around him a lot.

He wrote me this letter and gave me this pen that he said he wrote a lot of good songs with. And he said, 'I know it's got some good juju left in it.' I'd give away my World Series ring before I give away that pen.

What would you need to do musically to stand on par with your achievements in baseball?

I can't get there. My experiences with the Red Sox – going from losing in the playoffs to the Yankees on that Aaron Boone homerun in '03, to being the first team to ever come back from three games to none in '04 – is at the pinnacle of sports history. It's definitely in the top 10 (sports moments) of all time.

So it's just not going to happen to me musically, especially at this age. The only way you could even compare it is if I rewound myself to be a 20-year-old kid who turned out to be the lead singer of Pearl Jam, or The Who, or to be Bruce Springsteen. To go all the way to the mountaintop in two different things is going to be almost impossible.

I am super happy to play for 150 people at a rock club and just get it off my chest, man. And I don't need to go to the mountaintop musically at all. I don't aspire to, because I just know it's not reality. Baseball-wise, I felt like it was a reality to get there. And even that was a stroke of luck for me just being claimed by (former Red Sox general manager) Theo Epstein to get to the Red Sox. I could have still been in Pittsburgh at that time. So a little bit of luck had to play its way into that. And musically, it's the same thing. You have to be lucky enough to write some songs that that a mass of humans enjoy to still put 40,000 in a stadium 25 years after the inception of the band.

So I don't think about that on music level at all. I think the pinnacle of music for me is feeling like I just ripped a really nice set. And whoever happens to be in that crowd that day, whether it is 25 people or 500 people, leave saying, 'Wow man, that didn't seem like an ex-baseball player. That was a hell of a show.'

You're obviously extremely competitive, but is there a competition aspect of music for you?

My only competition musically is: Can I survive? It's almost like a marathon for me. Can I survive at the end of the race? I'm not really running against anybody else. I want to get to the end of the race, to sing 27 songs in a set and not look like I'm going to die.

What links the worlds of music and baseball for you?

It's all about going to the woodshed and just putting in the work. That really is where it's at. It actually feels good to me to be in that weight room when everyone else is on the All-Star break. And I'm just hitting the batting cage and working out. I love doing things when other people aren't doing them, when everybody has gone and nobody else wants to do the work.

There is a big similarity between that and coming down here in the basement at midnight, when everybody else is sleeping, and just absolutely rip for an hour and a half until I have nothing left. I'm so tired and my rib cage is hurt. I've come home after band practice and taken my temperature and it's like 102 F. Like, I was just getting after it. In a perfect world my voice holds up without me ever having to practice. But it's not reality. Just like it wasn't reality for me to pitch 200 innings 10 years in a row, and just take the whole offseason to go Jet Ski. So at some level, if I was going to do these things and it was going to take this much work, I would have to find a way to love the work. And I just do.

Lindsay Perry

Encinitas, California, September 2018

In life-size ads for Taylor Guitars, Lindsay Perry looks like the freckled all-American girl dressed in cutoff shorts and a cowboy hat. That's why it can be difficult to reconcile with the rocky family history that drove her to success.

At 18, Perry lost her mother and sister in a car accident and an aunt to murder. The teenager from Panama City, Florida had already been a keen guitarist and vocalist, but dove headfirst into surfing as a way to cope.

"My therapy was the ocean and surfing, to not think about the things that I had just gone through," she reflects. "So that's what saved me. Getting it out of you physically is probably the easiest way to deal with it."

Perry's surfing obsession led to competitions before a career in modeling surf clothing and equipment took off. For eight years she was featured on ads for Billabong and other leading brands. All the while, she was writing songs and developing her musicianship.

"I started writing music at 14," she says from her home in Cardiff-by-the-Sea, California, a coastal town north of San Diego. "I taught myself how to play guitar by ear. YouTube did not exist; I did not have music books. My (adoptive) dad had a Gibson guitar, and I would come home from school and pick it up and play. Apparently, I was playing chords, so that worked out."

In 2017, Perry made her mark with her album *The Dark Revival*, which debuted at No. 1 on the iTunes blues charts. Her third album, *All The Pretty Boys*, is in production at the time of writing.

One thing that strikes me about Perry during our interview is that she is very much her own boss. Now retired from pro surfing, she divides her time obsessing over her music, fulfilling her modeling obligations, being a brand ambassador and the head of her own creative firm Distinctive Noise..

"I'm freelance for everything which is kind of how I prefer it, because as you can attest to, it's hard to get me to settle on a time," Perry tells me over a candid lengthy talk, which had been rescheduled several times to work around a music video she was shooting. "My schedule changes by the flight of the wind."

Funny enough, Perry's role as a brand ambassador does not mean she is a fan of being labeled. The last thing she wants is to be pigeonholed as cute girl making surf music. Not that she has anything against fellow surfers who softly strum guitars by the beach ("I think Jack Johnson is the coolest human for sure"), but it's just not her style.

"In the surfing world, it's a much more pretty Hollywood thing, so therefore you're going to get your chipper kind of music and ukuleles," she says. "That's not real life for most people … in my case, I'm a blues musician covered in tattoos who comes from a surfing background. I like to make authentic music. I'm from the South, so it's a much different demographic."

Tell me about growing up in Florida.

I grew up in Panama City, Florida, the Redneck Riviera (*laughs*). I moved out of my parents' house, I got adopted (by my half-brother's father) at 13, and then I moved out of my adopted parents' house as 16. I moved to Satellite Beach on the east coast (of Florida) when I was 16, on my own.

So what happened there?

It certainly wasn't anything to do with me as a kid. I came from a pretty broken home when I was young. I would get free clothes and shoes from the church, and had menial backing.

So things just kind of came to a head at 13 and my mom went one way and I didn't want to go that way, so I kind of took my own route. My mom did the best that she could; it just didn't work for me at the time, and I got adopted by my brother's family. (My brother and I) have the same mom and different dad.

So that worked for me for three years, and I felt like I was capable and ready to be on my own as an adult at 16 — like a dingdong — and so I did that, and I didn't have the opportunity or option to turn back. I just had to pursue my music and my surfing as my career path. That is what I set out to do, that's why I moved out, and that was the option that I was left with. So I made it my job.

And when did you first get into surfing?

I moved out of my adopted parents' house, because I wanted to surf and they were really good conservative parents. And they were conservative about going surfing (and worried about) drowning … and I was like, 'I know more than they do.' (*Deep breath*) So I left home to be a surfer.

Then at 18, my family passed away, my mom that had separated with me, she and my sister passed away in the same car accident — and then my aunt was murdered five weeks later. I had been on my own for two years, so that was pretty wild, and then I jumped headfirst into surfing. That was my therapy, surfing.

I can't imagine the trauma you went through. How many hours were you putting in the water at this point?

All the hours? (*Laughs*) Because I was overstimulating. Like, my therapy was the ocean and surfing. It helped me to not think about the things that I had just gone through. So that's what saved me.

At that point I had been playing guitar for four years — but I put that down to get obsessed with surfing. So I got obsessed with guitar and then surfing. I'm sure you've lost people you love, so getting it out of you physically is probably the easiest way to deal with it. (Whether it's) running or whatever.

How did you get sponsored as a surfer?

I taught myself basic HTML when I was 12 and a half, I'd always been into computers, and when all that stuff was going on with my mom at 13, I carried through with computers as another therapy channel for me — like web design and so forth.

Fast forward to 16 and 17, I was surfing all day, and then at night I taught myself graphic design and web design, whatever I could do to stay busy. When I was 18, I started putting up editorial content and graphic-rich pieces on my blog, and by some grace of God, Billabong stumbled upon it when I was 22. They figured out that I surf and play music. They didn't even know anything else. It just checked all the boxes, so that's how we found each other.

What is your relationship with surfing now?

I made a healthy income from surfing by being an advocate towards the brands and marrying in the music to the surfing. I had six sponsors at one point. I'm no longer a professional surfer, which is really nice. It was a good, fun run.

So you had six surf-related sponsors at the same time; did you feel pressure?

Yeah, kind of. I'm glad that I did what I did – and I'm glad that's over. Every day you wake up and you're like, 'Am I wearing this right?' Or, 'Let me check this shirt.' And then it's like, 'Oh my God, do I have a new wrinkle? Oh shit.' Like everything that you do and are as a human being is dictated by: 'Are you on brand?' And that's a very, very difficult mindset to live in.

So some athletes don't tolerate that thought at all, and they prosper quite well. But then the ones that are super humble – we get eaten alive by that sort of mindset. Because we are so thankful to be where we are that we are just trying to acquiesce and appease the brand that we get paid by.

I can speak candidly about this now, but it was a pretty mentally daunting and tiring thing, and it's not a particular sponsor or anything like that, it's just the whole gamut. It's not like cool carefree peace signs at the ocean, it's not that at all. Because nobody's paying you to kick it.

To be an athlete and then perform music in front of crowds, there is a stigma that you have to battle. But the people I have spoken to all have one thing in common: They have no fear of failure, and if they do fail, they are like, 'Well, screw it.' Can you describe that?

Yes, that is actually a really brilliant way to position that. The best way I can describe it – not in a narcissistic manner – but I was naturally talented at something that came easy to me that I loved more than anything in the entire world, and all I wanted to do was just get to this one particular level, and I could have that notoriety and that validity and I would be there as a sponsored athlete.

So I get there and I'm like, 'Holy shit'. As soon as I put that sticker on my board, it made me nervous. My surfing became different, it became less confident, and I wasn't quite the same anymore.

But what it gave me in return was that I figured out that a stage is where I am supposed to be on, and music is what I am supposed to do. And that is my fearless most confident (place). I know where I stand in life because you learn through these athletic channels how to thrive and to fail, and then you get to find your passion and thrive from that.

I found out how to be so confident in my music through my surfing channel. Because surfing put me on these big (music) stages. I was performing at the Billabong Pipe House and the Stone Pony and these huge venues in front of a lot of people – thank goodness for my surfing career and thank God for Billabong.

Can you describe the thrill you felt when you signed with Billabong?

The greatest feeling of all time. I literally don't think that I can ever recreate that wonderful ... Oh my goodness, holy moly, yeah... I manifested that whole situation, which is really bizarre. I manifested that at 19 and it happened at 22.

Describe that. Did you visualize it first?

So at 19, after my family had passed away, my best friend called me and he said 'There is a poster of you at (surf retail store) Ron Jon.' I drove 19 miles to Cocoa Beach to go look at it. I looked at it and thought, 'Fuckin' a, the chick looks exactly like me.' So I said to my best friend that I will be surfing and modeling for Billabong by the time I am 25 and I will be on a billboard and I will be in Foam magazine and Nylon magazine. At the time they were both huge.

Well you had the drive and the determination and you put the hours in, right?

Yeah, and manifestation is one healthy thing. People don't know about that.

When you had all these sponsors, how much actual surfing were you doing, and how much was required by the sponsors?

For the longest time I was surfing a lot. But to be honest with you – and you're the first person that I've interviewed with that I will go on the record to say this – when I moved to California three and a half years ago (and first became sponsored), that really took my affection for surfing away. I just got intimidated by surfing and started shying away from it, I don't know why or how. I don't know if other athletes have felt that way, but it's a very common thing, I feel. I would end up retreating to the mountains and snowboard from November and April.

Would you say you felt anxiety from surfing?

Yeah, I would say anxiety, and once your thing that you like to do becomes the thing that you are collecting a paycheck for, it's (different). But music is not like that for me.

Do you get nerves in big waves?

Yes. I am afraid of drowning. It's a big thing that I've just learned about myself in the past few years, and I think it's because of the way I learned how to swim. I was thrown into a creek at four years old, and I'm pretty certain I just had to doggie paddle and figure that shit out. So that does not make you equipped for big waves. I wasn't taught to swim properly. Sure, I can surf fine in Florida, and if (the wave is) head high, neat, you get rumbled and you come up. But that's not like anywhere else.

That only came to light in the last few years?

I only allowed myself to think about that ... because I don't surf big waves. I don't like big waves, no thank you. But I will sit myself down more often now and think: 'OK why do you not like this?' And I came to the realization, and I was like, 'Oh, that's why.'

So for the past few years you haven't really surfed much at all?

No I haven't, and it's sad. So what I do now to rebuild my relationship with surfing in the ocean is every morning I have a regimen. I get up and swim in the ocean every morning. I'm trying to rebuild my relationship with the ocean, because I was so disconnected.

But something about surfing – everything got fucking convoluted for me. And now I'm so excited, I'm just now building my relationship with surfing and I cannot wait to paddle around a board that has no stickers on it and just go surfing. Like, that's my new thing right now.

Do you feel you get stereotyped as a laid-back surfer who plays music?

At times, yes … up until I actually play the music. I just gracefully ended an eight-year relationship with Billabong; I loved the company and they loved me, there are no qualms. It's just that I'm 30 years old now, and I want to do different things and they are moving in different directions.

When I released my first album, I was 25 or 26 and it was a very Billabong branded thing. I am super grateful for the platform that Billabong and my record label gave me to release such a rad thing. But how most surfing musicians feel is that you're capped in this industry – because it's not a music industry, it's a surf industry. Your music still has to reflect the brand that you are representing.

So no matter what music you want to play, if you're sponsored by an athletics company, you feel your music has to reflect that brand's culture and, in a sense, match the perceived culture of the sport you play in.

At the moment you have zero surf-related sponsors, right?

Yes, and I am so happy about it. All my (sponsors) are just music related.

What is your greatest achievement professionally?

I'd say that the best was *The Dark Revival*, my second album, going No. 1 on the iTunes Blues Chart in the first 15 minutes, and being on the phone with the CEO and the president of the record label. It's a mom and pop label, and on the phone they're like, 'It's No. 10! It's No. 5! It's No. 2! Holy shit this is so cool!'

I had left this Billabong meeting (ending a long term sponsorship deal) and got this tattoo that said: 'The Dark Revival.' So *The Dark Revival* is a coming of age album — all things that are dark will come to the light.

For me, it was processing shit that I saw when I was a kid and all the things that I went through, and my mom and my sister passing away and like growing up in a trailer and being fucking poor and (going through) crazy shitty fucked up things, and just letting all of those things go till the darkness comes to the light.

And so for that to be rewarded by the universe — like to go straight to No. 1 so fast, that was so lovely to me, because it was my mom smiling down on me. I felt a nod from the universe, just a nice, sweet nod from my mom or somebody, and that's the best feeling ever.

How do you combat nerves on stage?

Nervousness and excitement are the same thing; the most comfortable human being I am is on stage. Singing I get nervous, but guitar playing I cannot ever get nervous, I'm cruising.

You have such a wonderful voice, so I'm surprised.

Thank you.

What's your bigger thrill, riding that wave or being in front of a crowd playing your music?

A high is a high. Your adrenaline is your adrenaline. Now the adrenaline I get is being on a stage in front of a full crowd. I can substitute missing out on surfing for that high that I get from a crowd. I kind of feel like I conquered all of that fear and feeling (of playing to crowds). It could be like 300 people or 30,000 people, I am equipped for this. But I need to get back to that fun nervous feeling of surfing, because that is the most ultimate high ever.

More than music?

Yeah absolutely, because nature is what you are battling against, and nature changes so rapidly. You're in God's playground dancing on something that God made. Like, a stage is cool. But the ocean changes so rapidly you have to adapt, it's not adapting to you.

Can you wipe out playing music in the same way you wipe out on a surfboard?

Oh my God yeah, shit can go super awry. But the worst part about it is you're still on the same stage and the people are still there, for like 15 to 30 minutes later. They are there the whole time. So if you are surfing and you just shit the bed, you get to restart. You don't get to do that with music. You're just there and it's just weird. It's awkward. Thankfully enough, I'm good at bouncing back from fucking awkward things.

What is the current state of your modeling career? (Perry modeled globally for Billabong, ESW, Teva Guitars, Nixon watches and Spy, among other brands.)

I just started kicking back modeling again, because I did not miss that at all. I did that for 10 years. That was a whole other monetary career. Modeling was my least favorite thing to do, but now I'm having fun with it. I'm having fun with being selective. Like, I'm just happy. I'm the happiest I've ever been in my life and I feel the most radiant.

I guess that social media comes into play with that too?

(*Makes gagging sound.*)

You're not a fan of social media?

No I'm not actually, I think it's really, really bad for young gals to feel like that they need to emulate anything on that platform in order to be accepted. So I'm trying to continue to set a proper example, that you can be talented and a good person and still have a following.

Ok let's talk about the new album (*All The Pretty Boys*). You were recording in San Diego, how is it going and what is the process at the moment?

I'm doing a super cool like '60s Bond girl feel with this new album and I'm having the most fun time ever.

And you play all the instruments?

I play most of the instruments on my albums, it's really important to me.

What other instruments?

If I have to do something in the studio, I will definitely learn it for the day — like even a banjo, I will learn it on that day. Or a bass guitar, keyboards, whatever I have to learn to put on the track.

Can you describe your writing process?

It can be a thorn in my side. It's super compulsive, like I have to get it out now! I will literally be in the middle something and just have to write. So I have to lock myself in my office and be super manic and work on a song for 12 hours just to get it done.

How does that creative process with music compare to the creative process on the surfboard? Is there a connection for you?

I have always kept them entirely different. Surfing and music have no correlation to me. I am not doing Jack Johnson or any sort of surf rocky kind of thing.

What about the drive and determination that it took to be good at both, and to be professional, where did you get it from?

When my mom passed away, she was 40 and she was not able to do a lot of things. I want to be the best at anything I can be so that I can create a legacy for her. She didn't get to do any of that stuff. She didn't get to see any of those things. I didn't even know my mom wanted to be a model, I had no idea. So it's pretty cool. I get to fulfil my mom's dreams and start new ones. I am very driven to just excel at all of my personal passions and the things that I love the most, because my mom can see all the things through my eyes.

So you are doing it for both of you in a way?

I am 100 percent doing it for the both of us.

Bernie Williams

Hartford, Connecticut, February 2019

Before Bernie Williams played a vital role in four New York Yankees championships, he was a quiet kid perfecting classical guitar skills at a performing arts high school in Puerto Rico.

"Why are you playing baseball?" his puzzled guitar teacher would ask. "Don't you know that will mess up your hands?"

That teacher can be forgiven for trying to steer Williams away from the sport that would make him a legend in New York. After all, no one had a clue that the skinny 14-year-old would become a professional athlete – least of all the player himself.

"Music and sports were basically a means to an end for us," says Williams, whose mother Rufina was a high school principal and educator for 40 years. To her, those pursuits were simply not legitimate careers.

Instead, Williams had serious ambitions to become a doctor, graduating high school with a 3.8 GPA and passing the required board exam for medical school. Then baseball got in the way. Williams was spotted by a Yankees scout and shipped off to the minors just days after graduating high school at 17.

Remarkably, Rufina enrolled her son in medical school anyway, a year into his minor league start with the Yankees. "My mom still had this desire for me to get at least a college degree," he says. "She didn't realize that it was going to be way too hard to become a doctor (while playing baseball), and I didn't realize that as well at the time."

Undeterred, Williams would return to Puerto Rico to complete three semesters of course-work during his off-seasons, but was understandably falling behind. He finally reached an agreement with the dean of the medical school.

"I have this problem," Williams explained. "I cannot perform to my best abilities with my mind divided on two very demanding things."

The dean told him to pursue his dreams, while leaving the door open if things didn't work out with the Yankees. "That shifted my focus solely onto baseball. By that point I was already in Double A," Williams recalls.

'The ultimate experience'

His five-plus years in the minors were no picnic, it turned out. Williams encountered racism in parts of the mainland that had never been apparent in Puerto Rico.

"I'd never really experienced anything like that," he says, "but my parents taught me to not talk too much about myself and do my talking on the field. I would internalize a lot of stuff that was said to me and get mad, but I was able to channel all that energy. It made me a better player because it fueled my motivation."

The discipline honed from four years of music school was also on his side. Throughout his baseball career, Williams leaned on his guitar playing for comfort. "It was something that I really needed to have in my life constantly," he says.

With the Yankees, he would play along with music videos on MTV before games, or jam with teammate Paul O'Neal on drums during rain delays. On the road, Williams would test acoustics at visiting clubhouses and fingerpick intricate songs in the tunnels (the sound in Anaheim was particularly good, he says).

Known for his quiet leadership and valuable production, Williams played center field and batted cleanup for much of his long tenure in pinstripes. That was no small feat, considering he was part of some of the greatest line-ups in baseball history – including a 1998 team that won a then-record 114 games before taking the first of three straight World Series titles.

Among his numerous accolades are a 1998 American League batting title and 1996 ALCS MVP award. Williams also remains the MLB leader in career postseason RBI and is second in post-season hits and home runs. Although he played his final game in 2006, Williams did not officially retire until 2015, a quirky act of defiance against the Yankees for not being guaranteed a spot in his twilight.

"I didn't leave on the best terms with the team," he admits, clarifying his beef was with the Yankees front office and never its fans or teammates. "I was like, 'You know what? If they don't want me, I don't have anything to prove.'"

After a two-year self-imposed exodus, Williams returned to the old Yankee Stadium for a ceremony marking its final game before being torn down. Trailing the great Yogi Berra, Williams was the last announced honoree, receiving an ovation that lasted nearly two minutes from the Bronx faithful.

"It doesn't matter how you slice it, being the center fielder of the New York Yankees for 16 years – there aren't a lot of things that I can compare that with," he says. "It's just the ultimate experience in my head."

In 2015, the Yankees bestowed Williams with its highest honor, retiring his No. 51 jersey in a plaque in Monument Park, accompanying fellow Yankee center fielders Mickey Mantle and Joe DiMaggio.

The funny thing is, Williams is not so sure he hasn't reached greater heights off the field. His guitar playing has brought him to the stages of Carnegie Hall and the White House, and has garnered sessions alongside some of the greatest talents in jazz and rock. His second album *Moving Forward* was nominated for a Latin Grammy.

He even earned the college diploma that eluded him in his youth, a Bachelor of Music from the prestigious Manhattan School of Music – perhaps his proudest achievement of all. "They didn't even care who I was," he beams. "They said, 'It doesn't matter how many home runs you hit, that is not going to help you now.'"

'A palpable buzz'

The morning after a winter gig in Hartford, Connecticut, Williams meets me at the business center of the Marriott across the street from the venue. Now 50, he is dressed casually with his head closely shorn to hide his greys. In person, he is exactly how I pictured him, gracious in spirit and thoughtful with his words.

To my ears, his performance at the 350-capacity Infinity Hall went without a hitch. The audience chanted his name as he strolled onto the stage, as though he was stepping up to face Pedro Martinez in his heyday. The former slugger toyed with the crowd, asking if there were any Red Sox fans in the house.

Then the first chords were struck and a palpable buzz took over for 90 minutes. He improvised jazz solos on electric and acoustic guitars, playing off a talented group of musicians gathered that night as the Bernie Williams Collective (he also gigs with the Bernie Williams All-Star band).

Afterward, the meet and greet line stretched to a two-hour wait. Always the gentleman, Williams flashed every fan a smile while politely soaking in their adulation.

Bernie and I budget two hours for the interview but extend to nearly three, covering the most pivotal life moments that have shaped his dual-careers.

They include his relief efforts for Hurricane Maria, the 2017 storm that devastated Puerto Rico. Nearly 3,000 were killed and much of the island was stranded without power. Two years later, Williams was still making two trips a month from his home in New York to support his motherland, following the example of his baseball idol Roberto Clemente.

Around the same time that I conceptualized this book, I realized Williams co-wrote his own book on the topic: *Rhythms of the Game: The Link Between Musical and Athletic Performance*. It's a fascinating read delving further into the science of performance, getting into terms like alpha state and beta state.

This book would simply not be complete without his involvement. I can't count the number of times I described its premise to people, only to hear back, 'Have you spoken to Bernie Williams?'

As a matter of fact, I have.

Some athletes who take on music say they have to work two or three times as hard to convince people their music is legit. They almost have to overcome their past; have you experienced that?

I've thought about that numerous times. And the one thing that I realize is that there are two types of crowds. The people that support and follow you because of what you did before, they'll be fine with whatever you present to them. But then there's another type of audience that comes to see the shows, and they are the skeptics — the people that come in saying, 'Let me see what this guy has. What is this buzz about?' And those are the people that you try to convince with what you do. But at the same time, if you think too much about that, then I think it robs you from the joy of actually performing.

Music has this great thing that I find so interesting. For instance, if you look at a painting, you have all the time in the world to admire it and see all the details. There's no time limit. With music, you can enjoy it as it comes in time, and it's those moments in time that that you live for as a musician. Because when it's right, dude, there's nothing like it in the world.

There's nothing like it in the world — except maybe hitting two World Series home runs?

Well yeah, that is true (*big smile*). But that is such a really quick moment in time. The amount of time that I spent actually enjoying that particular moment was probably less than a minute or two. You hit the ball, you run the bases, you're elated, and then it's over. You have to think about the next play, the next at-bat, the next game, the next year.

So it's just that little snippet of time that you kind of get in your heart and you keep it there for you to reminisce. But in terms of the actual moment in time when you're enjoying the thing that you're doing? Music is definitely a lot more vast and a lot more complex.

How much of your playing was improvised yesterday?

A lot of it was. The only thing that I have to memorize is what I would call the head. Like the initial melody that hooks people — and then everything after that is just improvising on those chord structures and those chord progressions. So a lot of my playing relies on me knowing how to navigate through chord changes within this kind of music.

I don't really play too much of the melodies when I'm practicing, but I do try to play my scales and my arpeggios and my pentatonics and try to connect the dots. I try to have this spatial awareness of my musical dexterity, because I can apply that knowledge to any kind of music that I go into.

I know about the story of your father being a merchant marine who came home with a Spanish guitar and taught himself to play from a book. At what point did you start to learn guitar?

I asked him to teach me how to play, so he taught me my first couple of chords. And when I was probably 7 or 8 years old I showed tremendous affinity for it. It's like something lit inside me. So I spent a lot of my childhood pursuing music after that first encounter with a guitar. I took lessons with the neighborhood teacher, and then spent four years in a performing arts high school.

I was astounded when I first heard about that.

Yeah, I took (the encouragement) from my mom, it was all a means to an end. She believed in a well-rounded educated person and tried to raise us that way [ED: Williams' older brother Hiram is also a musician]. She wasn't really musically inclined or sports inclined, even though she had two brothers who played baseball, one professionally. My dad was never a sports person, but he was a very athletic person, so they were basically trying to give us all kinds of options as we were growing up.

What was it like at that school?

I was playing guitar. They made me audition to see if I had the aptitude to learn music in an organized way. The ability to know the difference between a minor or major chord, and recognize different pitches. Sort of general stuff that a kid would notice.

So that got me into the school, but it didn't have a physical education program in its curriculum. I had to rely on outside sources to keep exercising. The first half of the day from 7:30 a.m. to 12:30 p.m. we took all the academic classes, English, Spanish literature, science, mathematics, and one fundamentals of music theory or harmony. The other half of the day you would break into groups. I would go with the guitar players and the kids playing a Puerto Rican instrument called a cuatro. It's kind of a mandolin with a lower register. It was a very immersive experience in music for a high school.

And how did baseball and track and field come into play?[1]

They were extracurricular activities. My education was over for the day at 3 p.m., then it was all athletics. I would go into a baseball field or track field or basketball court and play organized sports.

After that I would go home — which was about an hour away from the school — by 8:30 or 9 p.m., exhausted. We would get something to eat, finish a little bit of homework, and be ready to wake up at 5 a.m. the next day to do the whole thing again.

At that point was your biggest passion music or sports?

I loved them both equally. I felt excited to do both; in hindsight I can't really tell.

While at performing arts school, did you think you could become a professional musician?

No, I never did, and I think it was because of the insistence of my mom. In her eyes, she never envisioned sports or music as legitimate ways of making a living (*laughs*). In her mind, she was presenting us with a lot of options to become a good doctor or a good engineer or a good architect or a good lawyer.

So baseball presented itself as a pro career earlier than music?

Yes, pursuing baseball was more of a function of the opportunity presented to me at that time. Music was never in the picture. It happened when I was about 15 or 16. I was playing at a higher level in baseball. Back then you had all the scouts that would come to the island to sign people up that young.

---

1. Williams won three golds in the 1984 Central Caribbean and Caribbean Junior Championships in sprinting events.

Williams hits a home run in the 2003 World Series as Florida Marlins catcher Ivan Rodriguez looks on.

You got scouted by the Yankees at 16. How did that feel?

I was a little nervous, because at that time I wasn't even the best player on my team.

Really?

That's absolutely correct. Juan Gonzalez and I grew up together and played on the same team. He was playing right field and I was playing center field. And most of the scouts on the island went to watch us because they wanted to see that guy play (*laughs*).[2]

And, for some reason, the scout that the Yankees sent – a Puerto Rican guy named Roberto Rivera – he took a look at Juan Gonzalez and Juan seemed a little bit distracted at the time, just kind of mingling with the girls on the side, and dancing to the music and being a bit distracted. And he saw me really focused with my game face, and he said from that time on he shifted his attention to me. And then he went full-on pursuing me to sign with the Yankees.

---

2. Gonzalez, a two-time American League MVP, is in the Texas Rangers Hall of Fame.

You left Puerto Rico at 17 and didn't get into the big leagues till you were 22, so you bounced around the minors for more than five seasons, which I've heard little about. What cities were you in?

I was in Fort Lauderdale, Florida, in Sarasota, Florida, in Albany, New York, in Columbus, Ohio, and Prince William in Virginia.

Was that tough for a kid from San Juan to go to those small towns on the mainland?

Yes, at the beginning it was really tough because I didn't have any experience dealing (with that environment). That was basically my college experience, what people would call coming into age and becoming an adult. I had to do it through my minor league experience.

The responsibility for taking care of myself, paying bills, having roommates, having teammates, cooking, surviving, and still having this focus of trying to make it through the ladder to be a Major League Baseball player at 17.

I credit my success in that process to my parents. They were relentless. And they were very supportive. I think they realized that they still had a kid out there. They went to the States at least once or twice a year during the season to make sure that I was fine. Those first couple of years they were very present in my process.

I read that (former Puerto Rican Yankee teammate) Jorge Posada got into a bunch of fights as he was coming up through the system in Alabama. Did those kinds of things happen to you in the minors?

No, I never really got into squabbles with people. I was more of a non-confrontational person. If you were in the South, obviously you were going to be exposed to a lot of racism and things that I was never really exposed to in Puerto Rico. There's racism everywhere, but so blatantly open – I'd never really experienced anything like that.

But my parents taught me to not talk too much about myself, and do my talking on the field. I would internalize a lot of stuff that was said to me and get mad. But I channeled all that in a positive way, even though maybe it was not the ideal way to get into the process. Coming up as a young player, it was really educational. I had to learn when to speak, when to actually stand up for myself and when to be wise and say, 'You know what, I'll prove it to you on the field.'

As a baseball player, you don't want to be so confrontational that you are deemed a problem, a troublemaker. That would put you in a in a corner and stop your progress – but at the same time you don't want people to walk all over you. So there's always a grey line, a balance that you have to keep. And navigating those waters at 17, 18, 19 years old it was a really interesting experience to go through.

Did you have your guitar with you in the minors on the road?

All the time. I had a Spanish guitar; it just became just part of who I was.

There was talk of getting traded in the first few years with the Yankees.

Oh, yeah.

How did that feel?

It didn't feel good. But there are a lot of life lessons that I learned in that process. There are two sides to being a professional athlete: the business side and then the actual playing side, which is the thing that people would kill for – and that was the one thing that I was so grateful to have the opportunity to do that nobody could take away from me.

So I used to focus on that side. This is what brings me joy, the competition, playing the game, just interacting with my teammates and going into psychological battles. That made the game so special to me.

The business side was something that I learned not to take personally. I knew that I had the control of that narrative by the way that I played. There was no reacting to comments. If you let that get in your head, then it will impact the way that you play.

At what point did you feel secure with your spot on the Yankees?

Probably when I signed my long-term deal (in 1998, after becoming a free agent for the first time and receiving offers from other teams). At the end of the day I decided, if it ain't broken why try to fix it?

You were also playing with some pretty good players.

Yeah, we had a good thing going after the '98 season. It's a great thing that I was able to stay in New York.[3]

But you didn't officially retire until 2015!

Well, I technically stopped playing in 2006. That's the more accurate expression, I stopped playing. I considered offers from other teams, but at that point I didn't want to sacrifice two or three more years playing for a team that I didn't know. It was time to come back and focus on my family.

And I didn't leave on the best terms with the (Yankees). They offered me a minor league deal; (that's) the business aspect of it. And I was like, 'You know what? If they don't want me, I don't have anything to prove. I think this relationship has run its course.'

I also had the music thing going and was feeling excited about the possibility of just starting something new and different in music. So that was another trigger.

Walking away from the game must have been difficult.

It was difficult – but would have been a lot more difficult had I not had music in my life – something to fall back on after playing baseball.

It doesn't matter how you slice it, being the center fielder of the New York Yankees for 16 years, there aren't a lot of things that I can compare that with, you know? It's just the ultimate experience in my head.

But like any other thing that you're accustomed to doing for years and years, when you stop doing it, people stop calling. They stop considering you as a player, they say maybe you're over the hill, you're old. It's like this grieving process you go through, like losing your best friend.

I can't imagine the people that don't have anything else to fall back on. They have to basically

---

3. After Williams signed his deal in 1998, the Yankees made the playoffs every season until his last in 2006.

linger around the game, whether as a broadcaster or a coach or somebody involved with the team – because they don't have anything else to focus on. That's all they have. And even then, you're going through this process. Depending on your personality, you can get into a lot of trouble – because this adrenaline rush that you feel for the game of baseball, it's all or nothing.

Especially playing in New York with the whole atmosphere, it's like everything happening at the same time. Every day you go a hundred thousand miles an hour. You can be the goat of the game or you can be the hero of the game, and there's nothing in between.

So that's where music came into play. It replaced that zeal that I have for the rush for the game – because with music I didn't see a ceiling. There's no way that you can stop learning. And that really motivated to me to think, I can put the same focus and the same intensity and the same passion that I did into baseball and still not even come close to Beethoven.

So you had a long transition.

The whole putting an end to the actual mindset of being a player happened about two years after I stopped playing, probably in 2008.

And is that when you decided to get your degree in music?

I initially took classes at the State University of New York in Purchase, two years after I stopped playing. I wasn't really focused on getting a degree, but at that point, my life just kind of went upside down. I got divorced and it kind of put a stop to that process.

I needed to get my life together again, see where I was going to stand with my kids and my whole relationship and all that. So it wasn't until seven years after I stopped playing that I auditioned for the Manhattan School of Music.

What made you decide to enroll?

I always have this thing with my mom in the back of my head saying, 'You need to get your education. It doesn't matter how much money you have. It doesn't matter how much fame and popularity you have, you still need your degree.'

So I thought, why not put all the credits together – the ones from 20 years ago in medical school and ones from SUNY Purchase – and see what's left for me to get a degree?

So I called the department of admissions at The Manhattan School of Music and they didn't take me seriously at all. They thought it was a crank call! Eventually, they gave me an audition in front of a panel of instructors. They were like, 'OK, what you got?'

How did the nervousness of being in front of that panel compare to the nervousness of playing in in the Yankee Stadium for the first time?

Oh very comparable, because I didn't know what to expect, and I didn't know if I had what it took. That was probably partly fear in both cases. I tend to underrate myself. If I'm going to make an error, I'm going to err on the side of being too cautious.

But once I got in, and I had a general idea of what the whole thing was about, then I could develop a plan of action. And once that process of preparation gets in place, then it's a lot easier to navigate anything that you set your mind to.

I saw a video of you graduating in a cap and gown in 2016, you had this huge smile.

Oh, that was great.

You were obviously very proud. Why was that so important to you?

It was probably one of the hardest things that I've ever had to do after my baseball career. This is the stuff that kids do when they're young, when they have the energy and all the time in the world, and I was coming into it deep in my 40s. Most of the kids there, I could have been their father.

You know, they didn't even care who I was. They said, 'It doesn't matter how many home runs you hit, that is not going to help you now.'

So I was like any other person. (My background) didn't even catch up to them until my last semester. They were whispering, 'That's the baseball guy.' Before that, it was a process of learning at a very high intensity level with people that could run laps around me, because many of these kids were on scholarships as musical geniuses.

There were people coming from all over the world who started at 3 or 4 years old. By the time they're 18 or 19 they were already savants, and I was coming in like, 'I'm gonna be in trouble here.'

But that raised your game.

It did, and it made me realize that in order for me to function in the school socially I had to earn their respect, in a weird way. So I took the intensity that I had in my preparation as a baseball player and moved it right into music. Before, it was throwing, hitting, batting practice, soft toss and all these drills, then it all shifted into arpeggios, harmonics, theory, ear training and all that stuff. I really got into it, and it was a beautiful process.

After two years, I started earning their respect. These other kids would ask me to jam, and I felt like, 'Oh, I am part of this thing. Yeah!'

It was like proving yourself back in the minors all over again.

Yeah, exactly. That was the same process.

You mentioned that the realities of the baseball business hit you a few times. Have you faced any pressures in the music industry since your transition?

I had a lot of things in my favor going into music at the age that I was, mainly: I already had a career. I didn't have to rely on music to make a living. That freed a whole world of possibilities. I didn't have to tour 300 days out of the year and play weddings and bar mitzvahs or do all these things that working musicians usually have to do.

So I was in a unique position to choose the things that I wanted to do in the music industry, because I already had a built-in audience and following. I didn't have to go through the whole process of becoming a new and upcoming artist — but at the same time, I'm not there yet, you know. It's like this place somewhere in between.

My whole intention for being a musician was not necessarily to be the guy in front of the band living this rock star life. I wanted to be a real musician. I wanted to be able to go to Siberia and play some Russian music, I wanted to go to the Middle East and play with all those people. I wanted to go to Boston and play with the Boston Pops – so it's like being an eloquent speaker that knows different languages. Because if you're good at music, it's the same language everywhere. You hit the first note and you're already talking.

But (being a front man) was something that never appealed to me.

You say that, but I saw you yesterday and you had a great rapport with the crowd.

Yeah, that has been a process. It didn't start that way.

How did you develop that?

Two things: one, the preparation and feeling secure enough in my playing that I didn't have to worry about every note – being so worried about my performance that it would take away from the joy of actually enjoying it. And two, repetition. The more I did it, the more I realized that it wasn't a baseball game. It was like half of the people in the crowd are not actually rooting for me to strike out (*laughs*), they actually want a good show. So they're rooting for me to do well. Knowing that there's a lot of great energy and goodwill and a desire to be entertained and have a good time, it really lifted a lot of pressure off me. Because even the mistakes were thought of as funny moments in the show, funny and unique.

Do you watch videos of Freddie Mercury at Live Aid or things like that to learn to be a frontman?

I do, I do.

Please share what you've learned.

There's a certain aspect of showmanship that has to be thought of and looked at as genuine. I'm not faking this, what I'm doing right here, this is not a show. This is who I am. As long as I am able to give them that, then I think that's a really good exchange.

The process is twofold. It's the ability to engage a crowd into what you're doing and bring them into your world, and have enough confidence in your ability to make it seem effortless. Like, the playing is just what I do and I'm just kind of chilling here. But what they don't see is the amount of man hours that it takes to get to that level.

Once you are on stage, you don't want to be seen like a guy working really hard at something really tough. You want to be seen as this guy who was born for this. Look at him. He's just having the time of his life. He's got total control of what he's doing.

I recently saw the Grammys and a lot of those performances were done with such reckless abandon, just going for it without a safety net. They were (thinking), I'm daring myself to do this, and I dare you to listen to what I'm saying. As long as I'm in the mindset to get to that point, I'll keep working on my craft relentlessly.

What is the World Series of music for you? How do you envision that?

That's a difficult question because, it was easy for me to measure my success in baseball. Success is about your numbers; everything is tangible. It is about your production and your stats. Playing at that level requires you to have this default sense of your skill level. Baseball was straight up competition in a very highly intense dramatic, nerve-racking environment. And it was all based on production. It has great perks, but psychologically it wears you down. Music, however, is a very different thing, because there are no stats for notes played. There are no stats for bad concerts.

Thank God.

Exactly! It's just about people being entertained and having a good time. I measure my success in music by the places that I get to play in and the people that I get to play with. Money is an afterthought at this point.

So it's like, who do I get to play with? Is it James Taylor? Is it Bruce Springsteen? Is it the Brecker Brothers? Is it Will Lee? Are they calling you back to play with them because they liked what you bring to the table?

If you get to play Jazz at Lincoln Center, you get to play Carnegie Hall, Radio City Music Hall and all these places, it's because they think that you have the ability. To me that's a sign of success.

Let's talk about being in a zone. You were clearly there in the '96 ALCS, when you hit three home runs in two days off the Texas Rangers, including one from each side of the plate on the same day.[4]

Yeah, I remember that day.

Describe that mindset.

I call it effortless mastery. You have a perfect storm of the mental aspect of preparation. One, being secure in the fact that you've done everything you can to be ready for this particular part of the season; two, having the confidence of not having any lingering injuries that would limit your performance. And three, you have the intangible breaks that happen because you've put yourself in that situation to be successful. To have that confidence, and to have that preparation knowing that you're ready, and then have all these breaks happening at the same time is insane.

At that point the game really slows down. You still have less than a second to make a decision to swing at a ball or not, but it seems like you have five seconds. And the ball is coming at you in this sort of slow motion kind of thing, and you're able to see every stitch of the ball come in the rotation, and you are able to recognize the pitch.

It's a curveball, it's inside, it's outside, and you still have enough presence of mind of thinking, 'I'm going to wait and to hit the ball at the right time, wherever it's pitched.' Everything is happening within a second, and you have this great mental awareness. I don't know if I can explain it any better than that.

Do you feel the same way about music?

No, I did not. This is what's so interesting. With music I would have what I would describe as 'sparks of brilliance.' There's a moment within the course of a tune when I play a run, and I will say, 'Whoa, I love that.' But then I have to forget about it, because I need to think about the next chord. I need to think about the next song. And I need to think about what I am going to say to the audience after the song is done, or what joke I'm going to tell. So it's a little different.

---

4. ESPN has ranked Williams as the seventh greatest switch hitter in MLB history.

But I am finding that those sparks of brilliance are becoming more common the more I play. Maybe I would have one in every five concerts, and now every time I play, I find that there's that point in the concert.

How do you conquer anxiety? Did you ever even have to?

Oh yeah, anxiety is good. I think anxiety is basically one of two emotions that you feel – either anxiety or excitement – that correlate directly to your level of preparation. If you feel like you're prepared and you have control of what you're playing and you feel comfortable, then what you feel is not anxiety. It's more like the jitters. Like, 'Yeah, I'm ready to do this. I'm excited. I'm ready to go.'

It's like adrenaline?

Yeah, it's like an adrenaline rush. And it's very intense. But if you're not prepared, you feel like you're lacking or you're unsure what's the outcome is going to be, then the excitement is not excitement. And that can be unnerving.

Do you use visualization techniques?

Yeah, all the time. Especially when I was playing baseball. There were rumors of me falling asleep before the games, but that was basically me closing my eyes and trying to picture myself in a situation in which I was facing the ultimate success.

I would have a whole movie (in my head), almost in slow motion. Getting ready, the pitcher staring, then throwing the pitch at me, cocking back and making contact, hitting the ball right there. Making contact and seeing the ball going out of the stadium and me running the bases.

I would just slow it down with the whole atmosphere of the crowd jumping up and down, cheering —and it's all in this slow-motion highlight kind of thing. It would take me three, four or five minutes to get through the whole process, because I'd slow it down to almost frame by frame and then wake up from that sort of trance-like state and I'll be like, 'I'm ready to go. I got this.'

And then I would go into the game and most likely encounter a situation in which my performance would determine the outcome. I think every player has that opportunity within the course of the game where you feel like the game is on your court right now.

It could be a diving catch in the first inning. That might have been the play that saved the game. It's a matter of getting yourself mentally prepared once you know that you're physically prepared. You have to trust your preparation. It's that process of just saying to yourself – literally – 'I've done the preparation, I know what it takes, and I'm ready to take this on.'

Like a mantra.

Yeah, I had to say it to myself many times. Sometimes it flowed, sometimes you have to sort of nudge yourself a little bit, but it's part of being a professional player.

Were there any big concert visualization moments?

I don't know if you know this, but there's footage of me playing *Take Me Out to the Ball Game* at Fenway Park (in Boston), and they made this as a tribute to (long time Yankee captain) Derek

Jeter's last season.[5]

I saw that, I didn't realize it was in Fenway. Oh boy.

That was the first time that I wasn't booed at Fenway!

That's like being in the Roman Colosseum with the lions!

Yeah exactly, and to me that was a pressure-packed situation. And I had to rely on the only thing that I could: my preparation. I literally was able to play that tune (at any time). I would wake up at 2, 2:30, 3 in the morning and I could grab my guitar and out of the blue play the tune perfectly.

That's the level of proficiency that I needed to play that tune in Fenway Park. That was one of the ultimate things that I did, and it was all live. There was no tape. No nothing. It was like: You have to perform.

What is the achievement you're most proud of in baseball?

To be part of the healing process of the nation after 9/11. That's one of my proudest moments of being a professional athlete.[6]

I didn't think that we were even important, and I didn't really find any meaning to my profession. Like, we need doctors here. We need law enforcement. We need medical staff and support people that can help try to bring us back to normalcy.

I never in a million years considered that our presence — being able to play baseball and reinstate (a routine) — was going to have such an impact on people's attitude towards rebuilding. Even though we lost, it just took people away from all that craziness. And for a moment in time they were like, 'Wow, maybe we can enjoy something that we were always able to enjoy. And these people are not going to take that away from us.'

Finally, what links the two worlds for you, sports and music?

It's the process that you go through in any discipline that you get into. There are a couple of default things you need to be successful. You need to pay attention to detail, you need to have a plan of action. You need to have spatial awareness and the elasticity of mind to make adjustments — sometimes on the run, sometimes from at-bat to at-bat.

If you strike out on a blown inside pitch, then at the next at bat, you know for sure that he's going to try to throw it to you again. Making the adjustment shows that you have this elastic mind, like a high performance computer that can refresh itself.[7]

---

5. Williams has composed an intricate acoustic version of *Take Me Out to the Ball Game* which he performs at his shows as an encore.

6. The Yankees played in the 2001 World Series just seven weeks after 9/11, losing to the Arizona Diamondbacks in seven games.

7. The elastic mind Williams describes is tied to cognitive flexibility, a quality that Professor Martin Norgaard of Georgia State University discovered is enhanced by learning musical improvisation as a teenager. This is described in greater detail in on pages 12 to 14.

Rony Seikaly

Miami, February 2019

It's 7:30 a.m. on a Sunday morning in Downtown Miami.

Most sensible people are still lying in bed, but Rony Seikaly is halfway through a scorching DJ set at the roof deck of Club Space. Three thousand revelers in sunglasses and colorful gear groove to pulsating beats under smoke effects that obscure a glorious Florida sunrise.

Only a few are aware that the near-seven-footer behind the decks was once a dominant force in basketball, an NBA star with the ability to post 40 points on Michael Jordan's Bulls and still hold the Miami Heat team record of 34 rebounds in a game.

And that's exactly how he likes it.

Back when Seikaly was carving a name for himself in house music, long before he secured a hit radio show with SiriusXM and flew to Ibiza and Dubai for gigs, the Beirut-native would pretend to be someone else behind the decks — as unlikely as that may seem.

"I'd tell people, 'No, he's my brother,' or something like that," he recalls of his attempts at anonymity during the first stages of his professional DJ career. "It's just that I wanted people to judge me on the music that they were hearing and not who I am. And that was a struggle. That's when the overdrive kicked in. I said, 'You know what? I'm going to keep doing this to prove to everybody that I am my own guy. And I'm not doing this for anything else besides the love of the music.'"

In the few hours I spent with Seikaly in his beautiful Miami waterfront home, it was clear that he was indeed his own man. This is, after all, the same college grad who told the Charlotte Hornets not to pick him in the 1988 NBA Draft because he was determined to move to Miami, warning them he would play in Greece instead.

"You do those crazy, stupid things when you're a kid," Seikaly shrugs. His bravado turned out to be a blessing as he fell in love with the city and led the Heat to a playoff berth in just its fourth year of existence.

That individuality came into play again early in his career, after Magic Johnson contracted HIV. Seikaly challenged the retired Lakers great to a physical game of one-on-one in front of teammates, just as NBA peers voiced concern about Johnson's participation in the 1992 All-Star Game. "I wanted Magic to feel he was one of us," he told Sports Illustrated. "Just because he was infected didn't mean he wasn't a human being."

'Changing the barrier to entry'

Seikaly flourished in his four years at Syracuse University, where his number is now retired, calling them the best years of his life. He played in the most competitive era of Big East basketball, holding his own against the likes of Georgetown's Patrick Ewing and leading the team's magical run to the 1987 Final Four.

He arrived in Syracuse by accident, walking into the school's summer basketball camp only because he was bored after visiting his brother at nearby Colgate University. When legendary coach Jim Boeheim saw him dunking and blocking shots against the camp's councilors – all of whom were either active or former players for the Orange – he thought someone had played a prank on him. How could a high school prospect with that size and ability go unnoticed by scouts? When he could not find any hidden cameras, Boeheim pulled out a letter of intent on the spot and committed Seikaly to a four-year scholarship.

As a Lebanese citizen who grew up in Greece, Seikaly was an anomaly at a time when there were only a few foreign-born players in the NBA – and none from the Middle East. He found himself trying to please fans from his birth country and adopted country, while struggling with the me-first culture that pervades certain NBA locker rooms.

"Outside the basketball court, I felt a little bit like people didn't accept me being from Lebanon. It was really hard. The press, the majority of people thinking I'm from Lebanon automatically assumed me to be a bad guy," Seikaly explained to CU360.

"I was this guy changing the barrier of entry. I was this foreigner … Like, 'This guy's from another planet.' It wasn't easy. People didn't understand. You don't have the information that you have today."

Seikaly's family sent him to Athens at the age of 11, after one too many brushes with danger – including a bomb that went off in his apartment block. While playing at Syracuse, his uncle was kidnapped and reporters flocked to campus to speak to him. It was all a little "too close to home" for some, says Seikaly, who revealed that he was called "a terrorist" and other epithets during his playing days. "This is the stigma I came with," he sighed.

Seikaly's jarring childhood memories from the Lebanese civil war came rushing back in August 2020, after the huge explosion that flattened Beirut's port nearly killed his parents, who were staying in their nearby home. The determination that made him a star NBA player and a hero to lovers of house music came into play with a fundraising effort that has collected nearly $600,000 to date on behalf of the thousands left homeless in the city.

'An artist's mind trapped in an athlete's body.'

While Seikaly logs hours each week creating music, he maintains a third career as an in-demand real estate developer. After a stint of owning restaurants and nightclubs — mostly for enjoyment and to listen to great music — he now builds luxury homes catered to the Miami elite.

"I do have a very architectural mind," he says, lounging in his ultra-modern house which he designed and decorated with fine art by the likes of Rashid Johnson. Along with balancing all his interests, Seikaly is mindful of having quality time with his family. He is a father to teenager Mila, an avid tennis player, and toddler Aya with his second wife, the Brazilian model and businesswoman Martha Graeff. They also welcomed a goldendoodle puppy named Boris into the family.

After our interview, Seikaly showed me his custom-built nightclub — complete with an extra-high platform for his decks — where he hosts late-night events for friends. The practice began as a gangly high schooler at the American Community School of Athens, where he would throw parties for players of visiting teams in his converted parents' garage.

"I have an artist's mind trapped in an athlete's body," he says, noting that he has produced enough original music to fill 500 albums. "I'm not sure what it is, but I love creating and seeing where it goes."

'To me, music is about the story that you're telling,' Seikaly says.

What's a day in the life of Ronnie Seikaly?

I like to make my music, so it depends on how late those nights go. I get really creative between midnight and 6 a.m. when everybody's asleep. So no phones are ringing, nobody's asking any questions. I'm focused; I'm in my own little cocoon. Sometimes I get into that inspired mode in my music room and I'll knock out a track every single day.

And then the first thing I do when I wake up is go work out. Sports and music go hand in hand for me. If I don't do both, I get stressed out.

So you're a nocturnal person?

That's when I get the most creative because you don't have the disruptions. You know, the worst thing when you're focused and onto something is somebody going 'Hey, excuse me...' and then it all goes away. To me, it's more like meditation. So I'm in the moment.

Can you get to that moment when you're DJing in clubs?

In the clubs, it's different. You try to portray a story that you've just spent so many hours creating and see how the story resonates with the people that are in front of you. And that is the joy. To me, music is about the story that you're telling.

A lot of people don't understand house music. They think it all sounds the same, but house music is a little bit like classical music. It's all the intricate sounds. There are no vocals in classical music, there is no catchy stuff. It's the strength of the actual sounds and what the story is and how dramatic it is. So that's more my vibe. The nice thing about house music is that there are no rules to making that music. It is whatever you're feeling. And the stuff that I put out is what I feel.

Do you use any visualization techniques to get yourself in the mood to DJ at big clubs?

No. I think the training that I got from basketball, playing in front of so many people and the pressure of dealing with that for so many years became so second nature that going up in front of 1,000 people a club is kind of like nothing. I used to play in front of 30,000 spectators and millions of people on TV, with reporters on the sidelines criticizing every move I made. So that was more pressure. This is just a story now. Music is so subjective. There is no right or wrong; it's whether you like it or not. And if your music can attract more than just a very niche market, then that's what your sound is.

Did you get nervous on the basketball court?

When you're playing in athletic competitions and it's a big game, you always have the butterflies in your stomach because there's so much at stake. Not only are you playing for the name on the back of the jersey, which is your name, but you're also playing for your team, for your city, for your college or whatever it is. So you are representing a whole bunch of people.

Which leads to some pressure.

Sure. Yeah, it leads to some pressure. Sometimes I look back now, and I don't know how I did it.

Right: The crowd at Club Space Miami revels to Seikaly's sunrise set.

Really?

Yeah, I tell you honestly, I don't know how I did it. I see the pressure; I watch all these games in different sporting events played in front of all these people yelling and screaming at you. And the fact that you just tune everything out. In college, we played in the NCAA Finals against Indiana and there were 64,000 people in the stadium.[1]

And now I think about it and say, 'Wow, how did I even walk out there?' But back then, it just kind of seemed like nothing. You just had those butterflies in your stomach. But never any kind of extra nervousness in any way. It's just butterflies.

What do you remember about growing up in Beirut during the civil war?

What do I remember? Nothing good. None of the memories of that time are good. I would just hear the sound of machine guns, the sound of bombs. We had a bomb go off in our building. There was an office for a (targeted) magazine editor on the second floor of the building where we used to live. And every day, I would run up the stairs because we lived on the third floor. That day, I went up the stairs and as soon as I walked in and went into the hallway, there was a big vacuum. I still see it in slow motion, 40-something years later. Everything came in and just went boom.

How did you not get taken with the blast?

Luck. It was just a matter of seconds. Now, if I had been three steps back that door would have blown up on me, or had I still been walking up the steps, I would have died.

Was that when your parents decided to leave the country?

Well, no. Actually, everybody was still hopeful then. When you're in a civil war, you always think that they're going to resolve the issues, that it's just a temporary thing. And where are we going to go? This is where my dad had his business. You can't just pick up and go.

I read that you had friends who were killed during the war.

That's just part of the experience. The reason why I left Lebanon is because I started getting involved in the war itself. There was this guy who worked for my dad, and he figured that, to make me a man, I needed to go and witness fighting up close. He would take me to the danger zones of Beirut and make me watch the street fights between this building and that building. So the memory of that is just crazy. Getting there and getting out. And shooting from close range. So at some point — you're young, you're fearless, you don't know what you're doing — I said, 'Oh, this looks cool. I want to be involved.' And as soon as I got involved, I was holding a machine gun. And we had a roadblock on one of the streets in Beirut, in the Hamra area. And I stopped a car that happened to belong to a friend of my mom's, and she said, 'You're that guy!' And I said, 'No, I'm not. Go.' And 15 minutes later, my dad and a bunch of people came there, threw me in the back of the car and shook me up.

How old were you?

I was 10.

---

1. Syracuse lost the 1987 championship game by one point at the Louisiana Superdome.

Do you have any mental scars from those days?

I have mental images, but not mental scars.

When did music first take off for you?

My dad was a music fanatic. He had lot of LPs. I remember as a kid that my dad had the sickest sound systems; the stereo in the house was always state-of-the-art. And every Sunday he would blast classical music. It was heaven for him and my mom. Obviously, to me, I was just going to jump off the balcony listening to classical music. But that's what I grew up on. So I think I got the musical DNA from my dad. We had a garage in our house in a suburb of Athens, and I asked him if I could turn it into a little room for myself so I could play the music that I like. So with some equipment that he wasn't using, I made a makeshift club.

And when we used to play against opposing teams — we were 14 or 15 years old, so we couldn't go to clubs — I would invite all these kids to come over to my club and charge them $1 or whatever, it was just minimal stuff. And whatever I made for the night I would use to upgrade my sound system to the point where it became like a real club, with lights, speakers, turntables, a mixer, the whole thing. That's where the evolution of having a club in the house started. And 40 years later, there hasn't been a house that I've built that that doesn't have a club in it.

You resisted playing basketball to rebel against people's expectations because of your height. But a chance meeting with Greek basketball legend Takis Koroneos at his sporting goods store changed your mind. Can you describe discovering your love for the game?

When you have talent for anything, things come easier. You don't have to try too hard and you keep improving all the time. I've been playing tennis all the time and my improvement is (flat). I can't get up there because I don't have the talent for it. With basketball, every time I played until the last day, I felt like I was improving. So the day I started playing basketball it didn't feel weird to me. He didn't have to explain any of the drills to me. I don't know if it was my athletic ability, but it just came easy to me.

I started playing street ball and became addicted. I wanted to be the best player on the (high school) team. At the time, we had a lot of players from the American (military) bases, and those guys were always good and tough. So my goal was to be better than all those guys. And that didn't take that long. When you have a talent for something and you find it, it's a nice thing.

When did you realistically think you could become a professional?

As soon as I focused in on basketball, I said, 'I'm in,' and my goal was to make the NBA.

How did your parents feel about that? When I told my parents I wanted to write, they looked at me like I was crazy. That's just our culture.

Well my parents still think I'm crazy. Because not only did they not want me to play basketball, and they never came to watch me play a game of basketball in high school or anything else, but also it was, 'Enough with this dribbling the ball. You've got to get to school, you got to get an education. You got to be a doctor, an engineer.' I was like (waves his hand), 'OK, I'm going to play basketball.' And then as soon as I stopped playing basketball and got into the music, they had a second episode of like, 'Are you kidding me? Aren't you old enough already to stop this and start getting serious?' I'm like, 'This is serious' (laughs).

You reached your goal of making it to the NBA by being the first-ever draft pick for Miami Heat, who chose you at No. 9 in 1988. Did you feel pressure because of that?

No. I just didn't know what pressure was. It's a funny thing. When you're young, you have that kind of fearless mentality in a way that it's a challenge more than pressure.

Maybe just the benefit of youth naivety?

Probably.

You were recognized as the NBA's most improved player in your second season and won the NBA's Player of the Week award twice (once by averaging 30 points and 20 rebounds in a week). Playing in an era of so many quality big men, how much work did it take to get that good?

You know, I can only relate it to what I see with my own daughter. She's on the tennis team, and I go to practice with her and she's working hard to be a good tennis player. But I felt she wasn't working hard enough. I said, 'For the next five minutes, I want you to give me everything you've got. I want to see you with your tongue out, with you sweating and exhausted in the next sequence of hitting balls.' So she did it and she exaggerated it to show me that she was really trying. She came back sweating, her face was red. I said, 'Now you're working hard, and that's what you gotta do for the whole session.' She looked at me said, 'That's impossible.' So working hard and working hard (consistently) are two different worlds. And I worked really hard.

Where did you get that drive to put the hours in the gym and the weight room?

I think that I'm just a very driven person. And the more people that doubt me, the more I get a drive to prove them wrong. When I left Greece to go play at Syracuse, people were telling me, 'You're crazy to go play in college in the states. Just sign with (leading Greek club) Panathinaikos right now, you'll be the big fish in this small little pond. What are you going to do there?' When I heard that, that's all I wanted to do. And then when I finished college, it happened again. The Greek teams that wanted me to play for them said, 'You're never going to play in the NBA. They'll eat you up alive.' At the time there were very few foreign-born players in the league.

Is there a common thread to being successful in sports and other facets of life?

There is a thread. When you play sports, you're instilled with that competitiveness, that drive that wills you on. Just being smart isn't enough anymore. To be smart and driven is the formula for success.

You've said "Sometimes I'm too competitive. I take it personally; I take a loss home with me and that can be a problem." Does that competitive spirit play out in your music career?

It does. At first, I had real doubts about wanting to play my music to the public. I always made music for the love of it. I didn't want to be judged and open myself to criticism of people saying, 'What is this guy doing? He used to play basketball. Now he's a DJ. What's happened to him?'

But a DJ friend heard my music and told me I had a unique sound that I really should be sharing. The first time I played to a crowd was at the Miami Winter Music Conference in 2007. And it resonated really well. That was the beginning of the voyage of my second career. But I got so much shit for it.

From the press?

From everybody. People that are in the music business that could care less about my basketball career automatically judged me. By around 2009, when electronic music became big in the US and EDM came in, they thought that I jumped on the bandwagon because I wanted to be this famous DJ. Like, I just couldn't let go of the limelight. And they had it all wrong.

Was that a similar experience to having to prove it as a foreign-born player in the NBA?

Different. Music is a solo journey, it's not a team sport. In sports, you can have a great game and then follow it up with a bad game. But you're only as good as your last game. Whereas in music, if I go into a club and please 50 percent of the people there, I've done a great job. In sports, you've got to make sure that 100 percent of the people think that you've worked hard and did everything you could to win the game.

In an odd way, it must be a good feeling to play in rooms now and have the majority of people not be aware of how important a basketball player you were in Miami. That's got to be a sense of accomplishment.

Here's the thing, people that are over 35 today remember me as a basketball player. Those that are 35 and younger know me for my music. So the kid that just watched me play music goes home and tells his dad, 'Oh, I just want went to see Ronnie Seikaly DJing at that club and it was great. We had a blast.' And the dad will say, 'Rony Seikaly? That sounds like the basketball player. How did he get into music? What does he know about music?' And that's where the struggle is.

I always say, I wish being a DJ was like it was back in the day, where that person was not the focal point of the party. The party was the dancefloor and the DJ was just somewhere in the room playing the music. I wish people would just judge it based on that.

Where do you get the stamina to stand on your feet from 5 a.m. until the afternoon spinning records?

I can stand for 12 hours and play music. But I can't stand in a store when my wife goes shopping for more than five minutes. My back hurts, my knees hurt, I gotta sit down. I'm in a bad mood.

How many hours do you put in each week to create your radio show?[2]

The show is a combination of original music that I create and other people's music that I find. Nothing is ever repeated. Finding the music that I like and want to put on the radio show is the problem. It's virtually impossible for anybody to put out quality every single week for six years straight, because there is not that much quality out there for you to get. So that's the homework.

---

2. Seikaly's Sugar Free Radio show on SiriusXM ended its run in 2020. The streams are available on Soundcloud.

And those are where the hours are spent — looking for music that nobody has that are the gems.

Can you describe the process of making your own music?

It's taken me years to perfect my skill. Because I'm not a musician by nature. I've never done music theory. I don't play any instruments. So everything I do is by ear. It's what sounds good to me.

Does that give you a level of freedom in creating music?

That's a great point. What I used to think is that if I learned to be a musician and play instruments, creating my music would be a breeze. But the guy that taught me how to produce music told me it was the contrary. Now I have the freedom of doing whatever I want because I don't know how to play. But if I did learn, I'd end up spending hours doing complex melodies and stuff that I'm never going to use. So the simplicity of it, of doing things by ear, is what helps me.

Can you go over your process?

I've got every instrument known to man all on one device. There's a lot of music in my head. The challenge is, how do I get this stuff from my head onto paper? So house music is not like regular music, where you write out the song and then you play the song as you write it. It's kind of the other way around, you stumble on something that sounds good. Sometimes it's a mistake, but it's a good mistake. So you're kind of painting on a white canvas with no rules. If I have a clear melody or a chord sequence in my head that I want to build a track around, or a vocal — whatever it is that I like — I start with that and build all the pieces around it.

You seldom use vocals, but when you do, are you bringing in vocalists or using samples?

It's stuff that I'm mixing in. Vocals in our genre of music is a very, very delicate situation. Because if you have the right vocal, it could make the track. And if you have a great track and you put the wrong vocal, it'll kill the track. I can take a great track and make it cheesy just by the vocals.

What kind of rush does it give you to get a party going with thousands of people bouncing around to tunes that you created?

It's a very satisfying feeling. It's something that I call 'capturing the moment,' and every DJ, every musician out there performing wants to achieve that. And at one point when you capture the moment you feel like all of a sudden everybody's on the same wavelength. Everybody's in the same vibe. And that's what capturing the moment is. And I live for that. If I can capture the mo-ment, everybody's one. We're all feeling the same vibe and everybody's happy. I'm happy. They're happy. They're feeling the music, I'm feeling the music — everybody's together. That's capturing the moment, and that's the high of the performance.

How often do you get that when you're playing?

The purpose is to get it every time you play. That's what I thrive for.

So that capturing the moment feeling, how can you describe that versus having a huge game in the NBA?

There's nothing that comes close to the euphoria you get from sports versus DJing or music or connecting to 2,000 people. It's completely apples and oranges. The thrill of sports is the highest of any thrill you could possibly feel.

What is your biggest thrill you've had so far with music?

Honestly, I think that the biggest thrill I've had is playing in clubs that I used to be a customer at and thinking, 'Wow, what a dream it would be to play in a club like this,' and then getting the opportunity to play at them. Places like Amnesia or Pacha in Ibiza, Garten in Beirut and Space in Miami. I would wish those things secretly, and then when they came through I was like, 'Yes!'

Doing something that you love doing – that you would do for free and you get paid for it – that is insane.

You had some monster games against the Chicago Bulls when they were at their peak. February 13, 1990. Do you remember that day?

No.

You posted a career-high 40 points and 17 rebounds. That was one of several big games you had against them. What did it feel like facing those Bulls teams?

It was a circus. In the sense that Michael Jordan's aura was bigger than life. I tell people that there were only three players that I played against where you felt their presence on the court at all times. And that was Magic, Larry Bird and Michael Jordan. Because you knew that – no matter whether they're playing good or not – somehow they'll make that winning pass or the winning shot. Whatever it is, you just had to keep an eye on them at all times.

How does it feel to post 40 points against Michael Jordan and the Bulls? I know he wasn't guarding you most of the time but …

No, but he was coming down on the double team. Unfortunately, I would probably be dwelling on the basket that I missed or the rebound that I missed, instead of enjoying the 40 points that I did score. So that's the way I've always been. I never focused on the good stuff, I always dwelled on the bad stuff.

Even when I grabbed 34 rebounds in that one game.[3] I got pulled out with five minutes left and I was thinking, 'If they just left me in, I could have gotten 40.' I don't know if it's a competitive spirit or whatever it is that's inside of me, but nothing's ever enough.

You got traded from Miami, the city you loved, to the Golden State Warriors in Oakland. But it just didn't click there. What happened?

Yes, I was kind of hurt that I got traded, but I got traded to a contender. But as soon as I got there, the team was decimated by injuries, and that's when it started getting bad. Sometimes you go through a situation where everything's supposed to be great and it turns out to be a disaster. And that was a disastrous two years for me. This isn't an individual sport. This is a team sport, so if you don't have chemistry with your teammates then it's a waste of time.

---

3. Seikaly's 34 rebounds came in a victory against the Washington Bullets in March 1993.

Seikaly takes instructions from Syracuse coach Jim Boeheim during an NCAA game in 1985.

Was that your low point?

Yeah, no doubt.

I read you gave up $8.5 million guaranteed money to get out of there, is that true?

Yes.

That's a lot of money.

Yes, but I knew that the situation was just not satisfying to me on a professional level. And with the direction they were going in, I was just going to get stuck in mud for a while. And I wanted to move back to Florida. And when the Orlando thing came up, I would do anything to go to Orlando. And that meant giving up $8 million.

You then got to play on another talented team in Orlando that was a few seasons removed from being in the NBA Finals. But you were partly asked to fill the Magic's loss of Shaquille O'Neal.

That's when I felt pressure, filling the void left by Shaq. He's not only a basketball player, he carried the persona of Shaq and the dominance of his play. I knew that I could not be what he was. But I did everything I could to play as well as I could and give ourselves the best chance we could. And I felt liberated after leaving Golden State. That's when my career went right back to averaging 17 points and close to 10 rebounds a game.

There is a documentary about Shaq leaving Orlando which mentions you, have you seen it?[4]

Yes.

A former coach says that your teammates were jealous of you because of the attention you got from women. Were you aware of this?

That's why I told you earlier that in college, you play for the jersey, in the NBA you're kind of playing for the jersey and yourself — but mostly you're playing for yourself. And when a player comes in and steals some of the limelight off those guys — especially when Shaq left, they thought that they were going to get to another level in notoriety and stardom — and somebody comes in and kind of takes some of the spotlight away, it creates a little bit of jealousy. And the way my lifestyle was didn't help. It kind of irritated them even more because of the way I lived my life.

These were the players in Orlando or Golden State?

No, there were two different stories. In Golden State it was a chemistry problem (on the court). In Orlando, I didn't have a chemistry problem on the court. I had a chemistry problem off the court.

You clearly learned it was a business in the NBA. Did that take some of the joy out of the game for you?

Absolutely. It's a ruthless business. It's not a fun business. And you're treated like cattle, like a race-horse. They'll squeeze everything out of you. When you've got nothing else, they'll just throw you away. So it's a cruel business, and if you understand that going in — that you've got to do what's best for you as well — then you can equalize that. But when you come in giving your heart to that team or that business thinking that they've got your back, then you're wrong. It's happened to everybody.

Now the music business can also be ruthless.

It's not ruthless, no. In the music business you're dealing with scumbags, it's a different story.

And you're not in the NBA?

No.

Agents can be scumbags.

Agents could be scumbags. But the NBA is a proper business. It's clean, it's not dirty. It's just ruthless. In clubs, you're not dealing with a businessman, with somebody that says, 'Listen, let's meet at 5 p.m. and let's have a sit down.' The guy may show up, he may not show up. You're dealing with a completely different strand of person. One has discipline, one does not.

---

4. In an ESPN documentary about the Orlando Magic, former Magic assistant coach Richie Adubato quotes Golden State Warriors coach Bob Lanier as saying, "We have to trade Rony Seikaly because he's too good looking. All the players are jealous of him. He has women everywhere that you can't believe."

What about business pressure in music? Do you face that?

It's relaxing. I don't see playing music as pressure. Let's be realistic. You go to play a set and the music doesn't resonate. So you go home, then you go to sleep. And everybody says, 'It was OK,' or 'It was shitty.' No big deal. But you have that game in the NBA. And you've got every magazine, every reporter, every writer … the general manager already wants to trade you. It's a whole different animal.

And also with music, there's a lot more hype that drives some of the biggest DJs in the world. Some of these DJs are not that good. It's just that the hype behind them. And it's about being cool.

How do you look back on your accomplishments in basketball?

I've played in some amazing games against amazing players. I've dunked on everybody and I've been dunked on by everybody. But somehow, I don't really dwell on all that stuff. I just kind of I think life is like a basketball game. You've got four quarters. I think the first quarter was great, the second quarter was great, the third quarter … we're in it now, and that's what it's all about.

Kyle Turley

Costa Mesa, California, April 2019

Kyle Turley was jamming with his band at a music studio in Nashville when he saw an alarming news report. His friend Junior Seau, who had recently ended one of the greatest careers in NFL history, had just committed suicide.

"We had just taken a break from rehearsing," he recalls, "and I just collapsed, I fell into my chair and sat there like, damn. You know, I'm dealing with this shit at the same time."

Since Turley retired from the NFL in 2007, the 325-pound former offensive lineman moved to Nashville and was making a name for himself as a formidable country music singer, opening for the likes of George Jones and Lynyrd Skynyrd.

But Turley was also battling demons, including seizures, rage, vertigo, depression and suicidal thoughts caused by more than 100 concussions he says he sustained playing football.

Now Seau's suicide brought everything to the forefront.

"This guy's a first ballot Hall of Famer, the best to ever do what he did," he says. "Knowing all that was going on (with me), that was just a roller coaster of emotions."

Shortly after the incident, Turley pushed for the NFL to implement a suicide prevention hotline to help steady current or former players struggling with those thoughts.

Little did he know he would be calling that line himself soon after it went live – sitting in his truck in an empty parking lot, inches away from a loaded gun in the glove compartment.

Incredibly, the call went unanswered. It eventually took three tries to get through to a person with enough therapy experience to calm Turley down.

'It was a free for all'

Ironically, Turley's frustration with the hotline gave the former All-Pro a greater sense of purpose to help his fellow NFL retirees with their struggles. From his own experiences, Turley knew much of those issues stemmed from the opioids willingly prescribed by doctors to athletes in his day.

Offensive linemen aren't normally shown on ESPN highlights, but Turley made national news with the New Orleans Saints in 2001 when he was ejected for ripping the helmet off the New York Jets' Damien Robinson and throwing it downfield. He was instructed to see an anger management specialist. The therapist turned out to be a Saints fan and applauded his aggression.

As his career took off with Pro Bowl honors and a Sports Illustrated cover, Turley says he was given a cocktail of drugs to treat pain and vertigo, including Valium, Vioxx, Darvocet and Vicodin. "Doctors were giving that shit out," he says, admitting he kept 5,000 Vicodin stashed in a safe in his house. "It was a free for all."

After retirement, Turley continued to face difficulty. Despite his budding music career in Nashville, his dependency on pharmaceuticals did not wane.

He would experience vertigo almost daily, suffer bouts of extreme rage, and at least one seizure that required hospitalization. One thing that helped was the routine of being on the road as a musician, which included stints in his experimental heavy metal duo Delta Doom.

"To have someone who is used to having his entire life planned out for him go to nothing and then sit in that kind of (idle) environment – it was horrific to watch," Turley's wife Stacy recalls. "I felt sorry for him."

"I don't know if there are many women who would be like, 'Go on the road for four months,'" she adds. "But he needed (the structure). You could see it just building inside of him. Then he'd go out on the road and get into his groove and do his thing, and when he'd come back, he was all better for a while. But then you could see it building again."

'Fortune and Pain'

Months before Seau's death, Turley was performing at a bar in New Orleans when his best friend and former Saints teammate Steve Gleason told him he was diagnosed with ALS, the degenerative motor neuron disease.

In 10 minutes, Turley wrote one of his best songs, *Fortune and Pain*, about the suffering that NFL players go through to play the sport they love. "All my friends are dying, and all I feel is pain. Sitting here broken, never dreamed it this way," he wrote, describing the words as "all just spilling onto the page."

It was a deep moment of reflection for one of the self-confessed "nastiest players in NFL history," one that would trigger a decade-long recovery process.

Turley and I met not far from his home in Southern California, where he settled in 2014 with Stacy and their two teenage children. For now, he's taking a break from his life as a musician, instead focusing on growing his CBD business, Neuro XPF.

Turley credits the cannabis derivative, also known as cannabidiol, for eliminating the pain, inflammation and psychological toll caused by his long NFL career, and wants to spread its benefits to the masses. (The sentiment is shared by other former players, including ex-San Francisco 49ers Super Bowl winner Gary Plummer.)

It should be noted that there is currently no conclusive research that confirms CBD provides measurable relief for symptoms of pain, inflammation and depression in humans, but its impact on Turley is hard to understate. Throughout our meeting he appeared at peace with himself and lucid. He was also motivated to share his findings that brought him out of the abyss – a far cry from the day he made that desperate call from his truck.

What was the greater thrill for you, lining up for a big NFL game, or opening for Lynyrd Skynyrd in front of a packed arena?

Nothing compares to the NFL, nothing. There is not one thing I've ever done. I've surfed waves bigger than this building. My buddies are all surfers and for the first two years of retirement I traveled around and did big wave surfing, and then I did music.

And nothing has compared – nothing will ever compare – to the NFL. Of running out of the tunnel about to participate in this alpha male sport, in this gladiator environment with 100,000 people screaming for you. And you've made yourself into being one of the guys that they know and love, and they've got your jerseys in the stands and all that? No … I was looking for it in music, and I thought when I did open up for Lynyrd Skynyrd in that big arena show in St. Louis, it was still only 10,000 people (*laughs*).

Even though that's a huge number, right?

It's big, it's a huge number. I'd love to sell out 500-seat venues in all the House of Blues around the country. Now that would be a huge successful tour. But even if you sold out all of those House of Blues – like 50 of them – it wouldn't fill half of an NFL stadium.

Did you enjoy being on the road more with your NFL teammates or with your band?

You weren't really on the road in football. You're at home, and you go out on the road and would be in and out. What I liked about (football) – and it's the same with music too – was being an offensive lineman and coming from the offensive line position, you're a unit. You really have to work together, unlike the defense where you just go out and tackle people. You've got to hold the gap there.

All five of you have to coordinate this effort to get this play done. Because if the line doesn't work, then likely the play isn't going to work. And you know, that's the deciding factor in most NFL plays: Whose line is better?

That comes from that camaraderie and that bond that you develop in training camp. You're together, you're a unit and everyone has to get their work in. Music is same way. Everybody has to pull their load to get their shit done. That's why music was so awesome for me and why I committed to it for that long, because it brought that back for me.

How did you get started with music?

I went to college in San Diego[1] and picked up a $10 guitar at the (Mexican) border. I just kept it around and killed my roommates' ears playing and trying to learn. I'd just pick things up. I never had a music lesson for guitar, but I had a passion for it. And so when I got a guitar finally, I just kept trying and trying and trying.

And then I got to the NFL and got money. Every training camp we would be there for about a month, but you needed something to take yourself away from the game. And in training camp time, there's nothing.

They would be held in these tiny college towns. We'd be in these old dormitories, so I'd ask the coaches to give me a room where I could go down in the basement and play. And then I'd go to the local music store and rent every instrument they had. If some day they surprised me with a new instrument, I'd try and learn how to play it.

I did this in New Orleans and in St Louis. By the time I got to Kansas City with the Chiefs, we had a lot of musical talent on the team. There was (six-time Pro Bowler) Tamba Hali, who is now a dancehall reggae star in Liberia, and Dwayne Bowe who was into hip hop. If the Chiefs went to the Super Bowl, we had it arranged. We're going to perform together. That would have been cool.

At what point during your playing career did you feel you could perform publicly.

I started doing charity benefit concerts in New Orleans (where Turley played for the first five years of his career) to give back to the inner city. We sold out the House of Blues two years in a row for our music event. It was fun.

New Orleans is a special place for music. As soon as I got there in my rookie year, I was just exposed to all this unbelievable music. Heavy metal was my passion – and it's easy to play distorted guitar to make it sound like you know what you're doing. You can get together and jam with some guys and make it sound good. But why I did country music is because you can always come back to country. I can't go back play heavy metal at 60.

Was that the first time you got the rush of performing in front of an audience?

No, I got that from my buddies in metal. I was a huge heavy metal fan when I was in college. I had worked security from '93 to '97 in Southern California. That era of music was fucking on fire. The punk rock scene erupted. That was when Green Day sold out in the early '90s. I was there, so I got to work for all the big bands and got to know all these guys.

Then I found out that some of my favorite bands were from New Orleans, like Pantera, Soylent Green, Crowbar, Eyehategod, all these huge metal bands that toured around the world, that were massive in Europe. And these guys are all huge Saints fans. So I got to go on stage with Pantera and grab the mic and yell at the crowd and announce songs. I was also up there with Slayer and The Deftones.

You created a CBD business; how did it start?

Music really brought me here. Because we were living in Nashville and I was trying to fill my time

---

1. At San Diego State University, where Turley was a consensus All-American and the No. 7 pick of the 1998 NFL draft.

and my energy after what I was dealing with physically and mentally with the game of football, what it does to your body with all the pills and synthetics I was addicted to. In Nashville I was touring constantly, I was full time. I did 100 shows or more every year for five years, coast to coast. And I was using (marijuana) to kind of get away from a lot of health issues.

Including mental health issues?

Big time. Just life post-football. Music is a great escape, but it doesn't take away the damage it does to your brain. Until I discovered CBD and moved back to California, which is what we had to do to get everything in order with our lives and our family at the time, I would go out and do tours, and come back. And then it was just hit or miss that I'd be (ready to be) with my family.

Then I left music and I came out (to California) and I resolved all these issues, for the most part. They're still there – you deal with everyday life stuff – but nothing has resolved these things more than cannabis. I had been talking about it and then created a company that's helping people. So I've got to keep pushing until we get it everywhere. My mission is to really get this message across, because even now everybody wants to discount (the effects of CBD).

You have said you suffered 100 concussions in your playing days; that is an alarming number.

Now we know what concussions are ... I don't like it that people say that (number) because they're not documented. I've only had two documented ones. But every hit that you take to your head is a concussion. You bang your head into that wall right now you get a concussion. And on the offensive line in football, every play is that. Every play you're taking your head and slamming on the table as hard as you can. You have your helmet on, but that doesn't stop the laws of motion.

And your brain – as we understand it now – is floating in this space and rattles (in your head) and you get these concussive blows and subconcussive blows that add up to this big thing that we now understand is CTE.[2]

And how did you deal with it while you were playing?

Nobody talked about it back then. The concussion thing happened after I left. It was shortly after that when it got exposed, '07 was my last year.

Have you been involved in the player lawsuits against the NFL? (One federal lawsuit filed by 1,800 former players cites long-term health problems from illegally prescribed opioid painkillers by team doctors.)

Yeah, that's still ongoing. I've been to four different doctor's visits, at least. Each one of those takes six hours because they give me this litany of tests for neurocognitive issues and Alzheimer's. I've been diagnosed with stage two progressive dementia.

Were you hooked on painkillers in the pros?

All of them, yeah. In the late 1990s, early 2000s. One day our dog ate one of the bottles. (Stacy)

---

2. Chronic traumatic encephalopathy, known as CTE, is a degenerative brain disease caused by head injuries.

ran to a store get the ipecac to make her throw up. We were given those things like candy. I was making deals left and right. I had 5,000 Vicodin in a safe in my house.

So you had your own guy who was a dealer?

Doctors were giving that shit out. You can find crooked doctors everywhere that would get you 5,000 Vicodin.

And this carried on after your time in NFL?

Oh yeah.

For how long?

Until we moved (to California) five years ago.

Throughout Nashville years.

Oh yeah. In Nashville I ramped up to psych meds. Because of my neurological issues and vertigo that started to escalate at the end of my career. It was constant by retirement, all day. Almost every day I would get vertigo. I had a seizure one time; I had four nurses holding me down for the MRI machine.

I put everybody through hell for 10 years after my career ended. That didn't stop 'till four and a half years ago when I got rid of all those pills and found the strands (of CBD).

Did you ever really love football and the NFL? Some people just do the sport because they're big and they're good at it and it pays well.

You didn't go through with that if you didn't love it — especially in that era. That was like abuse that you had to endure. I mean, two-a-day practices in the heat of Louisiana, 150 degrees Fahrenheit on the heat index. And you're out there in the swamp surrounded by sugar canes, no wind with all that humidity. You're out there in the morning, then three hours in the afternoon every day for a month.

We got paid well, but the sacrifices (we put) on our bodies are responsible for those 10 years we just talked about. And they are responsible for all these (retired NFL players) that are continuing to have all these issues. My love for the game of football, my passion for the game of football, is the culprit for those 10 years — and still to this day, even on my bad days, I want to be back there.

As hard as it was, and as much as we had to go through with all the struggle and all the pain, if I could step back out on a football field and continue to do what I wanted to do, do what my passion was and play the game, I wouldn't have any problems doing it again.

You dealt with some serious injuries as a pro; I'm sure retirement must have been difficult.

What if you couldn't write anymore? You wake up every day (thinking): What am I doing? Where am I going? That's gonna make anybody struggle. And then you add on the orthopedic injuries. Now, not only can you not write anymore, but they just took 40 bone chips out of your left shoulder, your lower back discs are all deteriorating, you've had one surgery already and need another. They want to talk about fusing your right ankle with plates and screws, you need your left one reconstructed. They say you need two new knees and a new right hip.

And you've got a bad brain injury on top of that which is making you depressed and not able to be in public situations, and you're developing vertigo and light sensitivity to boot. Imagine not being able to do what you do and deal with all that. That's the average life of the NFL football player.

And how did you deal with it?

Drugs. Pills. I went to the doctors, I tried to get answers, they gave me pills. They gave me all these drugs and made it worse, they made my pain worse. They made my mind worse. They made everything worse.

And I understand you had suicidal thoughts. This is a terrible question, but what does it feel like to have a suicidal thought?

I don't know how to explain that to anybody — unless you have been there, you don't know. I don't know what it's like to kill myself because I didn't do it. But I know what it's like to be in that moment. And I know what it's like to think, I need to make this call (to the NFL suicide prevention line) right now.

That was a point in time where I had no control. I was hopeless. My mind was being controlled by all these synthetic medications that were manifesting all these crazy things — and I don't experience those anymore.

I mean, literally, I'm back to being an average human in those regards. I get angry and I get agitated, just like everybody else does. I'm still alpha, you know ... but I didn't have control before I got rid of those things.

Did playing music help at all with these issues related to your mental health?

That's why I did it. It's the only thing that helped.

Did you start writing songs?

Immediately. With my background of loving music, I wanted to do something that I was passionate about.

Were the crowds aware that you were this big NFL guy?

No, not in Nashville. I did all of the spots there. I did Bluebird Café, and I played all the Broadway bars.

Was it preferable for you to maintain that anonymity? To keep the NFL thing away so that you didn't have the baggage of people thinking, 'Oh that's some NFL dude who's trying to play'?

I did the work. I went out on the road. I played the small bars. I know every road and every little bar in almost every little town. I know I can book a show right now in any city in America.

It's a fine line to walk because that is just perception and you're not taken seriously. Yeah, it was hard. I ended up opening up for a lot of guys. Eric Church told me, 'Kyle you're one of the best opening acts I've ever played with.' That was massive.

Hank Williams III was the first guy I ever played with. And I did tours with my dad's heroes. I opened up for George Jones before he died and did three tours with David Allan Coe. And then I did metal tours (with Delta Doom). I played drums.

Did the anxiety and vertigo that you experienced in the NFL follow you on stage, or did that just go away?

No (I didn't experience it). I think just because of the energy exertion and my frame of mind mentally. Stress is what aggravates disease. Whatever that is, if you have a disease and you put that added stress on it, then it's going to make it worse.

But music (and touring) gave me what was missing after football. It gave me that structure again and allowed me to go out and accomplish something as well. I didn't have to think about what was going on. I knew where I was going. I needed to get to the venue. That's what it allowed me to tap back into (functionality). When I was off the road, I was stagnant, just sitting around just losing it and going crazy.

That's why football players are not able to assimilate outside of the arena — or athletes in general, or military people, because they're in these groups where you don't have to think. You go on regiment, you've got practices.

What would you say your greatest achievements were in music?

Just that I did it and I accomplished that goal. I've made albums. I wrote songs. I did everything I dreamed of doing as a musician. I opened up for the biggest bands in country music, and some of the greatest bands in music history. All because I've taken what I learned in football and work ethic in sports and applied it to that arena and made it happen.

Left: Turley, in action for the St Louis Rams, battles Michael Haynes of the Chicago Bears in 2003.

Kevin Walker

Stockholm, December 2019

Kevin Walker is having one of the best weeks of his remarkable life.

Only days after the 30-year-old midfielder wins the Swedish football championship with his club Djurgårdens IF, he is due to unveil his new hit single on national television.

Winning the league in a nail-biter on the final day of the season allows Walker, who was born to a Swedish mother and Irish father, to hoist the Swedish league trophy for the first time in his roller-coaster career.

But Walker has little time to celebrate. Instead of partying with his teammates, he prepares for the TV performance of his track *You Let Me Go* before rushing to a studio to produce the accompanying music video.

For the past seven years this has been his life, a situation he compares to living like Batman and his alter ego Bruce Wayne. One day he performs as a veteran leader in Sweden's top tier of football, and the next as one of the county's most endearing singer-songwriters, whose debut album *Belong* went platinum.

In 2013, a teammate of Walker's asked him to fill in at an open mic session at a nearby casino. A local filmed Walker's performance, then shared the footage with the producers of Sweden's *Pop Idol* who invited him to audition. The rest is history.

"I had the day off, so I'm very glad that I took that decision," Walker reflects. "I wasn't sure they were going to accept me as a footballer. I took it as a fun thing; I was sure they were going to kick me out eventually."

Instead, Walker beat out thousands of hopefuls to make it all the way to the finals, which was also broadcast in Ireland. The Swedish public voted him in as winner, earning him a contract with Universal Records. Not a bad showing for someone who had only picked up a guitar and began performing four years earlier.

While rehearsing for the show, Walker also scored three key goals in his former team GIF Sundsvall's run for promotion into the top league (they eventually lost in a playoff match).

"A lot of people probably don't have the stamina to do two things," says Walker, who alternates between a charming Irish accent and fluent Swedish, "so that's something I'm very proud of."

After winning the competition, he capped off the experience by singing a duet with British popstar Robbie Williams – a known football fanatic who told Walker he was living his dream.

"It was unreal, unbelievable," Walker recalls. "He was asking me questions backstage about football and he'd heard about my story. Before rehearsing with Robbie, I was the most nervous I'd ever been. And then once I said hello to him, it was fine. He was such a top man. It was a big moment for me to meet him."

In the ensuing years, Walker started a family, raising two children while progressing with his dual passions of football and music.

His 2016 song *The Wind* has over 2.7 million streams on Spotify to date, and his 2020 release *Humbled By Life* continues to make waves. The song's title is also a fitting one to describe Walker's down-to-earth character.

In December 2020, Walker signed a three-year deal with former club Örebro SK, sealing his position in Sweden's top league into his mid-30s. With further music in the works, Walker's Batman and Bruce Wayne identity swap is set to last for some time.

How do you switch from the mindset of being a competitor on the pitch to, all of a sudden, having to perform on TV in front of the entire country and create a music video?

I'm not sure I switch between the two. It's different to compete in football and perform on stage, so I don't really need to switch. I need to be focused; I need to be well prepared. All these things are similar, but when you're standing on stage it's about delivering feeling. Music is interpreted and it's all feelings.

I would say going up against opponents is the big difference. You're trying to express yourself in football as well, but you're trying to win ultimately. It's difficult to win in music, I suppose.

It's safe to say you're the only person in history to win major football trophies and a major singing competition all in one career. Can you compare the thrills?

Not really. You share the joy and the euphoric moments when you win together with a team differently than when you win a music talent show. There are a lot of people that help you around the music as well, but ultimately, you're there on your own on stage and it can be overwhelming.

But sharing the joy with my team who I'm working hard with every day to achieve things together, I think that is something that will live forever in my memory. When you win things together with a team, it's quite special.

Walker began writing hit songs only a few years after learning guitar. 'Everything that has interested me, I've really committed to it,' he says.

You picked up the guitar when you went down with an unfortunate blood infection about 10 years ago. Were you musically inclined before that?

I always loved music and had a deep interest for it. So I would go looking for music and try to listen to a lot of stuff, and I was influenced by a lot of different artists and genres and styles. I wouldn't cling to one thing only.

Eventually when my blood poisoning hit, I got fed up with playing video games all day as a 19 or 20-year-old footballer and I felt like I needed to do something with my time. So I bought a guitar and tried to play John Mayer songs and they were very hard to learn, so I would start writing down (my own songs) pretty early.

Did you find that playing guitar was like therapy for you while you were forced to be away from the sport?

Oh definitely. It helped me so much. It's easy to get down on yourself. I was flying football-wise; I was playing for a big club (Örebro SK) and I got blood poisoning during my trip with the Under-21 national team.

We were going to play in Belgium and it was a big blow for me – I'm not gonna hide behind that. It was very tough on me mentally, but (*big sigh*) you know, I feel like I've often come through challenges like that in my life, and this was one of them. Probably the biggest one, really.

The music definitely helped me through it all. It was a new interest and a new calling, you could say. I loved music before, but after that it just grew stronger.

Walker in competition for Djurgårdens IF during their championship season in 2019.

Did you have any formal training in in guitar or singing? How did you develop your talents?

I would love singing when I was younger. My mother used to play in what they call a guitar ensemble here in Sweden. And my father, being from Ireland, would get everybody having a sing-along at home. So that's probably where my musical interest grew from.

You've really taken them far. I'm assuming you've had some training along the way?

Not really. I learned from YouTube how to play basic chords and stuff like that when I bought a guitar in 2009. So that's how I started out.

You won *Pop Idol* only four years after picking up a guitar for the first time, so the trajectory is pretty remarkable. How much time were you putting into music at that point?

I'd be done with training sessions around lunchtime every day and then go home and play the guitar until I got tired … and then I'd keep working at it. I'm still doing the same today.

During my life, everything that has interested me, I've really committed to it. It's been fun to watch my development in music and be able to use things that I've learned in sports (to help me along the way). Things like being organized and taking care of myself and being sharp and staying in the learning process. Always being open to learning new things has helped me a lot with music.

How scary was it the first time you went on stage for *Pop Idol*?

Very scary. But it was fun as well. I knew I had a profession to fall back on. A lot of people that go in there probably see it as the turning point in their life, and I didn't have that kind of pressure going in there. I had an 'I'll give it a go' sort of attitude, and I tried to enjoy the moment.

It was a few weeks into the actual live shows that I started to feel the pressure and started to feel like … this could really be something. Then I got really nervous, because then everything was live on TV and I felt a bit out of my depth, to be honest.

How many people were watching you at that point?

About 1.3 or 1.4 million every Friday.

Can you compare the nerves you felt playing in front of over a million people, versus having to take a penalty in a tournament match in a big stadium?

Yeah, I actually took a penalty this year and I missed it! But we ended up winning the match anyway. It was a shootout in the Swedish Cup in the quarterfinal.

Are there any sort of breathing techniques you do in either case?

No, it's all about the hours you put in on the football field. You don't feel that sort of pressurized climate, you know? When I was going to take that penalty, I felt like I was going to score. What happened to me was I slipped on the AstroTurf; it can be pretty slippery.

So let's just pick up on *Pop Idol*. You got to the final stage and the whole country was watching you. At what point did you think, 'I can actually make a career out of this if I want to'?

Towards the end, I started to feel like the public really took to me and my story. I was making big headlines. There was a lot of talk like about football matches being postponed for my involvement – which wasn't true. And (the production company) were sort of twisting the tabloids a bit to suit them. So they would leak stuff to the media, and there were quite a number of articles on me every week.

But it helped me grow my popularity. Everybody seemed to take to my journey and I felt my following steadily rising. The public were voting for me even though maybe technically there were better, more experienced contestants left in the competition.

I was very grateful for that and tried to stay true to who I was, in terms of not getting carried away. And I felt like, this could be something after football if I play my cards right.

It's interesting that you actually had to make a decision after you won, because you won a recording contract in the competition. And having recovered from your illness, you were then playing in the second tier of Swedish football with GIF Sundsvall. So by then your music career had eclipsed your football career in an odd way.

Yeah. I felt like we were very close to winning promotion the year I was involved with *Pop Idol*, and the year after it we won promotion to the top league again. My football was going the way I wanted to.

The whole point of moving to Sundsvall was to rebuild my career after my blood poisoning and get games under my belt. I ended up staying there a few more years than I might have planned from the beginning. But everything happens for a reason. I ended up getting this chance in life to do music and I'm very grateful for my years up there (in Sundsvall). And then the team I play for now (Djurgårdens IF) came in and got me on a free transfer, and it felt like a really good challenge to play in the top flight again with a club in Stockholm.

So can you describe your decision-making process at that point?

It was never my intention to quit football. I grew up wanting to play for Manchester United and dreamed of that as a little kid – and that dream is still there.

I felt like my football was benefiting so much from learning about handling pressure and standing in front of audiences, and totally being out of my comfort zone. Doing something new helped me be more comfortable on the pitch. And I grew as a person, looking back on it.

I felt like I could do my music together with the football. I didn't feel like I had to choose. I could have gone all in on the music, I suppose, and quit football – but I think I would have regretted that for the rest of my life. You only have a good number of years you can play football and then it's gone. Hopefully, I can stay in the music business 'till I'm 70.

When did you realize you were benefiting as a footballer from your experiences on stage?

I remember playing some important matches when I was younger, but standing on stage and singing for a live audience on television was another sort of level of being nervous.

You know, if you play a match, it's not only you on the pitch, you have teammates you can lean on and it's a team sport. So all the focus isn't on you. But when you're singing on stage (in front of the entire country), it's a totally different ballgame.

It was very intense in *Pop Idol*. It's 12 weeks of live shows, and you're on air every Friday at 8 p.m. It's the best viewer time in Swedish television every week. In that sense, there are no other artists who get that kind of exposure every week.

If you don't feel 100 percent comfortable or calm or confident in what you do, then you get very nervous. I think I handled it quite well and benefitted from going through the big (Under-17 games against England and Germany) when I was younger.

It sounds like working on each craft helped build your confidence on stage and on the pitch.

Yes, although I was massively defensive towards doing *Pop Idol* because I was thinking, 'How is this going to affect my football? Am I going to drop in form? Am I going to lose focus? Is it going tire me out?' All those thoughts were creeping up.

But I had the support of the club and we made it work; I didn't miss one training session. I didn't want to jeopardize anything football-wise, but it turned out to be the total opposite. And the more I do musically, the better I feel about myself.

You have said that football helped you manage *Pop Idol* mentally, because you were used to handling criticism versus some of your competitors who really weren't.

Coming from the environment of a professional football player, you have to produce good things every day. You have to be fighting for your place on the team. You're scrutinized, you're under the microscope to perform every day. So I was used to getting criticism, from fans or whoever. Playing football, you know it's not always, 'You're the best in the world, we love you.' When you play football, you have to take the good with the bad.

I got my fair share of criticism in the music show as well. There were times when other contestants would get some (criticism) and they would be totally heartbroken from it. I wasn't all that interested in (winning). I was there to learn something from the journey and to try to enjoy the ride. So it helps to have lived a little before you get criticism.

What did your teammates think as you were rising in *Pop Idol*?

They were very supportive. There was never any banter on the pitch in practice or against opponents. Everybody thought it was a fun thing.

Did your music suit their tastes?

A few of the lads really like the latest song I've written. You know, there's a lot of hip hop being played in the speakers in the changing room. But they're quite open to all sorts of musical styles. I have to say it's not as stereotypical as you would think, at least in our changing room.

At the time you said you were living a Bruce Wayne lifestyle. You were Batman during the competition and Bruce Wayne in your day life as a footballer. Has that normalized now, six years on?

It's still often like that. My life revolves around football. I live like a footballer in the professional game and take care of my body. If I perform a gig somewhere, it's not like I have a few pints afterwards and stay out late. I make sure I get back in for training in the morning. So it's just worked for me. And then you'll hear the likes of (former Manchester United great) Roy Keane saying you can't be distracted from the club. That can be true, but (being distracted) wasn't the case for me.

I think our society's bending a little bit more towards people pursuing things they love and going outside of that (traditional) schedule where you work from Monday to Friday. Now you can actually commit to more things than one. A lot of people are balancing family with work and trying to have their interests mixed. I think it's an interesting equation to make the puzzle work.

For people with two professions like football and music, how does that even work to do both? It's pretty simple. I don't do both at the same time. You find time and you work around it. I have a family as well and obviously that's my priority in life, but I've cut out all the other things that would waste my time. I've got a hard time now just watching television. I feel like I'm wasting time. I'd rather be working on music or spending time with my family in another way.

Did you feel like you've had to work harder than other musicians to prove yourself because of your athletic background?

It's a complicated question. My brother and I went through having our father as our coach.[1] Having your father as your coach in a football team is probably mentally the toughest thing you can go through, in the sense that you're constantly trying to prove yourself to be better than others.

You're never going to get away from people thinking that you're getting picked because it's your father who's training your team. So the start of my career set me up for growing thick skin and realizing that there are jealous people out there. And that's going to be a big part of this career, not having that sort of thing affect me. I'm grateful having gone through it; down the line it's been massive in my career.

I was playing on the (Swedish Under-17 and Under-19) national teams, and people would still question it a bit. So, to answer your question, I don't do that musically, because I feel like my story is what makes me interesting. And I don't feel like I have to hide that at all.

It's not easy to write a hit song, yet you have done it a few times. That must be an incredible feeling to see songs that you've written streamed millions of times and doing very well.

It's unbelievable really. It's such a nice feeling. I'm all about trying to find really good songs and spending time on the lyrics and making them interesting. I love the storytelling in music, and making the melodies match up with the lyrics. It's quite fun to dive into.

I chose to go away from the record labels because they were all trying to make me do the Eurovision Song Contest. I couldn't get that to work around my football career, and I felt like it's better that I do my own thing. The (Spotify) streams that you're talking about are all (achieved) without any record label behind them. So it's quite nice to see that people out there want to listen to my music.

Are you a competitive person by nature? And how does that competitive streak translate off the pitch and into the music industry?

I'm very, very competitive when it comes to football. I want to win things. I'll make sure that I have the right sort of preparation for that so everything goes into winning.

With the music, it's all about self-development for me. I like to see how good I can become and how well I can write songs. And the competitiveness in that field is different. You can't say,

---

1. At Örebro SK, where Walker made his debut in the Swedish top flight. Though Walker has recently returned to the club, his father Patrick Walker no longer serves at the manager there.

'Next year I'm going to have a song that's going to have 10 million streams,' because it's another environment.

You can make a really good song, but if you don't back it up with good marketing (it may not go far). There's so much good music out there, so the competition to actually get into the headphones of people is pretty intense. But I have a few goals, and it will be fun to see if I can work towards them the next 10 years. I'm competitive with myself when it comes to the music.

I know that one of your goals is to play Madison Square Garden, which is phenomenal. What's your vision for your music career after you retire from football?

I said that as something to aim towards. It'd be some achievement to get one of my songs played in a big arena. Even if I don't reach it, I'll probably come further than if I didn't have that sort of ambition. If I'm able to make a living from music in the future, that's basically my goal with music. And to have achieved things that I've done now with music — like singing for the Swedish royal family or sharing a stage with a world-renowned artist like Robbie Williams — that I would never have dreamed of doing. It just pushes me forward to think positively.

How did it feel to hear Robbie Williams tell you that you were living his dream?

It was pretty unreal. It just shows you the sort of situation I was in, (given the option) to quit football or not. A lot of people would give a lot to have the opportunity to play football as an occupation. And luckily enough I had that my whole adult life now. So it's pretty nice.

Walker says the scrutiny he has faced as a footballer has helped his music career.

Mark Butcher

London, June 2019

Before Mark Butcher walked into my London apartment, I made sure to have a few pre-tuned guitars on display in my living room. Moments after saying hello, he was putting my Fender Stratocaster to far better use than I ever had.

Even though the former England and Surrey County cricket captain has a lot going on in in life – as an in-demand TV commentator, husband to wife Claire and father of four – he is clearly on top of his music game. He practices daily to "keep the fingers warm," he says while nonchalantly riffing off Steely Dan and Jimi Hendrix progressions.

That's good news, because his second solo album *Now Playing* is set to drop days after our meeting at a showcase gig with his band at the west London club Nell's.

That night Butcher is a musical triple-threat, displaying his formidable singing, stellar guitar playing and ability to write good songs. He penned 10 of the 13 tracks on the album, including the first single *Country*. The song makes a fiery political statement on how the children of immigrants are often viewed in the UK, peaking with the chorus: "I was born and raised in this country."

Butcher wrote it in 2013, "just after Great Britain hosted the Olympics, and we were all patting ourselves on the back of how inclusive and diverse we were," he says. "Subsequently things have happened like the Windrush scandal and Brexit. The events have caught up with the song."

As a biracial Englishman, Butcher can relate. His mother Elaine is a former gymnast of Jamaican heritage and his father Alan was a cricketer who broke into the England team and later coached Surrey. Butcher admits that he was not particularly active in speaking out for social causes during his playing days, in part because he was cocooned as the gifted son of a pro athlete.

"I think the fact that my dad played and is a white guy perhaps opened a lot of doors, in terms of people's perception of me," he reflects, "more than they might have done if my old man had been a Black guy."

Butcher looks back on his apathy towards former Surrey teammate Michael Carberry with some regret. Carberry, an outspoken critic of the England Cricketing Board's attitude towards racism, made his Test debut for England in 2010. At the time of writing he is still the most recent English-born Black player to do so.

"I didn't understand it very much. I thought he was seeing oppressions and wrongdoing where there weren't any," Butcher says. "But I think I see it better now. I see what he meant and what he was up against – the things that he would come up against that I didn't. And I feel slightly bad for not having been more of a support, because I didn't notice. But I now know it was there."

'Listen, this is going to stop'

Over the past few years Butcher has become a lively personality on Twitter, where he sometimes spars with other well-known figures on issues of race, immigration and politics.

"The more people that engage with it, the better off we will be," he remarks. "It just amazes me, the hatred that has been dished out on (athletes) for talking about police brutality. They're saying, 'Listen, this is going to stop.' If the highest profile, best paid athletes in country have no power to do anything about it, then what is the poor kid on the street going to do?"

As an international cricketer, Butcher had two long spells on the England squad between 1997 and 2004, when he played in 71 Test series and scored eight centuries. He captained the England team once in 1999, filling in for injured Nasser Hussain, but then suffered a dip in form which coincided with difficult spell in his personal life.

Our open conversation about that rocky time and his questionable process of reclaiming his status as a world class athlete by turning into a "ruthless bastard" makes this one of the most remarkable interviews I have conducted.

Butcher's journey as a professional musician began on a tragic note, after his England and Surrey teammate Ben Hollioake died in a car accident. He was inspired to write a song in memory of his close friend, then sang it at his memorial in front of a crowd that included former British prime minister John Major.

A year after retiring in 2009, Butcher released his first solo record, *Songs from the Sun House*. He then formed part of the blues supergroup The Boom Band which toured Europe and put out an eponymous album. He has played with the likes of the Rolling Stones' Bill Wyman on stage at the Royal Albert Hall, and his musicianship has even impressed cricket enthusiast and chum Eric Clapton.

"I've got no real set routine, which is something that I have strived for ever since I started playing," Butcher says. "If I can get away without having to do a proper day's work in the same place every day, then I'll have done OK."

Butcher, of course, works like mad. It's just that he makes everything seem so easy.

Butcher batting for England against Australia in the Ashes in 1999. The cricketer would have a song in his head to battle distraction during competition.

How did being raised as the son of two athletic parents shape your goals?

As I grew up, there was very little doubt that I would end up being a professional cricket player – in my mind anyway. It just never occurred to me that there might be something else that I'd do. Which wasn't arrogance, it was just that I was kind of good at it and I enjoyed it and it didn't really cross my mind that anything else could be possible.

My brother and sister and I enjoyed all sports, and there was always music played around the house. But we had no pressure from either of our parents to follow in their footsteps. It's just something that naturally happened.

Was it tough on your parents having an interracial marriage in those days?

Yeah, I think it was. You know in 1971 or 1972, it wasn't a normal thing – even in London. So I think that that my mum in particular probably got a hard time about it. I've never really spoken to my dad about it. Being a cricket player, Dad was away a lot, so she bore the brunt of whatever was going on. It wasn't straightforward.

Were you conscious of it?

Not really. I mean one of the incredible things that my mum did was to insulate us from that type of thing. It was something that snuck up on me later, realizing that there was something different about our family setup, something different about me and my skin color and my heritage. But we were largely protected from the worst side of that.

It didn't occur to me that other people would have an issue or were getting problems from that kind of stuff. And I think it was because my brother and I were both really good sportspeople. Being one of the best footballers or cricket players gives you an insulation from some of the abuse that some of the other kids might get if they don't look the same. And it's really weird. It dawned on me that that was the case. When you are able to do something that a lot of the other kids aspire to do, you have a superpower that protects you from people's prejudices.

What was your big passion first, singing or playing cricket?

My mum tells a story about me singing the Billy Joel album *The Stranger* in the bath at the top of my lungs as a kid – without the accompanying music, but getting the lyrics right from however old I was. So I think they were concurrent.

At what point did you ever think you could be a professional musician?

It was only much later on, after I'd already become a professional sportsperson, that I decided to take the songwriting and performing side of things more seriously. Now, had the cricket playing not worked out and I had gotten an injury, or just not been good enough, then who knows? I might have decided to dedicate myself to music, but that's not the way it turned out.

And you grew up playing guitar?

I got my first guitar when I was about 13, so I was a late starter. There were two events that shaped my guitar playing. Around that time I was on a cricket tour and we stopped at the service station for some petrol, and in one of the bargain bins was a cassette for like a pound. I'd heard the name Jimi Hendrix but had no idea about his music or anything. So I bought the cassette and stuck it in my powder blue Panasonic Walkman as the bus drove off and heard *Purple Haze*. And I'm just like, 'Oh my God. What the hell is that?' I had my mind blown.

And then I watched Queen during Live Aid in 1985. Seeing Brian May play his solos and then seeing Eric Clapton … suddenly I thought, 'I've got to have a guitar. I need to know how to do that!' So I saved up and got a Telecaster knock off from a place called Rock Bottom in West Croydon.

Let's talk about cricket. By the time you were 20, you rose to the top ranks of your county club Surrey. Five years later in 1997, you were selected to play for England for the first time. How did that feel?

It was quite something. It was an Ashes summer.[1] England had been pretty rubbish at this point, and Australia had held the Ashes since 1989. They had (Australian bowling legends) Shane Warne and Glenn McGrath playing for them and they were a damn good side. So it was with some trepidation, but I don't remember being quite as excited about it as I ought to have been.

Why didn't that thrill you?

Because I felt like it was inevitable, that it should have happened.

You went on to have a stellar career that included eight test centuries.[2] Can you describe the feeling of being in a groove when you're batting?

Yeah, a little. It happened so infrequently. I had a career for 20 years and I can almost remember every single time what it was like. You're incredibly focused. It's almost like you can hear the ball coming at you. Senses are heightened to that degree.

But you're also incredibly calm and relaxed. There's none of the outside noise or anybody else's business that's getting into your space. And everything seems to be happening in slow motion. That's basically it. You watch it, it comes. You can just make whatever decision you want to make. Hit it wherever you want it to go, know that it's going to go where you want it to. If I could bottle (that sense of awareness), it would have been much easier game.

Can you experience that level of being in a zone musically?

Yeah, I think so. Again, it's not something that happens all the time. I think. If you're singing something you wrote and you're absolutely engaged in it, then you close your eyes and away you go. But again, it's not an easy state for me to get into by playing music either. I'm not sure that it comes anywhere near as naturally to me as batting used to, and even then, it was hard to maintain that sort of thing. So the idea is to get into a state where you're not really conscious of anything.

---

1. The Ashes is a Test cricket series played between England and Australia at least every two years.

2. A cricket century is accomplished by scoring 100 runs in a single innings.

And it's not an easy state to get into or to maintain. You have fleeting moments of it, but that's the goal.

Did you use any mental techniques to get to that state?

I didn't, no. But perhaps the sport is much more enlightened now than it was then. And I think I'm probably more enlightened than I was then. So I wouldn't be embarrassed about trying to seek that out. But at the time so much in the sports world was very ego driven. And there was very little in the way of admitting to weaknesses in any way because you always felt that it would be used against you at some point – both by people who were on your side or people who weren't. So you tended to keep that stuff to yourself when you knew the better thing to do would be to talk to somebody about it and say, 'Listen, I'd like to be able to recreate this on a more regular basis.' It's not always going to be perfect. But if you can get close, then the likelihood is that you're going to be more successful more often. Obviously, that's done on a regular basis now.

Do you mean speaking to a mental coach?

Yeah. Or even a safe person to say, 'Listen, I'm wondering about this, this isn't right. This guy's got my number. What do I do?' Just actually saying it kind of makes it better. I used my dad quite a lot in terms of the technical side of the game. He was a brilliant batting coach and just having that sounding board there helped.

You were on a few teams that struggled, but were never able to reconcile with losing. Is that why you didn't get into coaching – to avoid bringing those losses home with you again?

From when I was a kid, I played on teams that hardly ever lost. We were good. Whether that was playing football, cricket or anything. So I wasn't a very good loser. By the end of my playing career at Surrey I was captain of the team and I'd take bad performances home with me in a bad way. I just didn't want to be around that anymore. The energy of it was just really bad.

So broadcasting means I get to be around the game that I love, that has done so much for me, and watch other people be amazingly good at it, and talk to people about it. But I don't give a damn who wins or loses, it's perfect.

Was your inability to let those losses go because of your competitive nature?

Yeah, I think so. It's one of the things about batting. I don't know if baseball players feel the same, but I once read every batting attempt described as being a mini-death. You build yourself up and practice, and you walk out in front of the crowd and TV cameras, and then you walk back having not made any (runs) and it hurts like hell. It's an indescribable kind of shame almost. And it's a difficult one for people to come to terms with. The psychological effect of failing as a batsman, some people can't deal with it at all. You're talking grown men throwing things around and smashing the place up. It has a real effect on people.

By the end I was more upset by the team results because I felt that was a reflection on me as a leader. And I wasn't so bothered about not scoring any runs, because – let's face it – I was a professional batsman for 20 years. You're going to get out. People are going to make mistakes. So I reconciled with that.

On that note, you went from being named England captain in the Test series against New Zealand in 1999 to getting dropped the next year. Your loss of form coincided with a divorce and the birth of two of your children in the span of 12 months. Did all the pressure just get to you?

There was a real personal issue with all of this. I was not a happy person. I messed up at home, cheated on my wife and I had a child with another woman that I had been seeing on the side. Everything was a real mess. And you couple that with trying somehow to maintain a career that requires a much steadier level of emotional competence. Unsurprisingly, I couldn't do any of those things. So there was a lot of alcohol and just bad behavior – shit behavior really. All of which culminated in me hating playing. I didn't want to play anymore, because – I didn't know this at the time – but I guess I didn't want to have to go face people.

Cricket is one of those games, because it lasts as long as it lasts, you can't lock away everything else that's going on, play the game, and then go back to it. Because the Test matches are five days. The first class games are three or four days. If things are terrible, they're terrible. And you're taking that with you. And there isn't anything you can do about it. I know a couple of people who were able to compartmentalize things and still be able to perform, and then go back to life once it's done. But I couldn't do that. So it dragged everything. Everything came down all at once.

How long did that feeling last? Would you say you were depressed?

Absolutely. And I was doing everything possible to harm myself and the people around me. So it was not very positive. It probably lasted about two years, from about the middle of 1999 to January 2001. I had an episode at a friend's house and I doubled over in pain. I couldn't get off the floor. Something was wrong with my stomach, so I went to the doctor. He said, 'You need to stop doing what you're doing, otherwise it's going to be bad.' So I got a massive jolt from that and I called my old man and said, 'Right, I need your help.'

The only thing that I knew how to ask him was, 'Can you help me bat properly?' It wasn't, 'I'm going to tell you what's going on in my life and can we have a talk about it?' It was teaching me how to bat as though I was 2 years old and never played the game before. That's what I asked him to do and that's what he did. And in doing that we had a two or three month period of contact through him being the teacher and me being the pupil that we'd really never had in our entire lives before. It was based solely on this. And my game went from hopeless to thinking, 'Oh hang on, I might actually enjoy playing again.' It wasn't, 'Oh, I'm going to play for England again,' or 'My career is going to take off again.' It was literally, 'I'll be able to enjoy this and we'll see what happens from there.'

Were you still playing for Surrey?

Yeah, although I'd been dropped from the first team there as well. I found myself on the outside of that side. You know you're on your way out when that happens. So yeah, it was an interesting time.

There is something incredibly fascinating about your process of coming back as a top level cricketer, which involved creating a nasty persona for yourself. You invented a character you described as 'a complete dickhead and a total cunt.' Who was that person?

Now, it just seems incredible, really. (I was) somebody who just paid little or no attention to anybody else's concerns. The weird thing is, what I identified as the problem was my inability to turn people down if it was to do with my time. Or being led into doing things in relationships that I didn't necessarily really want to do. I found it difficult to say no to people, and so the character was literally just going to please myself. That's it. I will do what I want to do when I want to do with whom I want to do it and see how long I can get away with it for. And for quite a long time it was successful. I was successful enough on the field for it not to have any sort of toll on me off it. It might have been having a toll on other people, but I was OK for a while. But it caught up with me in the end.

Is that because people tolerate bad behavior from sportsmen who are good at what they do?

Probably. I think back to when I was a youngster. I don't remember being sat down very often and told: 'No. That's no good.' I had this way of avoiding people (telling me), 'Seriously, you're going to behave like that?' And I guess I took it to the nth degree.

It didn't come naturally to you though. Was it a conscious decision to embrace this alter-ego?

Yeah, I was very aware of it.

Why did you feel you had to do that?

Because I don't think I was very confident that I'd be able to carry it off as myself. So I needed the arm of somebody else to carry it off. The thing is, if you asked my teammates at the time, I'm not sure that they would have noticed a great deal of difference. Because it wasn't necessarily in the environment of the team or in the dressing room or with the guys that I was playing cricket with that this character was a factor. It was outside of that. It was my friends and family and the relationships that I had – all with people that I would need but would keep very much at arm's length. I would use them when I needed them and then disregard them afterwards. And that went for my kids too. I didn't see them. I was missing for the early part of their lives. Because again, it felt like I'd be losing energy. I'd have to give too much of myself away in order to do what I wanted to do.

Apart from being selfish with your time, did being a bit abrasive with people also drum up some sort of confidence in you? Like, 'I'm like I'm a badass sportsman'?

Precisely that. The idea was to be so bulletproof from criticism, from the norms of what people would do – the rules that society would set for me and that I would normally set for myself – in order to then walk out there and feel like I could do whatever was possible and necessary when I was playing.

That's what it was about: trying to build myself and my self-confidence up to a point where I felt that I was invincible. And it would play out in weird ways off the field, you know, breaking the law, doing unspeakably dangerous things – that type of stuff. Because it was like, 'Well who's going to stop me?'

Reading that, some people might say, 'Well Christ, you went through all that and you still weren't that great, you know.' And it's true, but in my in my head, it was necessary to be able to get myself back into it. Now, what I didn't know was that once I got back to where I wanted to be, it should have been possible to roll it back a little and take everything, including myself, a bit more seriously. But I couldn't stop, and it got to the point where I started to eat myself from the inside out.

You said you were doing reckless things like drinking and driving. At that point were you still depressed?

No, but I don't think I was very well. I would class myself an alcoholic while all that was going on.

You played your last Test match for England in 2004 and then had a rash of injuries. You've said that you felt relief because you had grown weary of this character. Can you explain that?

I just got tired. I got this (wrist) injury which turned out to be much worse than they first thought. And I got to step away from it all for about six months. It was six months that cost me my career as an England player, because in that time, England won The Ashes for the first time in (18 years), and the team moved on from me. I was never gonna get back. My biggest career regret is that I couldn't be in the team that won that won The Ashes, but there you go.

But then once I stepped outside of that for a little while, I settled down and set a new goal. I captained Surrey, and wanted to see if we could go back to winning some trophies and bring on some of the young players. The focus was outside of myself. I was happy and I reconciled with all of that. I became normal again.

Does the act of inventing a character who distanced himself from regular people – for instance you refused to use public transportation because it was unbecoming of a celebrity – to a small degree still exist as a musician for you?

No it doesn't. The music side of it doesn't feel anywhere near as ego-driven as the sports side of it for me. I feel like it's more in service of the songs that you're playing than it is about me really. That is one of the things I like about writing (songs): You can be personal if you want. You can also veil personal things in a wider context. And then it just becomes about delivering them and being in sync with the other guys that you're playing with. It's more of a communal thing with the music and hoping that the people that you're playing it to are having a good time. And that's a pretty good place to be in, because it isn't about me anymore, which I think is a good thing.

A very sad moment in your life encouraged you to start your music career. It was when your teammate Ben Hollioake tragically died in a car accident. You wrote _You're Never Gone_, which you sang at his funeral. It was the first song you had written in years. How did that come about?

It was utterly devastating. I had known Ben since he was tiny because me and his brother were best friends from about 8, 9, 10 years old. The song just came out of me. It was the easiest thing in the world to write the lyrics and the melody. It just seemed to be there already. I'm not prolific when it comes to songwriting, and I don't have thousands of them stored up. But when they come, they almost come finished. They just they happen.

You must have been in the haze at the funeral. Did you feel anxious at all?

Yeah, it was pretty tough. Sitting right in front of me were his mum and dad. So it was pretty terrifying. It was at Southwark Cathedral; it's a big old place. And I got through it, anyway. I remember his dad smiling at one point, so that was pretty cool. Fortunately, that ceremony was a little way after the event itself. So we had enough time for the rawness of the moment to disappear, which I think was handy. I don't think I would have been able to do it otherwise.

And that got you into writing music regularly?

Yeah. I then had the opportunity to record it. We released it as a charity single to raise money for the Ben Hollioake fund. So I got back into the idea of playing and singing and performing. But you're right, it was Ben's death and the song that came out it that got me back into the idea of doing my own thing.

When athletes transition to music they can sometimes be opening themselves up to ridicule. Do you feel you have to go the extra mile to convince your audience that you are a legitimate musician?

I feel it every single time I perform. Every single time. I'm not comparing myself to what other musicians go through, because I know there are incredibly talent ones who for whatever reason cannot buy a sandwich at lunchtime. So guilt is not the right word, but I do feel as though I'm in a relatively privileged position because people know me already.

But that has its own terrifying side of it, because you've got a little bit of a leg up on a kid who's done everything in his life for music, but no one knows who he is. But also people know you as a cricket player and they're ready for you to be terrible. It can terrify you into being less free when performing. They'll say, 'Of course you're going to mess it up, you're a bloody cricket player, you're hopeless!' And that never goes away. It's not easy, but it sharpens you a little bit.

That's one of the things I love about touring, because in (continental) Europe there is no one out there who knows I played cricket. I'm just one of the band, so it's awesome. I don't have anything to prove, I just go out there and enjoy myself.

When you're batting in front of a huge crowd and another million on TV, do you think about it?

The first time I played a Test match at the Melbourne Cricket Ground there were 90,000 people there. I felt so tiny. Psychologically, when I was playing well, I'd walk out and feel like I was bigger than everybody else. It's a weird kind of thing. You're projecting a size or dominance. And when things weren't going so well, you'd feel like you could get squished by a blade of grass. And it's bloody intimidating.

How did you apply those experiences when you're on stage?

The interesting thing is, on stage I never, ever failed to be nervous. Whereas there were times when I was playing cricket, where I just didn't have the adrenaline and didn't get that kick. Maybe because I had done it for so long. But on stage I always have butterflies in my stomach, whether I'm playing for 10 people or a live TV audience.

You've spoken about the similarities between the musician's life and the cricketer's life, saying, 'you spend so much time hanging around waiting to do the thing you meant to do.' I think they're both a little brutal too, with how quickly you can be dismissed in either profession. Can you see the similarities?

Absolutely. One of the things about the American college sports system which is commendable is that it gives people tools. You have to major in something before you embark on your sporting career. And there's nothing like that (in England). I left school and wanted to get into my professional career as fast as I possibly could. And lots of professional athletes are exactly the same, with no qualifications. If you break a leg at 24, suddenly that's it. So yeah, there is a brutality to it.

The difference with sports is that, injury aside, a lot of it is in your control. You're not relying on the public or a critic's opinion on whether your songs are any good. You are in control of how you prepare yourself physically, mentally and technically. When you walk out there with your bat, it's in your power to score 100 runs. Nobody else is telling you that you can't. As a musician, you're very much at the whim of fashion or some critic you might upset. Maybe the production style on the album went out of fashion a month before and you're too late. There's so much more that is out of your control.

What links the two worlds for you, music and cricket?

Rhythm. When I was playing, if I was in a good place, I would have a song in my head, and that would be the only thing in my head. Because thought is the enemy of being able to play – or at least it was for me. Time and rhythm are both things that apply in equal measure in both pursuits.

You also have to be dedicated enough and single-minded enough to stick at something until you've got it. And it applies entirely to both. A lot of people get bored really easily, but I don't think you can as a sportsperson. If you're going to be really good, you need the mental capacity to do things over and over again. That's exactly the same with music, it takes repetition and time.

What is your career high in music?

That's really easy. When I was with The Boom Band, we were asked to be a house band for an unnamed artist for a charity gig. The week of the performance we found out it was Van Morrison. We got a setlist of about 10 songs, and we waited for Van to turn up for a quick sound check. We were all a bit apprehensive; you hear stories that he's an absolute nightmare. He comes in with his hat on and nods at everyone, then counts into his first number. He opens his mouth and I nearly dropped my guitar. I could not believe the sound of his voice, it was astonishing. It was like: *boom*! And I'm standing there thinking, 'This is epic.' It was a surprise gig at the Cranleigh Arts Centre in Surrey, so when he walked on the stage the roof came off. We played about an hour of his best known tunes and brought the house down. I thought, 'Well, if I never play again, that's cool.'

In 2001 you batted 173 not out against Australia in what has been described as one of the greatest innings in the history of The Ashes. How did walking off the field that day compare to your experience of jamming with Van Morrison?

The 173 (runs) was the culmination of everything that I had I wanted out of being a professional cricket player. It was one of those magical days. That was something that I had trained for forever, since I picked up my first bat around the time I could first walk. So that's still the high watermark.

One of my many weaknesses as a player was that I wasn't all that interested in scoring in the numbers. I wasn't very good at scoring runs for scoring runs sake. I was pretty good at being able to react to a certain sets of circumstances. I wanted to play beautifully. There was a level of vanity about it, I guess. I wanted to play perfectly and have everything look right and feel right. And on that day, it did. It had everything. So it has to be that, as much as playing with Van blew my mind.

Or even having a No. 1 album in the future, who knows.

You're one of the few people uniquely positioned to answer something like that. Between playing to a full crowd at The Ashes and the Royal Albert Hall, you've experienced incredible highs that only an infinitesimal number of people will ever have the thrill of experiencing.

Well, if you put it like that, it's pretty cool, huh?

Essence Carson

Washington, D.C., July 2020

Essence Carson is living her best life.

The six-foot WNBA All-Star and 2016 champion divides her time as a veteran floor leader in the league, an A&R manager with Motown Records, and a badass hip-hop artist, producer and multi-instrumentalist.

Carson grew up in Paterson, New Jersey, the gritty town she refers to often in the two albums she has released under her musical moniker Pr3pE. It was there where her father Joseph, once a promising athlete, fell into the drug scene and then got clean before dying of ALS when Essence was 11. Joseph was gone too soon, but left a mark on his girl by introducing her to two interests that would shape her life — basketball and rap music.

Carson was raised by her grandparents who steered her towards music and church, and shielded her from Paterson's rough streets. At age 12, she watched a neighbor die from a stray bullet outside their house.

Displaying the same youthful work ethic as Bernie Williams, Carson enrolled at the Rosa L. Parks School of Fine & Performing Arts, which was strong on academics but offered no sports programs. There she focused on piano, saxophone and electric bass, and engaged in fierce rap battles during lunch breaks. In the afternoons she would commute to Paterson's Eastside High

School, made famous by the film *Lean On Me*, where she developed into a star basketball and track athlete.

On Sundays she would take on a different persona, attending church regularly and lending her versatile talents to the band as a pianist and alternate drummer. "I just played where I fit in," she recalls. "I have always had a thirst for knowledge."

As her basketball skills progressed, Carson was heavily recruited by every major college women's basketball program in America. She chose Rutgers, a 20-minute drive from her home, and graduated with degrees in music and psychology.

In college, Carson became an Academic All-American and was a starter in the 2007 NCAA title game (a loss to Tennessee). She blossomed into the seventh overall pick in the 2008 WNBA draft, where she was selected by the New York Liberty.

It was during that run to the Final Four at Rutgers where she got her first taste as a public spokesperson for social justice, after shock jock Don Imus took racial jabs at her team on air.

Carson was vocal at the ensuing press conference, reminding the press that "before the student comes the daughter." New York Daily News columnist Mike Lupica gushed at Carson's poise, calling her "a basketball player and straight-A student and piano player and star of this day."

Looking back, that moment could be seen as a rite of passage for Carson, a figurehead for one of the world's most socially conscious sports leagues. "I'm the one who had to do all the interviews. I wasn't even a full-grown adult yet having to speak out against racism," she says.

In 2017, Carson was again at center stage when she and her Los Angeles Sparks teammates walked off the court before the national anthem during Game 1 of the WNBA finals, and chose to remain in the locker room during the rendition before the next three games.

"You're standing for what you believe in, bringing attention to something that needs attention brought to," Carson said days after the Sparks lost their title to the Minnesota Lynx in five games. "I felt like everyone is so focused on the flag, and it's not even about the flag. It's about racial inequality, criminal justice reform, police brutality, and everything along those lines."

'It helps you become inclusive of everyone'

Carson has gained added perspective as a world traveler, playing for teams in France, Spain, Italy, Hungary and Turkey during WNBA off-seasons. Not surprisingly, success followed her in Europe, as she won the French and Turkish league titles and the prestigious EuroCup in 2017.

She lists Madrid and Istanbul as two of her favorite cities, where she was able to embrace new musical genres and exchange experiences with teammates from mixed backgrounds.

"It definitely influenced my taste in music," she says of her travels. "And it helps you become inclusive of everyone, and I'm very appreciative of that. Despite what conflict is going on in the world, when music starts to play, it brings everyone together – just like sports."

Carson spends most of her time in Los Angeles, based out of the iconic Capital Records Building, where she handles label relations and nurtures artists for Motown. Although she works in Hollywood, she is still that girl from Paterson – a point reinforced by *Conversations Pt. 1*, the track released days after our interview.

We spoke via video conferencing, this book's first interview under travel restrictions caused by the coronavirus. Carson was in Washington D.C., getting ready for her 13th WNBA season which was played in a protective 'bubble' campus in Orlando.

What has your routine been like during this pandemic?

You really have to be very disciplined during this time. Not only athletes – I feel like that applies to a lot of people across the board. Because if you don't have the person next to you there to ensure that you're doing what you're supposed to do, then you take on all that responsibility. I actually enjoy being self-motivated, and I took that to another level. I'm also staying grounded and centered amongst all this chaos that has been going on in the outside world.

How do you juggle playing in the WNBA and working full-time at Motown Records?

It's not like I'm not focused. This is this is the only life I know. What a lot of people don't know is that I've been working full-time for Motown for three years – even throughout the season. I'm able to work remotely. But if I'm in (Los Angeles), I do stop by the office and make sure that I touch base with everyone.

What it has taught me is how to really be a great communicator. Because when you're traveling how I travel, in order for things not to get lost along the way you have to make sure your communication is up to par. So I've been able to hold it down on that front and still focus on basketball. But for me, that's not anything new. Because I've been playing music and basketball since I was a child. I started music when I was 9 and basketball when I was 11. If anything were to change, I would kind of be out of balance.

I know time management is crucial for you. How have you been managing your hours since you were a little kid?

To me, this is how life functions. To someone else, it might be too much. But this is why they're them, and this is what I'm me, right? It's all about how you look at these things. I feel that I have the capacity to handle both – it's just that you have to sacrifice other things, mostly some leisure time. Of course, you need to take time for yourself to center yourself, to get your thoughts together and create your own peace. But going out to party and stuff like that? I don't have time to do that. So what I am going to do is bypass that and take that time – those four or five hours – and dedicate that to something else. So that is how I look at it. It's really just about time management for what you ultimately care about.

Let's talk about your childhood growing up in Paterson, New Jersey. You saw a neighbor lying dead on the street. How did growing up in that environment impact you?

It goes back to your exposure. If that's the only thing you've been exposed to – I'm not saying that every day was filled with killing, because there were definitely some amazing memories that I have as a child in Patterson – but when that's your environment, you begin to believe that's the norm. And I believe that many of those that don't 'make it out' somehow lose sight of what's actually in front of them. They can only see what is literally around them. And they think that's all life has to offer.

Luckily, basketball was able to take me beyond the city limits, so I was able to see how other people lived, what other towns looked like, and what experiences were like for other children my age. And then I began to realize that their experiences were different. So once I realized that that there was so much room to grow (in Paterson), I made it a duty of mine to do all that I could as a child to give myself the best chance.

I started to realize that we didn't have opportunities. It wasn't that we didn't have the talent. It wasn't like we didn't have the determination. We didn't lack that, we just lacked that opportunity. And if you don't have opportunity, and you can't see that opportunity is there, you just give in and become someone that's part of the factory line. That's what it becomes.

And that's essentially what was around me. It was just people being products of their environment, surviving. And you can't blame any of them for that. Because at the end of the day, if they don't do what they have to do to survive, then what is the opposite of that?

I was blessed to be raised by my grandparents who had a whole other outlook on life, because they experienced life two times over by the time I came around. They knew of all the mistakes, and they tried to teach me about those mistakes and instill a certain grace and determination and grit in me that I can carry throughout life, and hopefully make something better of myself.

You went to a performing arts high school to study music while running track and playing basketball for Eastside High School, where you were a McDonald's All-American. Which pursuit was more of a passion growing up?

I honestly can't say, I loved both of them. It wasn't just basketball. I missed a game because I had to go to a piano recital. I missed a track meet to do a piano recital.

That must have been tough.

Of course, it was definitely tough. I was faced with decisions like that at early age, they didn't feel good. But what I learned is that you have to make hard decisions. You can't always have things your way or the way that you think is ideal. You have to make it make sense. So I learned that early.

When did you start thinking you could make a career out of either interest?

I always thought I could make a career out of music. Even as a young kid, just wanting to be a Quincy Jones. And then you fast forward to the hip-hop era, I want to be another Missy Elliott. Both of them are definitely innovators.

But on a basketball side, I didn't really know I could be a professional because the league came around when I was about 12. So before that, it was all about wanting to be the first girl to dribble the ball between her legs on TV, because I couldn't fathom there being a professional league.

Then once the WNBA came around, I was like, 'Oh, this can be a real thing.' There are women out here doing the same thing. It's not just me in Paterson doing this, it's this whole world. And by the time I got to college, I was like, 'Oh, a little closer to reality.' But by the time I was a senior, I was like, 'Oh, it's reality. This is probably going to happen.'

What did it feel like to get that scholarship letter from Rutgers?

I got my first letter when I was about 15 as a high school sophomore. I was like, 'Wow, people are watching me outside of this city. How did they know about me?' But then more letters kept coming. And then – I kid you not – I had trash bags full of letters. I'm talking about the black Glad heavy duty trash bags full of letters and they wouldn't stop coming. And they were from every school you can possibly think of. It felt good, there's no other way to explain it. You could say it was overwhelming. But at the end of the day, it just felt good. It felt good for someone to recognize your talent. Whatever it is, it could have been basket weaving. But if I got that many letters for basket weaving, I would still feel the same way.

I'm sure you also received offers from the powerhouse programs like Tennessee and the University of Connecticut. What made you decide to stay home and go to Rutgers?

There were a few factors. Rutgers had a really good music program, for one. And they had an amazing coach (Vivian Stringer) that had a lot of success on and off the floor, in terms of really raising her players to be amazing women. They didn't have the best record on the basketball court, but the camaraderie that they had off the floor was amazing. It was hands down the best out of the schools that I visited.

Going back to Coach Stringer, she was a woman of her word. Being a Hall of Fame coach that everyone respected, she had a schedule that was unlike any other with how busy she was. But she told me that if she played the first movement of *Moonlight Sonata*, I would have to come to Rutgers. I'm thinking, 'There's no way she's gonna do that. She just doesn't have time to learn how to play.'

She didn't study classical music or anything like that, but I guess she took piano lessons. I don't know for how long she took them, but she played the first movement. And I mean, at that point, I had no choice because she is a woman of her word, and I respected that.

'When everything's clicking on the court, it's like sweet music,' says Carson, in action for the Los Angeles Sparks in 2018.

In your 2016 championship season with the LA Sparks you began by winning 11 games in a row, and your first 20 out of 21 games. Describe that feeling of being unbeatable.

That was an amazing season. We were breaking records left and right. It was amazing in the way the defense moved that year. Teams couldn't score on us, and they couldn't stop our offense. We were high powered on both ends of the floor, and it just it felt really good. It seemed like nothing could go wrong and everything was in sync. Everything was in flow. Everything was working on all cylinders. And it moved quickly. The game itself moved in slow motion, so you could see every cut, every pass, every lane that you could steal the ball in. But as a season, it just seemed like it just went by so fast. You blink your eyes and before you know it, we are 20-1. It was like, 'Whoa, could that happen that quickly?' Um, but it did.

The Sparks had a roster full of stars that year, including Candace Parker. How did that affect team chemistry?

We all were in sync and there were no egos at that point. That is very important, because we all could have had huge egos. We all came from amazing basketball backgrounds; we all had accomplished plenty in our professional careers. But we put that aside to come together as one. We were all in lockstep with one another and all moved together. It was like a juggernaut.

So it sounds like you guys were all in a zone together throughout the season.

Yes, throughout the season.

How does being in that zone — when you feel like the game is in slow motion and you're invincible — compare to being in a zone musically for you?

Being in a zone musically feels like the opposite of pent-up emotions, or the point where you're like, 'Oh my gosh, I'm about to explode, I can't take anymore.' Being in a zone musically would be the complete opposite of that. It's just letting everything flow through you. It almost becomes your language, it becomes how you communicate with the world, with the listener. It doesn't matter what that emotion is that you're trying to convey, it just flows through you. I think one word that you will probably hear often is 'flow,' whether it's about music or sports. Flow exists in life outside of both of those realms, but I believe that it exists in its truest forms in each of those (activities).

Musically, it just feels like you're able to seamlessly communicate with the audience and you don't have to speak one word. They don't have to question what you're playing or question what you've said in your lyrics. They just get it. It's like everyone wants to be seen and everyone wants to be heard, and no one wants to be questioned. That's what it does.

It's just like basketball when everything's clicking on the court. It's like sweet music. I have a tattoo on my back that I got when I was 17. There is a basketball and a cross and it says: 'Sweet Music,' and the S is shaped as a treble clef. It's terrible art, but the concept is there. When you're playing the game of basketball the right way, it's almost like an orchestra. It's sweet music to your ears. You're watching everything flow together on offense, and it's just like when you hear a symphony. To me the two coincide, they always have.

You released your first album *Broken Diary* under the pseudonym Pr3pE in November 2013. I love the album, I think it is loaded with infectious tracks and I'm surprised I didn't hear about it earlier. Do you feel you're working against your career in basketball to make popular music? In other words, if you didn't have the label of Essence Carson WNBA player and just focused on your music that it would be more commercially successful?

I've asked myself that. I think at the time I did that album I probably thought so. But where I am in life now with the new music that I'm creating, it makes sense why it didn't move in that way. It's given me time to grow as an artist and, more importantly, as a person, and brought me to this place where I'm able to make the music I'm making now.[1]

I can say that the second mixtape that I did put out, *No Subs* (2016), is about what I was going through at that time and (served as my) musical therapy. There are a lot of emotions in that one. *Broken Diary* was a lot of storytelling, true stories. They are all true stories. Everything I write is pretty true. About 99.8 percent true.

Where do you record?

In LA, I actually found a studio that really like. When I just want to hibernate in a room and be locked by myself overnight, I head over to Hush Money Music studios in Koreatown.

Take me through that process. Can you just sit in a studio for 10 hours and let the creative juices flow and record?

Yeah. Um, I mean, there's some eating that happens within that (timeframe); I order some food or something like that. But yeah, I go in there, set up all this stuff. Sometimes I start with piano, with some keys and just play on the keys for a while and just vibe. I always turn the bright lights off, and there has to be like a nice easy hue, like a blue or a purple. Colors trigger certain things in your mind, you learn that in psychology, and blue and purple, and sometimes a little bit of pink helps. When it becomes orange, or yellow or white, I don't like how that makes me feel when I'm trying to create. So that's one thing I've got to set right, the mood with the lights.

This might sound monotonous to you, but I find something I like, then play it on the keys and I just let it loop. I'll find some other instruments that I like and just kind of work those instruments in there. And then, because of my writing process, I'll get up and I just walk. Walk, write it in my head and say it out loud. Walk, write it in my head, say it out loud, over and over again … until I get something that I feel is substantial enough to record. Kind of like a real reference point. And then I just keep building on top of it from there. And by the time the night is over or daylight comes, I might have a full song or two.

You've been very active with social justice both as a college player at Rutgers and as a WNBA player. Why has social justice been important to you as an athlete?

Because of this one simple thing: I've been Black all my life, so I know what it feels like. This isn't something that's new. People may acknowledge it now, but it's been a lifelong experience for people like myself. The fact that we have to even think of how we are going to make it in the real

---

1. Carson is releasing another self-produced album titled *Conversations* that addresses events that took place during the first half of 2020, including the killing of George Floyd and ensuing protests.

world is a problem. But here we are, it's all come to a head. It is very important that we use whatever platform that we (have) in order to voice that. I feel like I've been part of some moments in time that have forced me to speak up against certain things – starting at Rutgers. I wasn't even a full grown adult yet having to speak out against racism.

It's time that we take a stand, and I'm glad that we're doing so. People are tired of being tired and you're seeing the unrest. When you oppress people for a very long time, you can only expect an uprising at some point. It's been proven in history. That's what happened.

Why has the WNBA always been ahead of the curve in social protest?

One, we are a league of predominantly Black people.[2] Two, we are women. And if you go through history, women have always been on the front lines (of protest). I truly believe that it's innate, it really is. When it comes down to protecting what's ours, that's what we're going to do

What are your musical goals and where would you like to be positioned within the music industry?

I want to have a Grammy or two. And that could be as a contributor or as an artist, or producer or writer, or even as an executive where I help move parts. I look at the Grammys as the National Championship of it all. Of course, you don't just want your music to be heard, but also to be well received.

Has music helped your basketball career, and has basketball shaped your music?

Yes. They create balance for me. Those that know me as a basketball player know that I'm even-keeled. Not too many highs or getting too low. I keep a good head on. Despite what role I might take – whether it's defensive or offensive – I'm still going to come to the table and I'm going to bring a dish or two. And I'm going to do that with a certain poise. And I think that comes from music, because you have to be poised in order to play, right?

If you're at a recital and you're not poised and you're suffering, you're breaking down because of your anxiety – which can happen – you probably can't or won't perform your best. But you can be very anxious up until that moment you touch those keys when it's time to play. And that's when all silence falls upon you. And you overtake the moment, you don't let that moment overtake you. I learned that just from being able to study music for so long. That also helped me concentrate because you have to focus when you're learning to read music. So that helped to focus in basketball as well.

Basketball, in turn, gave me the competitive edge of wanting to be the best. So if you want to be the best, you're going to continue to sharpen your skills as a musician, as a songwriter, as a lyricist and as an artist. You're not going to become complacent. You're always going to be looking for new ways, new avenues to travel in order to create something better. So yes, the two definitely feed into each other.

---

2. Sixty-seven percent of WNBA players identified as Black or African-American in 2020, according to OnLabor.

Have you found the music world to be competitive?

Oh, yeah, for sure. Especially when you're talking about hip-hop. When you're talking about battle rap, that's a sport. So I'm going to have that competitive nature from competing at the highest levels in the world of athletics and then carry it over into music. I mean, whether you have the skill to back it up or not is a whole other conversation, but just having that competitive edge in itself, it helps.

Give me a glimpse into the thrill of playing to a crowd vibing to tracks you've created.

I did a show in the Flatiron District in New York at Toshi's Penthouse. It just felt euphoric, like floating on a cloud. You just kind of lose yourself. It felt good to be able to express all of that to the crowd.

You played lights-out in Game 3 of the 2016 WNBA championship in Los Angeles, hitting all four of your three-point shots and scoring 16 points. Can you ever achieve that feeling in music?

Yeah, I think that can. I think something huge would need to happen, maybe something that is a first of its kind. It would have to be something along those lines, but I think it's possible.

I could see that happening.

To me, it's just about what a person values in life. Some people are just happy to be able to wake up every morning and see the sunrise. Sometimes that's enough for people. Other people are not happy 'till they get $10 million in a bank account. It's just all perspective. But from my perspective, it would have to be something that was pretty great, a first of its kind.

You clearly set your goals very high.

I have to. It keeps me focused.

Daniela Hantuchova

London, August 2020

There is far more to Daniela Hantuchova than meets the eye.

Standing nearly six feet tall, the stylish Slovakian who speaks six languages could easily be mistaken for a secret agent from a James Bond film. But Dani, as she is known to her friends, is a former world class athlete, broadcaster and pianist who has accomplished more in her 37 years than most have in a lifetime.

Hantuchova retired from tennis in 2017, peaking at world No. 5 in both singles and women's doubles. As a mixed doubles player, she lifted all four Grand Slam trophies, becoming only the fifth female in history to do so. During her 17-year career, she represented Slovakia in three Olympics, won the Fed Cup and Hopman Cup for her country, and nabbed seven WTA singles titles – including the prestigious Indian Wells tournament twice.

Her post-tennis career is proving to be just as dynamic. With her infectious personality, Hantuchova transitioned seamlessly from the tennis courts to the TV booth. "Literally, the day that I announced my retirement I went straight to the studio," she says.

She features as a tennis analyst for Amazon Prime, Fox Sports and the Tennis Channel, and launched her podcast, *The Real DNA* in 2020. The show gets into the heads of tennis greats like Ivan Lendl, Chris Evert and Jim Courier, often focusing on the mental side of the game that became a strength for her as her career developed.

Hantuchova is also passionate about her music. From the ages of 6 to 14, she studied classical piano and credits the nerves she developed performing classical compositions as preparation for pressure-packed moments in her tennis career. "Ever since I was little, whatever I tried to do was with intensity," she says. "I always needed to have a purpose and a reason for doing things."

Studying piano was part of a rigorous academic schedule that required commitment at an early age. At 14, she moved to Florida to train at the famed Bollettieri Academy, but returned to her hometown of Poprad, Slovakia to take her high school exams. "Education for my parents was always the number one priority. It was school, piano and then tennis – that was the order of importance for them," she explains.

Despite turning pro a year later, the budding star graduated from high school and even enrolled in university back home before withdrawing due to the demands of the tour.

Now, with her broadcasting career firmly on track, Hantuchova is giving renewed focus to her musical training. She recently moved back to Slovakia and purchased a piano as a birthday present for her mother to share some of the joy that the instrument has given her.

"The thing I love most about piano is when I sit behind it, I just forget the rest of the world," she says.

You grew up in the former Czechoslovakia, which became an independent Slovakia when you were 9 years old. What do you remember about living under the restrictions of the Eastern Bloc?

They were crazy times. I remember the first time the borders were opened we went to Austria. Now we laugh about it, because it's a 20-minute drive from my house. But for my brother and me it was like we were going to New York – that's how far it felt. I remember little things like going to a supermarket in Austria and suddenly seeing all this candy and Coke. My brother and I saved our Coca-Cola until Christmas Eve to have it on the table as a special treat. That's how little there was. I think my work ethic and commitment came from those times when there was not much and we had to really fight for everything.

How did that affect the sports facilities and training in the country?

The first time I played in an indoor gym was when I went to Florida to train at the Bollettieri Academy. We have very cold winters in Slovakia, and before that I had to train under a bridge when it was snowing. But it was still below freezing outside. My trainer at the time tried to turn it into a fun game.

It's funny because during the coronavirus lockdown, I felt like we were back in the days when I was under the bridge training. So he was very creative and we got the job done. Now people see me traveling around the world and going to nice hotels and gyms, but there was none of that and we still made it work. And I was so happy; I didn't feel like I was missing out on anything, because that's just the way it was. Now, I tell younger players to be ready to put the work in no matter where they are. Whether it's an unbelievable gym with an AC or under a bridge.

Who was your tennis idol growing up?

It was Miloslav Mecir who won the 1988 Olympic gold medal for Slovakia.[1] That was the first

---

1. Mecir represented Czechoslovakia at the time.

time I saw tennis on TV. He was from the same (hometown) club as me, and was my main inspiration for playing tennis. We always had a special connection. Later he became the captain of my Olympic team, and having him around during my career meant a lot to me.

What was your routine like as a kid juggling academics, music and tennis?

It was a crazy schedule. I started my day at 6 in the morning on the tennis courts. Then I would go to school from 8 a.m. to 1:30 p.m. I would have piano lessons from 2 to 3 p.m. three times a week, then go to fitness from 3:30 to 4:30 p.m. Then go back to tennis from 5 to 8 p.m. and come back home and do my homework.

That's very telling that you still remember the exact time slots.

I do, it was my life. I loved every second of it. Some people might think it was crazy, but I wouldn't change anything about my childhood.

Is it true that your piano teacher didn't want you to play tennis?

Yes, she always complained that it was not good for my fingers and that it was going to make my hands stiff. She said I should consider stopping tennis because she thought I was good with the piano. She wanted me to keep studying music after high school. So yes, she probably didn't realize how important tennis was to me.

Did you have to come to a decision at one point whether to choose one or the other?

No, once I had to move to Florida to train, there was no question. But I absolutely love the piano. I have to say it's prepared me so much for what was coming on later in my tennis. Because, even though they were small concerts in Bratislava, every kid from my class had to play in front of their parents and grandparents and cousins. It was so much pressure that when I came to play on Centre Court in Wimbledon, it felt like nothing.

So that preparation for your piano recitals actually prepared you for high pressure situations in tennis?

Yes, I've said that many times. To this day, no matter what I've done – whether in my tennis or TV career – I've never, ever been as nervous as I was a couple of seconds before having to play in front of people. Because we had to play everything by memory, I was freaking out that I would just embarrass myself and sit on the chair and just forget everything. That happens – especially when you're 10 years old. So many of the kids from the same class would just sit there and not even be able to start. So it was nerve-racking.

What kind of music were you playing in those recitals?

It was classical music by composers like Beethoven, Bach, Mozart and Schumann. Back then, the teachers chose all the music that we were practicing. That's the only thing I regret. It's obviously beautiful, but it was only classical music. We were not allowed to play anything that came from the West.

Hantuchova poses after winning the Aegon Classic in Birmingham, England in 2013.

Did musical training help your tennis?

The thing I love most about piano is that when I sit behind it, I just forget the rest of the world. That's one of the great things my parents did. Practicing piano kept me grounded and made me feel like a normal kid; it was not all about tennis. It was like entering a different world and forgetting everything else.

Attending tennis camp in Florida while still being enrolled in high school in Slovakia was a big commitment at such a young age. What did that instill in you later in your career?

It's about how we grew up. I got that from my grandmother; she was a very strong person. She was my first tennis coach and she's been through so much in her life.[2]

   She was always so positive and had an unbelievable attitude about life. And she taught me so much. That work ethic definitely came from her. But most of the kids who played sports in Czechoslovakia were that way. The mentality we had was, once we're told to do something, we just do it. There's no 'Why?' or 'If' or whatever. So the way I was brought up helped me later on.

---

2. Hantuchova's grandmother lived through the struggles of World War II. She became the Czechoslovakian champion in doubles, playing alongside the mother of Ivan Lendl, but travel restrictions meant she could not compete internationally.

Your tennis breakthrough happened at age 18 when you won the singles title at Indian Wells, the tournament known as the fifth Grand Slam. At the time, you were the lowest ranked player to win the competition, and you beat your future doubles partner Martina Hingis. What was that feeling like?

It was a huge honor for me to play against Martina. She was one of my idols, and she was actually born a one-hour drive from where I was born (in Košice, Slovakia). So coming from the same part of the world, she inspired me big-time. She was a former world No. 1 and at the top of her game, so I don't know where that confidence came from. I woke up the day of the final and I just knew I was going to win. It never happened to me ever again. But it was a beautiful feeling and I played one of my best matches.

That's incredible. Why did that only happen once in your career?

I don't know. It was definitely a different feeling. I remember preparing the small speech of what I was going to say afterwards, and my parents told me, 'OK, Dani this is great, but try to prepare one for in case you lose.' And I got so mad at them. I said, 'I'm not going to lose!'

Would you call that youthful confidence?

I would say it was the naivety of things.

What are some of your favorite moments on the tennis court?

Winning the Fed Cup for my country in 2002. That's obviously so special, because you're not winning just for yourself but also for everyone at home. And then winning Indian Wells the second time in 2007, which was actually much tougher. I was much more aware of what it takes to win a tournament like that.[3]

And you played in three Olympics as well, including the 2012 London Olympics.

One of the most beautiful moments I had on a tennis court was when I got to play in the London Olympics. Watching Miloslav Mecir in the Olympics was why I started to play tennis. He was in my box as the Slovakian team captain, and I got to play on Centre Court in Wimbledon. So it was like a combination of everything. I was in tears before even stepping out on court.

As your tennis ranking improved, you had an opportunity to try new activities off the court, including modeling. Sometimes athletes open themselves to criticism when they get attention for things outside of their sport. How did you deal with that criticism?

In the beginning, I was taking everything personally, so I took it really hard. I just thought it was unfair to make comments that were not true. So it took me a while to get through that. Luckily with the people I surrounded myself with, they helped me understand that none of that is important. At the end of the day, it's the work you put in. And you can look at yourself in the mirror and know that you've done all you could (on the court). So that helped me get through it. Then, once I understood that it's just part of the business we are in, I never looked back. It hasn't really affected me since.

---

3. She defeated Svetlana Kuznetsova in straight sets in the final.

Were you making a statement by posing for the Sports Illustrated Swimsuit edition (in 2009) and the ESPN body edition (in 2012)?

When you get approached by Sports Illustrated or ESPN, you almost can't say no. They were beautiful photoshoots, especially the one for Sports Illustrated which took place in one of the most beautiful places I had been to (the Dominican Republic). It was very exciting.

You were known for a while as 'The Queen of the Three-Setters.' By 2014, you had played in more three-set matches (263) than anyone else on the women's tour and won nearly 70 percent of them. What was the secret of your success in three-setters?

Well, I don't know if you can call being in so many three-set matches a success. Because, let's face it, I should have won most of them in two sets. But for some reason, I enjoyed making it more complicated for everyone. So my family is very grateful for that. I think they went through a lot of stress thanks to me.

But for sure the endurance helped me to get through those. My former trainer Nigel Sears used to do the Ironman competition. So coming from that kind of training during the offseason, I was physically ready at the beginning of my career. Later the girls got so much more powerful, but early on that was one of my strengths. I knew that if we would get to three sets, I was going to have the edge. I felt like I could last for five or six hours out there.

How much of what separates the top players in tennis due to mental strength?

Mental strength is what separates the best from the rest. It's everything in sports. Everyone can hit forehands and backhands at this level, but the difference is between the ears — who wants it and believes in it more. I would say up to 70 to 80 percent is mental. Of course, work ethic, commitment, willingness and humbleness to always improve no matter how good you already are is a must. Without that you can't be anywhere near the top 10.

You once said: 'The tennis you can't control, because it's either there or it's not. But the fighting is something you can control.' Can you explain that mentality?

My coach Eduardo Nicolas told me that he didn't really care about how I was going to play, but he cared so much about always putting 100 percent in mentally. Every day is different. You're hardly ever going to hit all your shots the way you want to, but it's about how you approach the match mentally. And if you always give 100 percent out there, then you can end your career and have no regrets — which I don't. So it's an amazing feeling.

What did you learn towards the end of your career about the mental side of the game that you wish you would have known in the beginning?

Not taking it personally if I lose a match or if I miss a shot. At the beginning, it almost felt like I was a worse person just because I missed an easy forehand stroke or something. Whereas later on, my thinking was, 'OK, I just missed the shot.' I tried to understand why, but that was it, move on. There is nothing else. Nothing personal, no emotions involved with that. So it helped me separate my tennis from who I was as a person.

You reached world No. 5 in both singles and doubles, but you achieved more Grand Slam success in doubles. Which game did you prefer playing?

Singles, of course, was my priority. I always played doubles just for fun and to be able to be with my friends on the court. I really enjoyed mixed doubles as well. I got to play with the guys – who are generally much more relaxed – and got to practice the returns against their serves. It really helped me become much more reactive and helped my net game big-time. I always tell young players that it's good to play singles and doubles to have more variety in their game.

Was playing doubles 'just for fun' what allowed you to have greater success? Why could you not take the pressure off yourself in the singles game?

I think that is the question that every single player asks: Why can't we play without pressure? It's impossible. It's like asking, 'Why do you care so much for someone?' Well, because you love that person. In this case, you love the sport so much that it's impossible not to care. So yes, if I had the same attitude towards singles that I did in doubles and mixed doubles it would be probably another story. But at the same time, it was normal because I cared so much for it.

Let's talk about your rivalry with the Williams sisters. You once said: 'They kind of ruined my Grand Slam career in singles.' Although you may have struggled against them (3-19 overall) you did beat Serena twice, including once at the Australian Open. What was it like playing against them?

The number of times I had to play against them in the quarterfinals of the Slams was crazy.[4] Whenever I saw the draw, I was like, 'Really?' They deserve so much respect and credit for all the amazing things they have done for our sport.

Playing against Serena – who is the most competitive tennis player I have ever met – in a Slam was really tough. She is still playing unbelievable tennis now, but back in the day she could be unplayable. When she was serving aces and going for returns, it was really, really hard for me to do anything. I knew I had to go into long rallies with Serena (to have a chance), but it was almost impossible when she was having one of those good days.

It was very special when I got to beat her on Centre Court in Melbourne, because playing against her was so tough. But I always enjoyed our matches. Every time I faced her, I knew what I had to do to improve my training. Even though I may have lost, it helped me prepare for other players.

You mentioned your favorite moment in tennis was your Fed Cup win representing Slovakia. If you were to dream big about a moment equal to that in music, what would that be?

To have a piano session with Andrea Bocelli or with David Foster, both of whom I have had the pleasure of meeting. That would be a dream.

---

4. Hantuchova faced Venus or Serena Williams in 13 Grand Slam tournaments, including three quarterfinals.

Yannick Noah

Paris, October 2020

The night before Yannick Noah played the match of his life, he had a terrible nightmare. In painstaking detail, he dreamed he had just lost the French Open final in five sets, then broke down crying.

"It was in three-dimensions," he recalls. "And I lost. I made a couple of mistakes. And when the game was finished, I woke up. I felt terrible, because I just lost the finals."

Still dazed, Noah was awakened by his father asking if he was ready for the big day. "After a few seconds, I realized that it actually was a dream. And I tell you, when I woke up – to be able to have a second chance right away – I felt invincible."

The 23-year-old avenged his fantasy loss to Mats Wilander by defeating the defending champion in straight sets, making him still the only Frenchman to win at Roland Garros since 1946.

The emotional on-court celebration that followed the 1983 final is one Noah looks back on as "the perfect situation" because of its personal significance. It took place on the court where he trained relentlessly as a junior, with his family and friends in the stands and mentor Arthur Ashe in the TV booth. "The moment was so strong," he says.

Over a fascinating conversation, it becomes clear that Noah is one of the world's great storytellers, with tales accentuated by a voice that oozes charm. It's no wonder that his career as a stage performer took off: Noah is a natural showman.

He was born to Cameroonian father Zechariah, who played pro soccer in France, and French mother Marie-Claire, who taught philosophy while excelling in tennis and basketball. Noah grew up in Cameroon, playing tennis on one of the country's 11 courts. He was discovered by Ashe, who was on a good-will tour of Africa and gave the 11-year-old his first racket. The American great would become a beacon in the young prodigy's career, facilitating his move to the French Tennis Federation's academy. The two even played doubles together at Wimbledon in 1978.

Remarkably, they remain the only Black men in history to win Grand Slam singles titles. The significance is not lost on Noah, who also names Muhammad Ali as a hero. "It wasn't about how many games they won. That was secondary, because it was about what they did with it, and Arthur did unbelievable things for people (and) for injustice," he says. "You've got to feel blessed to be able to play tennis … But the most important thing is to make sure you don't forget where you're coming from. Don't forget the reality."

'This is it, I've made it. I can stop now.'

Just 10 days after Noah's Roland Garros victory, reality came crashing down from the highs he experienced on the court. The young champion who was crowned the 'King of Paris' felt so uneasy with the constant attention that he suffered a bout of depression. "I was not prepared," he reflects. "I did not like it at all." On impulse, he moved to New York with his wife, the former Miss Sweden Cecilia Rodhe, where they started a family.

The rest, as they say, is history. Noah returned to the French Open in 1984 to win the doubles title with best friend Henri Leconte and in 1986 reached his highest singles ranking of world No. 3, but he admits he never regained the drive it took to win another Grand Slam. He retired at 30, looking for new challenges when serendipity struck.

Noah's interest in music percolated on tour, as he provided vocals during off-hour jams with guitar-wielding pros John McEnroe, Jim Courier and the late Vitas Gerulaitis. After trying his hand at songwriting, Noah's musical career unexpectedly took off with hit single *Saga Africa*, a song reminiscing about his days growing up in Cameroon.

Around the same time, he was asked to captain France's 1991 Davis Cup team. As Noah turned mentor to buddies Leconte and Guy Forget, the duo upset Americans Pete Sampras and Andre Agassi in the final and became the first French Davis Cup winners in 59 years. The home crowd formed a conga line to the sounds of *Saga Africa*. Hollywood couldn't have written a better script.

Since then, Noah has fostered his dual career paths as coach and singer to spectacular success. Under his captaincy, France won the Davis Cup again in 1996, before he led the women's team to a Fed Cup victory the following year. After a long break to focus on his music, Noah returned to captain France in 2017 and his magic touch yielded another Davis Cup victory.

In the meantime, Noah has become a major pop star in France and neighboring countries, blending upbeat soul music with reggae. His 12 albums, including 2019 release *Bonheur indigo*, have sold millions of copies and are backed by 18-month world tours of up to 200 shows.

Being more well-known as an entertainer among France's millennials is a testament to Noah's music. Many would identify him as the father of longtime NBA center Joakim Noah before placing him as a Grand Slam winner.

Noah says his musical achievements — which were capped by a 2010 performance to a capacity crowd of 80,000 at Paris' Stade de France — were put in place by the mental grind he endured as a tennis pro.

"When you get onto a court, you're about to die," he says. "But I'm never nervous before going on stage. I'm excited. I'm happy, but no nerves."

Though he would finish his Hall of Fame tennis career with 23 singles and 16 doubles titles, one could argue that six No. 1 albums and a No. 1 hit single in France (the 2007 dance track *Aux arbres citoyens*) qualify Noah as a more successful musician than tennis pro.

But he's not buying any of it. For Noah, everything starts with that perfect win at Roland Garros. "Deep down inside, I still feel like a tennis player," he admits. "I think I've been surfing that wave for 37 years."

Take me through a day in the life of Yannick Noah.

A typical day doesn't exist for me. It really depends on the hat that I'm wearing, whether I'm coaching or playing music. I like to transmit. The transmission is the best part, which is actually the link with music. Because that's what we do really, is transmit some good energy towards whatever we're doing. I was always sensitive to the crowds (as a player) and transmitting to the players (as a coach), and now to my fans through my music. So those are the connections.

At what point did you start to take your interest in music seriously?

After the second Davis Cup win (in 1996), I decided to give myself a real chance and cut out tennis completely. I gave myself three years to really work on my music and put my heart and soul into it and see where it would lead. And I met the right people.

I was produced by Robert Goldman.[1] He said, 'I have a project for you,' but wanted me to sing in French. And for some reason it was easier for me to sing in English. When I started to work on my singing, I realized that as much as I was not shy on the court, when I was on stage I was very shy. So for me to sing in English was a form of protection.

Once I accepted that, I opened myself up to actually sing in French. I thought it was difficult at the time, but it worked. The therapy that I did with my singing coach was great, where we worked on me not being shy. And to be courageous enough to not have to always be who I was as a tennis player — trying to be the strongest, the baddest, the guy flexing his muscles.

All of a sudden, I was able to open up the other side, with a little shyness, and of course love and even some hesitations — all these delicate feelings that are not allowed on the tennis court. It was funny, because back in my playing days, I would jam with the friends on the circuit, and we were all about rock 'n' roll. 'That's what we do! Yeah we're bad!' It was great, that's who we were. We had to have that quality.

Sometimes they even talked about not having enough killer instinct. It works sometimes in certain areas — especially in sports — but not in (everyday) life and to continue on that path is definitely not what I wanted as an artist. So once I realized that, I recorded my first album in French, and it went to No. 1 and was on the charts for two years. We had a hit single, then another hit single and it went on.

---

1. Goldman is an accomplished French songwriter for the likes of Celine Dion.

Noah exults with a fan after defeating Mats Wilander (left) in the 1983 French Open final.

That must have come as a surprise to you.

I have to tell you the truth, not really.

Why not?

I've always been passionate about music. I always had like a little studio in my house, wherever I was, where I could jam with friends, professionals and amateurs. For some reason, I always felt I could do it.

The good thing I did was to go from playing on center court in tennis, or being the winning Davis Cup captain – being known as the King of Paris and so on – to playing cafes and bars and little clubs with 200 people. I really loved going from that pedestal back to a certain reality. So I really worked on learning how to handle the stage. And I felt that I could do it.

How did you turn your passion for music into a career?

It was just a matter for me having the songs that I needed. Because the first song that I wrote (*Saga Africa*) happened to be a big hit, but that was an accident. It was like a beautiful accident.

But after that, I had to learn. I went from town to town in buses with my friends and stayed in little hotels, and sometimes slept on the bus. I learned how to do it. But the thing that never changed was that I loved it so much. I was always worried about where all the passion I put into my tennis would go. I spent all my good years on it, from my youth to my adolescence and into my 30s. It was my life.

It was not me wondering, 'Am I going to make money? Am I going to be a successful businessman?' I didn't really worry about that part. I was worried about the fact that I wanted to have to do something that I love to do. It was my priority. Even though the first few years were low in terms of money, or in terms of recognition. It was, 'Of course, you're a tennis player, you'll never be able to be a singer.'

So people doubted you?

Oh yeah, of course; nothing mean, but just skeptical. And I liked that. I liked the challenge, but most of all, I loved rehearsing every day. I still feel this way. But I know that regardless of what I'll do in the years to come and what I did before in music, people are gonna go, 'He's the tennis player.'

Why do you think that is?

Maybe it's because I started out as a tennis player. That was my first dream as a child. And always – deep, deep, deep down inside – I still feel like a tennis player.

And the good part is that every time I'm on stage – I don't know how many thousands of concerts I've done – but I still feel privileged, lucky. Like, 'Wow, I can't believe I'm here in front of all these fans!' Even after 30 years, I never take any concert for granted. I still have the energy of an amateur. The energy I had when I was a child and went to play tennis.

As a performer who still feels like a tennis player at heart, are you able to go on stage and feel like you belong with some of the great artists who have influenced you?

No, I have too much respect for those people. I mean, I love Bob Marley and all these artists. But this is my life. I just look at it as my journey. And my journey was very different. You know, I see a lot of artists, and sometimes I'm a little shy to say that they are probably better than me. But none of them won a Grand Slam.

How did playing big tennis matches prepare you for performing to crowds in big stadiums?

My biggest show was at the Stade de France with 80,000 people. And people were like, 'Oh my God, you're going to be so nervous.' They don't know how it feels when you are about to get on center court.

(Playing stadiums) is nothing. Because when people buy the tickets to come to see you, they know the music. You are organizing this big concert, it's like a mass celebration of life. It's a happy thing, people come because they love you. And you really have to fuck up to have the people that come to see you disappointed. You really have to fuck up big time. It never happened (to me) to tell you the truth. Because I don't do drugs. I don't get drunk before a concert. So I know what I'm doing. I love what I do, and I don't take it for granted. But (being nervous) before going on stage? No way.

When you get onto a court, you're about to die. It hurts. Physically, mentally, it hurts. Playing a match is painful. It's not like I'm having a good time before a game. Before a game, you're stressed as hell. You know that you're going to play against this other guy and he wants you dead.

'As a player, I liked the show,' says Noah, pictured at a legends tournament in Budapest in 2009.

I've heard you say that competition in sports can be unhealthy, that you hated not speaking to your friends who are opponents before a big match. Do you think that that had something to do with you retiring so young at age 30?

I struggled with that for a while when I thought it all got too intense. Focusing on the result was too intense. I felt like journalists and the media were too intense. It felt like there was too much of a difference between sometimes being in a match when you play like shit and still win and losing a match when you played great. Losing was always, I felt, (overblown) and sometimes winning was overrated. People were just overreacting all the time. We were just playing tennis.

As a player, I liked the show. I liked that part of the game and I still do. Sometimes I hear people say 'Oh, you could have won more matches if you were not like that.' And I say, 'So? So what? So when I was (world) No. 3, I could have been No. 2? So what?'

You're at peace with that?

Oh totally. I mean, I had to work on the transition. Going from me, me, me, me, me, me all the time for 15 years since I was a child. Being the center of attention all the time. I really had to work to get that out of my system. It's not healthy.

I was so excited to become a (Davis Cup) captain because from that very moment it wasn't about me. I had to help with my experience, and most of all think about the other guys who were all my friends. All of a sudden I had to think about Guy Forget. How am I going to help him? How am I going to really help Leconte? A good coach has to really think about who his player is. Talk to him, listen to him, listen to his family, listen to his wife, look at his children, get to know him, his weaknesses, his strengths. And everybody is different. It was great.

How did it feel when people sang along to *Saga Africa* after you won that first Davis Cup in 1991?

I just saw so much joy. I thought, 'This is it. I've made it. I can stop now.' When I watch footage of us winning that Davis Cup, what I love to see is the reaction of the people. The people are so happy. To be able to participate and maybe be one of the reasons why people are so happy — that's what it's all about. You can do whatever you want in life, but if you don't have the possibility to help someone, then it's not complete. And I think that's why I chose music, because I really get very emotional about the opportunity to give joy to people.

And you have found that you get more joy out of victory as a coach than you did as a player?

Yeah, because I'm like a spectator. When you play, when you're the actor, you don't feel it in the same way.

Even when you won the French Open?

You know, I've won some tournaments, I've had some beautiful moments, plenty of them — the biggest of them being the French Open. That was, I believe, the most complete (set of circumstances) in terms of emotion of any Grand Slam I've seen. I was home in front of my entire family. My dad was on the court. My mom was crying in the stands. All my friends were there. I mean, I grew up there. I spent like a year and a half in that stadium, practically sleeping there, because I was one of the players who practiced there in the winter.

So it was just the perfect situation. That moment was so strong. It's been 37 years, and even today every time I walk (in public) people tell me about their reaction when it happened. 'My parents were screaming in front of the TV. We were all crying.' So what makes a moment special is the emotion. I mean, that's why I wanted to play, to be able to live these moments. This is how I was trying to motivate my guys. It's not about winning the match point – of course, you have to go through that in order to win the match – but it's what happens a few minutes after all of that, that's what it's all about.

I go crazy when I see certain events on TV where the minute the game is over, they go to commercials and I want to break my TV. Because this is why we play, you see. This is why we do this. So if you want to motivate and stimulate kids to play, it's not about having a good forehand down the line. No, it's about the emotion. It's about if you win a game, this is the way it's going to feel. You're going to be in the clouds. So please don't turn to commercials right away, give me those extra 10 minutes.

It is amazing that your parents shared that emotion with you at the French Open, and then you experienced that feeling twice as a parent when Joakim won the NCAA tournament with the University of Florida in 2006 and 2007. What was it like to experience victory as a parent?

I was so proud; you cannot even imagine. I was so proud because he's a great person and he's generous. Joakim was playing for the right reasons. He has always cared for people. And I like the fact that his career helped him develop as a person. Being a basketball player for Joakim is just a step, just like it was for me being a tennis player. I see that. He's real.

When he was a kid, he couldn't really play, but you would think, 'God he has the passion.' He didn't have the technique, but he had heart. So when he got the NBA Defensive Player of the year award (in 2014), I got very emotional.[2]

What is the feeling like in the dressing room going into a big match compared to playing to a big crowd?

I'll give you an anecdote. Before a concert, I'm never nervous but I'm concentrating. I don't like it when people are playing around like 20 minutes before. But for some reason, on one particular occasion I was nervous. I didn't know what was going on. I'm going up the stairs into the dressing room and I'm nervous. And I realized that I was nervous because it was the first time that I was playing a show in the same place where I had played in a tennis tournament. I realized that later. It was Bercy (home of the Paris Masters). And I always played like shit there. I was not good indoors or on that surface, but I also knew that I had to do better because I was playing at home in Paris.

So 20 years later, I felt all that stress again, and I didn't know where it was coming from. Something was wrong. Even in my beautiful dressing room, with my bottle of wine, nice flowers, a Buddha and candles, it smelled like I was in the massage room before a match. So I was like, 'Oh, that's what it is.' So yeah, there's a big difference between being in the same place as a tennis player and as a singer.

How is the preparation different for playing on the tennis tour to going on a big music tour?

Well, if I have to play a match, I have to be the best athlete in the world, so that's a lot of pres-

---

2. At the ceremony, Joakim Noah thanked Yannick, saying, "Dad, all the work ethic, it all comes from you."

sure. Technically I was a very mediocre player, except for my serve. But I worked really hard on my physique.

For me, a good concert is when people are happy and they dance. When they're sitting down, and all of a sudden they stand up for the rest of the concert singing and dancing – then I win. And it happens all the time. But in order to do that, I have to move. I have to dance, I have to take over the whole stage, go right, go left, take everybody with me.

Humbly, I'm trying to be inspired by greats like Mick Jagger, and I have to make sure that it happens. So physically, I have to be ready. Before I go on tour, I always prepare myself by jogging a lot and being in shape. Of course, now I'm 60 years old, it's not the same. There's much more wine (*laughs*). But at the end of the day, I enjoy being on stage. So if I really want to enjoy myself, I have to be in my best shape.

How is the connection with your fans different as a tennis player?

I think the majority of athletes all try to find recognition through the eyes of the public. Which is, in real life, a little unhealthy. But the better they are, you find out that there was less affection they had back home.

You mean growing up in their family?

Yeah, that's something that I found out as a coach. When I was working on my players, I found out that there was something about champions that was always missing. For most of them, I felt they were missing a little bit of affection. And for them (being on court) was a way to find affection through the public. The clapping, the cheers of 'Come on!', everything.

That applied to you as well?

Yes, I had that. When you saw me on the court, you'd say, 'Wow, this is a lion.' And then journalists would come and ask me questions, and I would be talking like a mouse. Very shy. When I was as a child, I remember going to parties with my friends at 14 or 15. I was always the one sitting there looking at this girl, trying to find out a way to talk to her but couldn't do it. And the only way for me to get her attention was to play tennis.

That maybe true, but what about just winning for the sake of competition? For trying to be the best? You saw the Michael Jordan documentary *The Last Dance*, he was super competitive. Did you not have that as well?

Of course. I saw Michael, but I didn't see Michael really. I saw a part of Michael – the part that is a competitor. But I didn't see the person. I don't know why he became a competitor. Why was he like that? That's the important part. And as a coach, (you need) to understand why he is a competitor. I would love to spend a week with Phil Jackson talking about that. He is my hero.

What is your musical writing process?

Well, I wrote my first three albums. The problem was the first one was a hit.

Why was that a problem?

Because I thought I could write. And sometimes you have some wins when it's actually better to lose, because you learn more from a loss. But I started with … Bingo! And I thought, 'Oh, I can do that easy.' So I became stubborn. The first album worked well because of the big song. But then the second one I wrote was kind of painful for me because it was very mediocre. OK, the third one was mediocre also. And I was happy with that, you know, I was happy with what we were doing. We were playing small gigs, and I didn't really have a plan.

And then, as I said, I decided to see how far I can really go (with music) and dropped everything else. Because I had a gut feeling that I could do more. I can go somewhere else with what I have. And that's exactly the moment when I met Robert Goldman. He said, 'I'm going to write for you. Do you agree?' I said, 'Of course, go ahead. I respect you so much. I'm gonna listen to the demos whenever they're ready.' So three months later, we listened to the demo and I was overwhelmed. It was like some of his words were written exactly the way I would have expressed certain feelings, some that I didn't even realize I had. It felt so right.

The album before that (*Zam Zam*, released in 1998), we sold 40,000 copies, which is good for a tennis player. But then on my first release with Robert, we sold 1.8 million records in France.[3]

That was very different, because from one year to the next we went from playing in front of 200 people to 8,000 or 10,000 day after day, four or five concerts a week. For that year, we just played and played, and that went on for 10 years. That was a big change. That's when my career went to another level. So yes, I realized it's very difficult for my ego to say that I cannot write.

---

3. The self-titled *Yannick Noah* released in 2000 achieved diamond status in France, platinum in Belgium, and gold in Switzerland.

What is your process of collaborating with Ronald Goldman?

It's a group of people. We talk and I give them a few ideas on direction. We always want to propose something positive, whatever topic we're focusing on. That is very important. We're not talking about the problems. Enough of the problems. This is not what I want to be the vehicle of. I want to propose something positive. And this is what we've been doing since.

You were 12 when you began playing junior tennis in France. You must have been one of the only people of African descent playing the sport?

Yeah, I didn't see any others.

Were you conscious that you were different?

The first time it became really obvious was when, by destiny, my first ATP tournament was a wildcard in Johannesburg. Arthur Ashe was my mentor, as you know. He helped me get this wild-card and I went with the French team. And when we arrived there during apartheid, that was an adventure. I realized then that I was African and I was Black, and the whole thing came together. But I was 18, it didn't affect me, but I realized that I was different.

And all these years later, you are still the only Black man to win the French Open. How does that make you feel?

Well, anything that's positive, I'll take. I think I've inspired a lot of kids to play. It brings a little smile to my face when I see that some players are named Yannick. It makes me feel really happy to know that Yannick is one of the most popular names in some countries in Africa. Yannick is a very French name from Brittany, so when I see all these Yannicks It makes me feel something.

How did it make you feel to see Naomi Osaka wearing the masks in support of Black Lives Matter in her win at the 2020 US Open?

I hear a lot people say athletes or artists should not participate. I think we are citizens. We see the same stuff. When I win a match, or when I won the Davis Cup as a captain, I liked the fact that people sang (French national anthem) *La Marseillaise*. And I know what I represent. Now more than that, of course as time goes by, I know that I represent not only the French and Cameroonian people, but I also (represent) Africa and Black people and also mixed people.

Being born from the love of a Black man to a white woman, my destiny is to make sure that my two cultures are together. When I won the French Open, it was the first time they gave a microphone to a player, so I didn't prepare myself. But I thanked my family from France and I thanked my family from Africa. So when (Osaka) did that, I thought it was very good. I was very happy that she did that. Very, very happy.

You have spoken about using visualization techniques before stepping out on the court. Were you able to do that before the French Open final, even after your bad dream?

Yeah, I never dreamed of any match, ever. The only time I've dreamt of a match was the night before the final. I tell you, when I woke up, to be able to have a second chance, right away I felt invincible.

Leading up to the tournament, I had been working on my visualization (process). It's very important to project yourself. Even though you're not on the court, you can project yourself through meditation. After the bad dream, I was lucky enough to have the perfect meditation session visualizing my match before going on court. And I didn't make any of the mistakes I did during the dream.

You have said your mentality was 'win or die' going into that final. Where did that come from?

You know, everything was aligned for me, everything. It was a beautiful day. I was healthy. I was playing great. I was feeling great. My whole family was there. All my friends from Paris were there, the people I grew up with. Everybody was ready. This is what I had been dreaming of my whole childhood. I didn't dream about Wimbledon. I didn't dream about the US Open. I was dreaming about the French Open. I used to come and practice on the empty stadium and run up and down the stairs. And I'd be saying, 'I hope one day I will at least play one final.' So I was so fired up. That was my moment. And it was just perfect, and I won.

And If I didn't win that one. I would have still searched for it after that. But because this one was so perfect, I didn't have the same drive (again). I practiced. I got my best ranking a few years later. But my priority totally changed. I had children. I was 25. I loved being a father. But I was not ready to die. No, I had to be there for my kids.

So you took your foot off the gas a little bit with your tennis career?

Yeah, mentally, because I was (still) putting as much time on the court, you know? But mentally it was different.

I know it was difficult to deal with all the expectations that came from winning the French Open while you were living in Paris. What happened?

I was living my life and, all of a sudden, one day later it totally changed. I couldn't do anything without being recognized and be the center of attention. It was so difficult, because it was love, you see. It was love; people were so happy. So there was no way I could have a little bit of peace, except when I stayed in my apartment. That was the only place. I was 23 and my phone number was still in the phonebook. I was not prepared. I didn't have 25 agents and bodyguards. It was just me.

(Leaving France) was my only way to survive, because I didn't want to be this fake star. I didn't want that life, it wasn't me. I want to be the actor, but I want to be the actor on the court, not an actor in everyday life. So no, I didn't like it at all. Also, I wanted to learn. I wanted to be able to sit on a bench in a park. I wanted to just have a normal life. And I found it in New York. And I love those years. They were the best years of my life. I love New York City in the '80s. It was perfect. Joakim and (second child) Yelena were born there.

With all your musical accomplishments, is there anything you could possibly do in music that could match winning the French Open?

Oh no, oh no. It's impossible. I mean, nothing comes close to this feeling when you win the match point of a Grand Slam. And I've only done it once, but I won it at home.

The feeling you get the second that you realize that you win – 'That's it! I did it!' – nothing beats that. Nothing. It doesn't last long though. It lasts for about 30 seconds. And then you surf the wave for a few days, you know? But I think I've been surfing that wave for 37 years.

What is your greatest thrill as a musician?

Oh (*deep breath*). The greatest feeling is when you start singing the first couple of lines and you have the whole stadium singing for you. This is it. You see these people, they believe you. They believe in this. And this is when you say, 'OK, now it's complete.'

And finally, what links the two worlds for you, tennis and music?

Passion.

Chelcee Grimes

Wales, November 2020

It's unlikely that anyone has experienced the highs and lows of the music industry quite like Chelcee Grimes.

As a fresh-faced 18-year-old playing catchy songs in local clubs, the Liverpudlian was signed with much fanfare to Sony's RCA Records. Six months later, she was promptly cast aside when the executive who discovered her was fired.

But unlike other young recording artists, Grimes was armed with a steeliness honed from a lifetime of playing club football as a striker for Liverpool F.C. Women. The challenges she faced on and off the pitch — including a difficult decision to drop her football career to pursue pop stardom — prepared her for the ruthlessness of the music industry.

"I think both (occupations) are very, very similar," she explains over a video call from a cabin in Wales, where she is holed up for creative inspiration during the travel restrictions of Covid-19. "It's dog eat dog wherever you go. You've got to be the best at what you do, whether it's in music or football, someone's snapping away at your heels to be where you are."

Though getting dropped from her label felt catastrophic, she now looks back on it as a blessing in disguise. "For the next two years I traveled, I made music, I made experiences. I lived a bit more, fell in and out of love, and I had more to write about," she reflects.

With her savings dwindling, Grimes was offered a lifeline with "a really small deal" by a publishing group to work as a songwriter. For her first assignment, she was sent to Denmark to collaborate with the producer Cutfather and penned a song for pop sensation Kylie Minogue on her first day in the studio.

That set her off on a path to writing dozens of tracks for some of the biggest names in music, including Dua Lipa, Kesha and Jonas Blue. Her writing credits appear on songs that have totaled over one billion streams, including the blockbuster *Love Again* on Dua Lipa's record-breaking album *Future Nostalgia*.

Grimes is now establishing herself as a performer and artist in her own right, releasing several singles, and appearing on Blue's bilingual hit *Wild*, which she co-penned. She is also a member of the dance music collaborative Vize Versa, which released its first single *Closure* in 2020.

'What have I done here?'

Not long after Grimes' songwriting career took off, she developed a serious itch to get back on the football pitch. It had been six years since she hung up her cleats to focus on music, and watching her former cohorts competing for England in the 2015 Women's World Cup was the final straw.

"I put the TV on and … boom. That hit me," she says of the agonizing situation. "It was just one of those days where I said, 'Mate, what have I done here?'"

Although she set out with low expectations, Grimes was given four tryouts and signed to prominent London clubs Tottenham Hotspur and then Fulham F.C., for whom she scored three goals in the FA Cup. In 2020, she became the first non-England squad woman to play in the annual charity game Soccer Aid, teaming up with Premier League winners Michael Essien and Patrice Evra at Manchester United's ground Old Trafford.

She now suits up for Tranmere Rovers in Liverpool, which competes in the fifth tier of English women's football, to better balance the commitments of her packed schedule.

"I do laugh and think about the audacity of me playing football from the age of 9 to 16, getting in a position of going pro, and then thinking: 'I know what I'll do, I'll go be a musician' – the second hardest job to get into," she says.

"But that's just how I live. I just think if anyone can do it, then I can do it as well. I just don't let anything hold me back. It's that hard-headed Scouser in me. When I put my mind to something – whether it takes me a week or a year – I will stay there until it's done."

Along with her football and music pursuits, Grimes is fast becoming an in-demand broadcaster. She presents the weekly BBC football show MOTDx and reported from the 2019 Women's World Cup in France. She also hosts the weekly podcast, *What We Coulda Been*, which explores the rollercoaster careers of sports figures, musicians and other professionals.

One episode focuses on former Liverpool midfielder Ryan Babel, whose music studio she recorded her first single in as a 16-year-old winner of a radio singing competition. That experience came full circle in 2019, when Grimes was asked to play the after-party for Liverpool's Champions League winning celebration in Madrid.

"It was like an insane dream," she says about the commotion of being huddled up in the players-only lounge and greeted by giddy Liverpool manager Jurgen Klopp, defender Andy Robertson and club great Steven Gerrard before going on stage.

The first time Liverpool won the Champions League during Chelcee's lifetime was in 2005, famously coming back from a 3-0 halftime deficit to defeat AC Milan on penalty kicks. That moment, Grimes says, taught her to never stop chasing her dreams.

"That is honestly the day that I started to believe in magic, I'm telling ya," she recalls of watching the game as a 13-year-old. That same year, she would score a goal for her Liverpool youth team in the 90th minute against Manchester City to take the match into extra time.

"I can remember crying as I was running back, I was so overwhelmed with emotion," she says. Naturally, Liverpool went on to win the game in penalties. "We were all like, 'How did we win that?' But we just didn't give up. I will always remember that game.

"I just believe anything's possible. Anything."

First of all, I want to say that you have the coolest name in both football and music. A person named Chelcee Grimes has got to be an athlete-musician, there's no other way.

It's crazy the amount of times I have to get my passport out and show people that it's my real name. People don't believe me!

You're obviously an extremely busy person. What's a typical day like for you?

It's forever changing, but I think that's why I love it so much. Because there's no same day in my life at all. One day I'm writing a song, one day I'm playing football, one day I'm doing an interview, one day I'm the interviewer.

How do you manage your time?

I've actually recently found out that I've got ADHD.[1] One of the ways it was diagnosed was because of my timekeeping. Living strictly through my diary has become a little bit obsessive, but I love being on time. I love waking up, looking at my calendar and knowing what I'm doing throughout the week or the month.

When it was diagnosed, they were saying, 'Well, to be honest, it works for you in your career. Some people struggle with ADHD, but for you, you've kind of excelled with it.'

It's opened my mind to so many things, and yet it's just nice to know there's nothing wrong with me.[2]

Why is it important to you to have more than one career to focus on? It seems that you could easily stick to working in music and be busy enough.

I just think it fascinates me and it keeps me feeling alive. I've never really been able to stick to one thing, which the ADHD probably had something to do with in my younger life. It makes me happiest when I'm doing everything across the board. I think if I had to stick to one thing, it wouldn't work for me at all.

And playing football is also important on a mental health level for me. I'm not getting paid crazy money to play football at all. I'm playing Division Three level, so it allows me to keep (TV) presenting and doing the music and songwriting and everything else. It's good for me to just take some space away from music. You know, if Britney Spears hasn't cut my song that week, or if I hav-

---

1. Attention deficit hyperactivity disorder is characterized by restlessness and difficulty in concentrating.
2. Research suggests that ADHD is more common in athletes than in the general population, according to the NFL Players Association, citing a 2011 report in *The Handbook of Sport Neuropsychology*.

en't got the cut that I really want and am hoping for, I'll go out for 90 minutes on the weekend and all I think about is getting the ball into the net. It's so simple, and everything else I forget about.

What got you started playing football?

Growing up, I was an only child until I was 16. So there was a lot of playing out alone to be done. I could kick a ball against the wall or the curb for hours on end. I live next door to four brothers and they played out a lot. So it was either stay in the house and do homework or go and play out with the boys, and I got good quickly. When I was 9, my granddad saw an article for a soccer school with (Liverpool legend) Ian Rush. I didn't know who Ian Rush was, but I was the only girl who turned up. And the stars kind of aligned, because the place where he held the soccer camp was where Liverpool F.C. Women trained and they were scouting. They saw me and invited me to a trial the next week. I didn't even own a pair of football boots, I turned up in trainers.

So I signed for Liverpool at the age of 9 and I was there until I was 16. So it was a bit of an 'all meant to be' kind of thing, but I loved it. I just remember that first day of training, turning up on a Wednesday seven o'clock on the Astroturf and seeing a sea of young girls, and I just felt like I'd found my little clique. I was this tomboy and only child. I didn't have that many close girlfriends and was feeling a bit lost. And then I found all these girls who enjoyed something which I did and my world exploded. So that's what made me fall more in love with it.

When did playing music start to take shape in your life?

That was a lot later. In secondary school, I was choosing my GCSEs[3] and I chose sports science in case I got an injury. I also chose music just to pass the time and I fell in love with it. The first assignment was to go and write a song on the weekend. I remember when I wrote lyrics that really meant something to me, it kind of gave me the same feeling as scoring a goal or getting a really good assist.

I never had that feeling outside of football, and it was something that I really enjoyed. It didn't feel like a job and I just kind of rolled with it. My music teacher was like, 'You're picking it up quick. Your lyrics are good, maybe you should start doing it a bit more seriously.' And I did. I started writing songs, I started playing publicly and getting my confidence up a bit at every open mic night that I could. As word started to travel, more and more people came to watch me and I felt confident. And once I had my confidence, I really thrived on it. So it just came about because it gave me the same feeling that football did.

Can you describe that feeling?

The closest thing I can say is it's like being in love. It's just that feeling inside you that is very content, like all your problems go away for a good few minutes. You know, when I'm focused on a game or on music, I'm enjoying it that much. It makes me forget about my problems. And I think that's when I know I'm enjoying something: when it takes me away from reality. And for that minute or two minutes or hour or whatever it is, I know I'm in love with it because I forget about everything else.

---

3. The General Certificate of Secondary Education, or GCSE, is taught to pupils aged 14 to 16 in the UK as part of the national curriculum.

Grimes celebrates after winning the Soccer Aid for UNICEF 2020 match in a penalty shootout at Old Trafford in Manchester.

Soon after you got into songwriting, you won a competition on the radio and got to cut a record at the home studio of Ryan Babel. What did that feel like?

That's the first break that I had. People in the city knew who I was after that. It was our biggest radio station called Juice FM, and I missed the first audition. It was another girl on my team at Liverpool who put me up for it. She entered me without me knowing, and I got a message on MySpace two weeks later from Ryan. I saw the blue verification tick, and I was like, 'Oh, my God, a Liverpool player's messaging me!' And he said, 'Hey, I'm doing this competition with Juice. You've missed the first audition. But we had a few dropouts. Why don't you come to the semifinals and see how you get on?' And I did. I turned up with my piano and my mum. They were all kids from LIPA, which is the big theater and music school here which Paul McCartney runs. I left school at 16 and didn't go to college or university or anything. I just wanted to go and be a musician and play and be poor.

And I turned up and ended up winning it. I sang my own song that I wrote called *Mannequin*. And everyone else was singing like Adele and Michael Jackson and Michael Bublé. It was just one of those situations where the stars aligned for me.

Honestly, I thought I couldn't do any more than that. Like, I get to go to Ryan Babel's house and make a record with all his amazing producers. I didn't even know what a backing vocal was at that point. They'd be like, 'Throw a backing vocal down – a BV.' And I was like, 'What's that?' So I learned so much. And then after we cut the song, I'd go to the games with his girlfriend and his family, and I was just living the life.

I take it since you were out of school at this point, you started having thoughts of becoming a professional in the music industry or perhaps in football?

Yeah, though at that point I think I was growing tired of football. I'm 28 now, so 12 years ago women's football was still at a point where even if you were professional in the English league, you had to have another job. And I just wanted the finer things then. I was 16. I'm going to Ryan Babel's house, which is like a mansion. I'm going through VIP entrances everywhere. I'm starting to sell out gigs. And football had gotten to a point where I felt like I was not going to make a living from it. So I needed to shift focus for that part in my life, because I'd played from the age of 9 to 16 with no money at all.

Just the fact that I could wear the Liverpool kit and be proud was amazing. And we'd get some perks, but there wasn't much in it for us really. And then I made music for like six, seven months and I had all these opportunities. Record deals are being handed out to me with money and checks, and I was like, 'Well this is great. I've done an eighth of the work and it's happening so fast … so maybe this is my calling.' So I stopped football at the age of 17 and it was all music for a few years after that.

It has to be said, if you were a guy at your level of football going through that, there would have been enough money to keep you going in the sport. Did that frustrate you?

Yeah, of course. We had family friends, and this kid was 13 and he played for Liverpool and was getting a retainer from them. He was getting looked after and the girls weren't. We played together and I was just as good as him growing up. It was disheartening. Just because I was a girl, it was different. But I knew that I couldn't change that on my own as a 16-year-old kid from Liverpool. So

I had to think fast and just make a decision that was going to benefit me for the rest of my career.

What happened after you signed your first record contract?

I got signed when I was 18 or 19 to Sony RCA for a really big four-album record deal. Beyoncé signed there, Britney Spears, Justin Timberlake … I thought, 'This is it.' And then the guy who signed me (got fired). It's very similar to football, I always say the similarities are so closely tied together. It's kind of like if a football manager signs a big striker and then he gets sacked and a new manager comes in and he wants a smaller, quicker player and you're not his cup of tea, then you're out the door. And it was kind of like that. The guy who signed me to Sony got sacked six months into making my album. A new guy comes in and he wants to change the whole vibe of the label. So I got dropped, but I got paid out. So for the next two years I traveled, I made music, I made experiences. I lived a bit more, fell in and out of love and I had more to write about. But I got down to like, my last three or four thousand pounds in the bank. My mom was like, 'OK Chel, you're about to turn 21. If you get through this amount of money, you're gonna have to go and get a job.' And I was like, 'Ehhhh.'

Luckily enough, a week before I was going to start looking for jobs, I got a new publishing deal offered to me by the only guy in the business who would touch me. His name is Peter McCamley, and he had signed the Spice Girls and Craig David, amazing acts. And he signed me to a really small deal, but he gave me a lifeline. That's when I became (solely) a songwriter for a bit, because I had to get a bit more credible again. So it was a mad journey. But again, when I talk about my career, just at the moment when I needed something to happen, it tended to happen.

I don't think that's a coincidence. Because of your spirit and positive attitude and your ambition, you made your own opportunities as well, right?

One hundred percent, yeah. I live by that. It's a weird thing, but you have to create your own luck.

On your path to getting that first deal, you said you were playing all these open mics and noticed that kids were getting tattoos of your lyrics. Was that true?

Yeah, it was. That's when I thought, 'OK, maybe I really can do this music thing.' Because at that point, I was playing gigs and there was hype in the city. People in Liverpool tend to really back you, and I started getting a name for myself. People started knowing who I was and I felt like it started to turn. I could feel more eyes on me; more people were coming in. There was a clan of like 10 to 15 kids; it started out as that, then it'd be 50, then it'd be 70, then it'd be 100. And they were getting tattoos of the songs I was singing, which (still) have never even been released. And I would literally say, 'Have you asked your mother that this is OK? Because this song may never come out.' But they were just so supportive. Now they're like 23 or 24. And they still message me and send me pictures of the tattoos. It's just crazy.

Soon after your publishing deal, you were sent to Denmark to collaborate with the producer Cutfather and his team. What happened on that trip?

Yeah, Peter had just signed me and he said, 'I think you're a great artist. I've listened through 300 of your songs. And I think that there are three huge records in there.' And I was trying to test him and be like, 'What about that song?' And he'd be like, 'Great bass, but the chorus I didn't like.' And

I was like, 'Damn, he's really listened to all 300 songs!'

Yeah, he's crazy like that. But he said, 'Listen, I'm going to set you up with a few sessions with big producers, they're going to give you a chance and you have to go in and prove yourself. Basically, you need to get a bit more credible in the writing world, because that's something that will never let you down. Artists come and go, but as a songwriter you'll still be needed when you're 50, just as you are at age 25, if you've got the lyrics and the melody.

So I started looking at it. He made a good reference, because I was so football-driven all the time. I was like, 'I'm ready though. I want to be a star. I want to be an artist.' And he said, 'It's kind of like when a kid's coming through the youth academy: You've got to sit out on the bench sometimes. I know you're ready, but you might come on for the first five minutes to show what you've got, and then you might get to start in a bit. Just get in and (make something of it).' And I was like, 'OK, cool.'

So I took a step back, went over to Copenhagen and I met the guys. I remember walking in and seeing all the plaques on the wall. They had so many hits with the likes of Pussycat Dolls, Britney Spears, and Kylie (Minogue). And I was just like, 'Oh my God, this is so cool.' And he said, 'Yeah, we're working on a new Kylie album. Do you want to have a go at writing for her?'

By this time I'm 21 turning 22. And I was like, 'OK, everyone knows who Kylie Minogue is, but how am I gonna write for her? I don't know what she wants to say. I've never met her.' But I ended up writing a song called *Million Miles Away*. They changed it to *Million Miles* at the end. But it was about me being really far from home. It was my first trip away from home as a songwriter who was being paid to fly out there. And I wrote the song in like 10 or 15 minutes and then cut it the next day. They were like, 'Yeah, we sent it to Kylie and she loves it. She's going to record it today.' And I was like, 'What?' and then they sent me the song that night.

I will never forget where I was and what I was doing. I was literally lying in the smallest, grossest hotel room, and I put my headphones on and heard that start: dah da dah, dah da dah. And then I heard the voice come in, and I was just like, 'Ahhh! I'm a songwriter!'

It was amazing. I was like, 'So this is what it feels like?' Because I used to ask everyone: 'What does it feel like when someone records your song? Is it the same feeling (as writing a hit for yourself)?' I didn't think it'd be the same. I felt like I had just matured and aged in that three minutes of listening to the song, because my whole perspective on having a career in music just shifted. And I felt like this is actually cool. OK, it's giving me the same feeling as if I was singing it. It was just such a proud moment for me. That was the first song I ever got cut, and I'll never ever forget that.

And you thought, 'Oh, this is easy!' right?

I did (*laughs*).

What is it normally like to write for someone else?

Yeah, I think I just got a bit of luck. Like I said, things tended to happen when I needed them to. I don't know if I would have carried on if I got a publishing deal and then didn't get a song cut for six to nine months. But it happened so fast. In my first session I write for Kylie Minogue, the album goes to No. 1 and it's me and Pharrell Williams and Sia and MNEK all on this album.[4] It was just like, boom! And then the phone started ringing for me to join all kinds of sessions.

---

4. Minogue's album *Kiss Me Once* peaked at No. 1 in Australia and No. 2 in the UK.

Sessions can be difficult. It's a weird thing to do. You're supposed to go in and meet someone who you've never met before and by the end of it, hopefully, have a great record that will make everyone money. It's strange. Sometimes it works, sometimes it doesn't. You might get an artist in the room who's very negative or not in the right headspace, or a bit jetlagged. Or you might get someone who's just not in the mood to write that day. Or they want to write about heartbreak, and you want to write about love. Everything has to merge into one to get a great record. So it doesn't always work out as easy as that one did.

Does playing football, where you're relying on 10 teammates on the pitch, help in your experiences collaborating as a songwriter?

Yeah, for sure. Because you might see this artist on TV and listen to their song and love it, but 95 percent of the time, they haven't written it. They are just kind of the face of it. And it's like they're the goal scorer but you forget about the goalkeeper, the center-back and the central defensive midfielder, who's putting in the tackle which is just as good as scoring the goal. So it is for sure about the whole team (and not) just the person who's scoring the goal, so to speak.

Songwriting is by nature a very generous process, in terms of writing for another artist or collaborating on a song with them. So is the process of splitting royalties. I know you have given half of a song's royalties to an artist in the past simply because they were in the same room with you, although they really were not contributing a whole lot. Yet you feel it was worth it to establish a working relationship with that artist. Can you explain that trade off?

It's one of those things. It's the business, although I've definitely said no and stood my ground. One really big artist actually, on Capitol Records in America … About two or three years ago, I wrote a song which I loved and it was supposed to be for me. But I was a massive fan of this girl as well. And yeah, they came in for it and said, 'It's going to be the next big single in America, it's going to be (big), and she wants 33 percent.' And I was like, 'No.'

(It would be) fair enough if she was in the room. And they were like, 'Well, that's just what she does.' And I was like, 'OK, well, she can do it somewhere else, but it's not happening here.' And I stood my ground on that one, and a lot of people said it was a brave move. And sometimes you think, 'Oh, maybe I shouldn't have let (the opportunity) go.' But it's not right. And I think more people need to stand up for themselves as songwriters, because a lot of people are afraid. They think, well if I don't give 30 percent of it, then the song's just gonna sit there and someone else will give them 30 percent. And 70 percent of something is better than 100 percent of nothing. Which I do understand, and maybe if I didn't have money now I might have said something different.

It's a trade-off that you have to be OK with, and at that point in my career I was OK to say, 'Actually, no. Not this time.' But it's a tricky situation. I think one rule does not fit all. So it just depends on the artist and on the songwriter.

What happened to the song?

I ended up keeping it. It's five years old now, but it's one of my favorite songs that I've ever written. We haven't got the production rights yet, so I don't know. It might come out in 10 years, it might come out in a year, nobody knows.

Grimes penned 300 songs before she was signed as a hitmaker. 'You have to create your own luck,' she says.

It's obviously killing me to know what the song is and who the artist is.

One day all will be revealed, if I release it.

What advice would you give to a young aspiring songwriter?

I'd say just keep writing. Nobody knows what song is gonna take off and what song is not. It's luck, literally. (You need) the right artist, the right time, the right kind of record. You just never know. These days with streaming, you just have to keep writing. Don't stop writing, even if you think you've just written the best song of the decade. There's no trick to songwriting at all, just believe in yourself and then start writing. That's it.

What's your process in songwriting? I've read that you bang out one song every day, is that true?

Yeah, I try to. I mean, the past month or two, I think I've only written like four songs. I haven't really been in writing mode at all, but I usually write every day – even if it's just a verse, or even if it's just the chorus. If I'm watching television, I pick up my guitar, because you never know what's going to come out. It might be Tuesday at 11:30 in the morning after a workout and I might just pop out something which is great. Or it might be a Saturday night out in a bar and I might just say something. So you never know when inspiration is going to strike.

Does the melody come to you at the same time you're writing the lyrics?

Usually I start with a lyric. I'm quite visually driven with songs. So if I start with a good title, that's always the best way. And then I can just make the story. OK, in this one, this is going to happen, and by the chorus, we get to the title. Then in verse two, we're going to say, 'Oh, it could have gone this way. It could have been that way.' In the middle eight, we're going to celebrate it, or say, 'I wish this would have happened' and then get back to it. I like the structure of having a story in place.

But it depends. It could start with a riff, it could start with just a title, or it could start with a melody that I'll just have in the shower or whatever. It's constantly changing.

Which experience is more thrilling for you, to write a big song for yourself or write for mega artists like Kylie and Dua Lipa?

It's so difficult that question, because I'm very aware that (with) Dua Lipa and Kylie, there's a much larger scale of people who are watching them. And also, let's be honest, they're gonna sell more records than I am, as it stands.

But then, Dua Lipa and (K-pop band) Blackpink recorded *Kiss and Make Up* (co-written by Grimes, with over 300 million Spotify streams). When Blackpink headlined Coachella, it became the first bilingual song ever performed there. Stuff like that is always amazing to be a part of. So … I think it's a tie.

When did you decide you missed playing football and wanted to get back to club level?

I was 23 watching the 2015 Women's World Cup, and I had played with everyone on that England Lionesses squad on some level. I was like, 'Oh my God, there's Alex Greenwood and there's Fara Williams!' I was so happy to watch them, but at the same time it was inspiring. For me at age 23 sitting on the sofa being a songwriter, it inspired me to get back and play.

I signed for Tottenham for the first season and that was amazing because the following season they ended up going to the (top tier) Women's Super League. But I quickly found out that the game had grown massively since I last played. I was doing songwriting as well, and if I was in a session with Dua Lipa, I couldn't really say 'Sorry babe, I'm going to training so do the chorus yourself.'

At that time music was supporting my lifestyle and paying my rent, and I couldn't keep up with the training. And if you miss one training session, you're in the reserves or you're on the bench. I was traveling two or three hours to training and it had just become too much. So I ended up leaving and joining Fulham, which is a lot less strict, shall I say? It was a league below that, but it got me back into playing at a high level again and absolutely loving it. And since then, I've carried on.

When you watched your teammates play for England, did you get a sense of dread that you had perhaps missed out on playing in the World Cup?

Yeah, I'm not gonna lie and say I didn't. I think it was one of those days where the music scene was a little quiet. Or I might not have got a song on the album that I wanted to get on that day. And then I put the TV on and … boom. That hit me. It was just one of those days where I said, 'Mate, what have I done here?'

You know, women's football is coming up now, and maybe I could have made money from it and had a good life. But it's all worked out, and it got me back playing. Thank God, because it's opened up so many doors for me now.

Does playing football provide a release from the pressures you face in the music industry?

For sure. I don't know how to explain it, but it's just so simple. Like, it's not overthought, there's no politics in it. It's literally about — if all of you do your job that day and you play well, you can come away with a result. And it's all in my hands and I love that. It's powerful to be able to (do something) that's down to me. Not, I write the song and then I give it to a publisher who then sends it to a record label who then sends it … There's so many moving parts in music, whereas in football, it's such simplicity for me and it's a lovely state to be in.

It's funny, because for nearly everybody else I've spoken to, the music is a release from the pressures of their athletic careers. But for where you are positioned in the music industry, it's the opposite. From your observation, is the music business more or less ruthless than the business of football?

I think both are very, very similar. You know, there's been girls I've seen play at a team for eight or nine years, and then the next season just got dropped like that. But same in music: People are signed for three or four albums, they have four Top 10 records, and then the next one doesn't chart Top 40 and they're gone. It's dog eat dog wherever you go. You've got to be the best at what you do, whether it's in music or football, someone's snapping away at your heels to be where you are. So honestly, I couldn't tell you. I think both are as bad as each other.

What's been your biggest thrill as a musician so far?

It was pretty special when I was in LA and I got to work with (multiple Grammy-winning producer) RedOne. Anyone who's listened to any interview of mine knows that Lady Gaga is it for me. I was obsessed with her when I was 16 and starting music. That first album, *The Fame* and the follow-up *The Fame Monster* were just huge records to me. I used to listen to them on repeat and learn what a verse was and what a pre (chorus) was and the chorus. I used to message RedOne on Twitter daily, being like, 'I'm gonna work with you one day.' At that point, I don't even think I'd written a full song. But I was so obsessed. And then two and a half years ago, I was in LA and I got an email saying RedOne's asking you to go to a studio and work with him. I just remember walking in and seeing the plaques on the wall. And he was saying, 'Yeah, when we wrote *Bad Romance* it went like this…' And I was just thinking, 'I used to sit in my bedroom in Liverpool and everyone thought I was crazy.'

And now I'm in LA — Los Angeles — The sun is shining and RedOne is sitting in front of me with his sunglasses on telling me how *Bad Romance* was made. This. Is. Fucking. Crazy! It felt like I was in a dream, because I had dreamed about that so much. That was a huge goal for me and I had done it. And I felt so far away when I used to say it, and then there I was, just doing it. I've had loads of experiences, but that just stood out for me.

What is your biggest dream in music?

Probably to win a Grammy. That's still on my list. I've been a part of No. 1 albums and songs all over the world. But I haven't had a Grammy nomination yet, so that would be nice.

And your biggest dream in football?

Just hoping that the women's game still grows and that I can be a part of that. I'd like to help the game grow for the next generation, because I get so many messages from young girls who see me on TV. I'm representing women in the sports field on television now and I don't do that lightly. I always try to make sure that everyone I speak about is important and is driving (the sport) forward.

How would you define yourself?

I wouldn't define myself ever. I think I'm forever changing. Who knows? I don't know what I'll be doing in five years. I would just say, I believe that anything can happen, and I will always believe in magic and the greatness in life. I would never give up on anything that I do.

Damian Lillard

Portland, November 2020

Damian Lillard will almost certainly go down as one of the greatest scorers in NBA history. But can he also leave his mark as one of the great rappers of his era?

Don't bet against it.

Lillard has overcome improbable odds on the way to becoming one of the most recognized athletes in the world — a perennial All-Star whose highlight reel consists of sinking outlandish half court shots to win big games, and whose record book entries are matched only by the names Wilt Chamberlain and Michael Jordan.

Growing up in the Brookfield section of in East Oakland, California, Lillard avoided the gun violence of his neighborhood by shooting baskets with his brother Houston on a hoop made from a milk crate stuck to a telephone pole. Without a backboard, Lillard learned to perfect his jumper so that it would drop through the square rim dead on every time.

Around the same time, Lillard's cousin Eugene 'Baby' Vasquez arrived from New York and would take Damian and Houston for spins in his car for as long as they could rap over instrumental beats. Damian embraced the rule and learned to make up verses that lasted entire rides, not even giving Houston a chance to get on the invisible mic.

That type of confidence would prove crucial to Lillard through trying times.

At age 12, his mother Gina Johnson came home stressed after a rough day at work. "We're gonna be alright," he told her. "I'm going to the NBA." Tears flowed down Gina's cheeks.

As a high school sophomore, however, Lillard's prospects looked dim when he was benched for an entire season. He recalls his basketball coach at St. Joseph Notre Dame (which produced Hall of Famer Jason Kidd) smirking in disbelief when the youngster told him of his NBA goal. Although he transferred the following year and had impressive junior and senior campaigns, major college programs were not interested.

Then, just before graduation, Lillard was robbed at gunpoint while waiting for a bus. The thugs ran off with just $15, but Lillard knew it was time for a new start somewhere else.

He accepted a scholarship to little-known Weber State University, which had not produced an NBA prospect in 23 years. For many college athletes, the NBA dream would have ended there. But Lillard remained undeterred.

"I never even thought like, 'Man, this is going to ruin my chances,'" he recalls, adding that the mental toughness fostered by his Oakland upbringing left him unfazed by the university's homogeneously white campus in Ogden, Utah. "It wasn't very diverse, and I moved around just fine. I was never uncomfortable."

After dominating the Big Sky Conference in his sophomore year at Weber State, the prospect of playing in the NBA seemed possible for the first time. But eight games into his junior season, Lillard broke his foot and NBA scouts lost interest.

Rather than sulk, the 20-year-old sat on a chair with his foot in a cast and took 400 shots a day during practice. He developed a high arc delivery which has served him well shooting over taller defenders in the pros.

Lillard resumed his point guard duties for his final college season and earned his second Big Sky Conference Player of the Year award. By then the secret was out, and he was selected sixth overall in the 2012 NBA Draft by the Portland Trailblazers.

Despite the hype on him before the draft, deep down Lillard still felt like the kid who got overlooked at St. Joseph Notre Dame. "It was like when I was in high school. I just couldn't wrap my head around actually being recruited because I didn't expect it," he recalls. "So I didn't believe them. I never believed anything until the actual draft night."

'Dame Time'

NBA fans had barely heard of Lillard before his first season, but he ran away with the 2013 Rookie of the Year award in a unanimous vote over celebrated big man Anthony Davis.

Since then, his stock has been rising exponentially. Lillard made his mark as a clutch performer when he eliminated the Houston Rockets with a last second three-point shot during the first round of the 2014 Playoffs.

He repeated the feat in 2019, when he eliminated the Oklahoma City Thunder with a 37-foot jump shot over an incredulous Paul George, joining Michael Jordan as the only other NBA player to end two playoff series with time-expiring shots. "That shot is 20 years old. I've been making it since 2001 on a milk crate on Beverly Ave," Lillard wrote in The Players' Tribune.

He dug further into the record books in 2020, becoming the only player other than Wilt Chamberlain to tally 60 or more points three times in one season. He has been mobbed by teammates so often that 'Game Time' will forever be known as 'Dame Time' in Portland.

Off the court, Lillard has been just as dependable. Three years after leaving college for the NBA, he kept his promise to his mom and graduated from Weber State with a degree in profesional sales. That financial savvy will serve him well, following a four-year $196 million extension signed with the Trailblazers in 2019 that places him as one of the highest earners in pro sports.

> 'I feel the tension risin', 1950, how we divided
> And I ain't even trippin' on how the season decided
> Racism pandemic is years ahead of the virus'
> *Blacklist* by Dame D.O.L.L.A.

For most of his life Lillard was able to avoid run-ins with police, but just before his final year at Weber State he was racially profiled while driving his new car from Oakland to Ogden. According to Lillard, Nevada police asked him if he was holding drugs, then tore up the vehicle's interior and broke a window before opening his suitcases and spraying his clothes across the road.

Personal experiences and observations of that nature would shape Lillard's views on social justice and influence his decision-making as an activist and musician. In June 2020, he marched in Portland, a center of Black Lives Matter protests after the killing of George Floyd, and penned the song *Blacklist* as a reaction.

Dame D.O.L.L.A. is Lillard's rap alias, with the acronym standing for 'different on levels the Lord allows'. D.O.L.L.A.'s career has been rising nearly as fast as Lillard's on the court, with the release of three albums in four years and collaborations with the likes of Snoop Dogg, Lil Wayne, Raphael Saadiq and Jamie Foxx.

It is clear that Lillard is not just another NBA player with a home recording studio. He founded the record label Front Page Music and has been hailed by critics and hip hop luminaries like Common as a talented rapper with an ear for infectious beats. His songs have appeared on TV shows like HBO's *Ballers*, while fresh tracks are strategically dropped throughout the year to keep Dame D.O.L.L.A. relevant during the hectic NBA schedule.

As a rapper, Lillard has shown a competitive streak which rivals his feud with Russell Westbrook on the basketball court.

Telling an interviewer that he was a better rapper than Shaquille O'Neal, who put out four albums in the '90s, led to an all-out rap battle in the fall of 2019. They released two diss tracks each, with Lillard writing both of his in a little over an hour. Rolling Stone wasted no time in declaring D.O.L.L.A. the winner, referring to "Lillard's lyrical evisceration of Shaq" as "devastating."[1]

"I know the history of athletes doing music, and I knew that I wasn't just like anybody else that did it," Lillard says. "I just want people to be like, 'This dude is really the best. There's never been a player who played at his level and could also rap at the level that he raps at.'"

Can you describe the East Oakland mentality you grew up with?

I think the best way to describe it is the toughness. You know, the mental toughness and fortitude and confidence to just be secure in yourself because of the environment you grew up in. I think that's my biggest takeaway from being from Oakland. I felt like I was prepared to go anywhere.

---

1. O'Neal and Lillard patched things up and have collaborated on a song for the next D.O.L.L.A. mixtape.

Lillard waves goodbye to the Oklahoma City Thunder after eliminating them from the 2019 Playoffs with a series-winning jump shot. 'When you hit a shot like that, it's like you're sticking your chest out,' he says.

You told your mom you were going to make it in the NBA when you were 12 years old after she had a bad day at work. Did you really believe that, or were you just trying to make her feel good?

No, I really meant it.

You ended up playing at Weber State in Utah and becoming their first NBA draft pick in 27 years. Did that belief you had as a kid ever waver on the path to getting drafted?

I would say it did. It's actually funny that in my sophomore year in high school I transferred to a private school in South Alameda (in Oakland), St. Joe's Notre Dame, and I just didn't play. The coach didn't play me the entire season.

And around that time, I was like, man, this is usually the time you start getting recruited, and you start figuring out where you're gonna go to school. I don't have any scholarship offers. I'm not even getting letters. So it started to seem like it was a little bit of a reach to really imagine myself being highly recruited.

And then the following summer (at AAU camp), I just blew up. I had a huge summer. And I received 25 to 30 offers, but there were all from mid-major to low-major schools, you know, St. Mary's College, Weber State, Montana State, Portland State, Sacramento State, those type of schools.

And that was when I was like, you know, maybe this is the level that I'm supposed to be at. Maybe this is how it's supposed to be. But I never (doubted my NBA chances). Once I got the scholarship, I was just like, 'I'm going to be the next mid-major small college player to make it.' I never even thought like, 'Man, this is going to ruin my chances.'

When I got to college, I kind of realized it was going to be a little bit harder than I thought. College (basketball) is hard. Guys are faster, stronger. And they were also trying to prove something themselves. But I still didn't waver from that. And I felt pretty good about the pace I was growing at when I got on campus. I was First Team All-Conference as a freshman and Big Sky Player of the Year as a sophomore. And I was finally getting scouted (by NBA teams).

Can you describe the mental challenge you had to face after breaking your foot in your junior season?

When I started to slowly get healthy, I was just like, this is it. I'm going all in. I'm going after it. I worked as hard as I ever did. I was eating better than I ever did. I was sleeping. I wasn't hanging out. I set my mind on: 'This is it.' My mom is (struggling). They trying to fire her from her job and she's having a hard time, so I was like, 'I'm just going to shoulder all of this, and I'm going to handle it and I'm going to do what I've got to do.'

I happened to be at your very first game as a pro, when you went up against the Lakers. I remember thinking, 'Wow, who is this guy?' They had a crazy starting five, with Kobe Bryant, Pau Gasol, Dwight Howard, Metta World Peace and Steve Nash. Were you nervous before tipoff?

I wouldn't say I was nervous. I was just really anxious. If it was a road game, I probably would have been a little nervous. But since we were at home, the crowd was rocking. And I figured, 'What do I have to lose?' Like, if I come out here and get my ass kicked, it's not going to be a shock or a surprise to anybody. So I literally didn't have any type of nerves or fear. I was just like, you know, Steve Nash is a little older. I was a huge fan of Steve Nash. But I was like, if anything I know I'm going to be able to get around him, so I just embraced it. Once we got to the tip, I didn't even feel it in my bones. I kind of saw Kobe and I was like, 'Damn, like, we're really about to play (against) Kobe.' But aside from that, I was good. I was just ready.[2]

Can you describe Dame Time to me?

Dame Time in my mind is just the opportunity to rise to the occasion.

At what point during one of your monster games do you feel like you're going to be able to dominate and have a historic night?

It depends. It's a different level of momentum when you start from the three-point shot, and then you start getting layups and twos. So when I'm making those threes, I know in the first quarter or second quarter.

In a game against Utah in my fifth year (April 8, 2017, when Lillard scored 26 points in the first quarter and finished with 59, making 9 of 14 three-pointers). I came out and I was hitting

---

2. On October 31, 2012, Lillard had 23 points and 11 assists in 35 minutes, leading the Blazers to a win in the first game of his rookie season.

threes. I was just making shot after shot after shot. And in the first half of that game, I was like, this is gonna be a long night for them. Like, I'm going to score all night. If I'm making shots from three early, then getting to the rim is (no problem).

But if I'm making twos and layups and I'm getting fouled, then I don't know if it's going to be going in from three. I've had games where, for example, against Dallas (on August 11, 2020, when Lillard had 61 points and 8 assists), I hit a couple threes in the first half, but I was making a lot of layups and pull-up jumpers, those kinds of shots. I knew I was gonna have a lot of points, but I didn't know it was gonna be 60 until the third quarter when I just started running off threes. Then I was like, 'I'm definitely gonna score in the 50s, maybe 60.'

Can you describe your confidence in your ability to take shots from nearly half court at crucial times in big games? Do you ever waver and think, 'OK, maybe this isn't the wisest shot to take'?

The only time I think about it is if it's in transition when I get the outlet. I'm thinking, 'Do I really want to shoot this one? I don't want to make my team to have to come from working on defense for 24 seconds, and then I shoot this deep three and we got to run back and play defense again (if I don't make it). That's the only time where I'm like, 'Should I do it?'

But it's a pretty comfortable shot for me. I train on that shot so much. I train on it at the beginning of workouts. I do it at the end of workouts when I'm dead tired, and I still get the shots off the right way and make them. It's a pretty easy shot for me now, so when I'm there I don't look at it like I'm so far. I've trained and I've done it for years and years.

What is the feeling like when you sink a game-winner to end a playoff series?

It's a really big moment. Because I think in the playoffs more than any other time, there is a lot of back and forth. Both teams are tired of each other. You're playing them every other day. The narrative keeps changing, where (the media is) saying, 'Alright, now this guy is outplaying that guy. Now these guys are outplaying those guys. Now this guy had a bad game, and that guy had a bad game.' And then on TV, they're picking this team to win the series. And then after they lose (one game), they pick the other team. There are just so many peaks and valleys in those five, six or seven games.

And there are so many emotions that you have toward the other team, because it starts to get chippy. So when you hit a shot like that, it's like you're sticking your chest out. Like, I just beat you in the most hurtful way.

So, the first time I did it (in 2014 against Houston), I was much younger, and I wasn't having a big game. We were down by two, so if I missed it we would have gone to Game 7 at Houston. I felt like my chest was really out, because I was letting them know that I don't have to have a great game to feel like I can make a game-winner. The score doesn't have to be tied with nothing to lose. Like, whatever the situation is, I will down you.

Do you get that competitive in hip hop too?

Sometimes.

When did you decide to take music seriously as a second career?

In 2013.

Did it cross your mind that a lot of NBA players before you had tried to release rap albums with mixed results? Were you thinking, 'OK, I'm going to be different, I'm going to succeed when they didn't'?

See, I wasn't ever thinking like that. I didn't look at it like, 'I'm gonna be different; I'm going to succeed.' I just looked at it like, I know the history of athletes doing music. And I knew that I just wasn't like anybody else that did it, because I was rapping before I knew I was going to be an NBA player.

Me and my friends used to drop mixtapes in college. When we came out to warm up for our games in high school, we came up with our own music. And my cousins were rapping when I was 8, 9, 10 years old and they used to make me rap.[3] I would always tell my stories in my raps, so I knew how to rap and I had a real story to tell.

So once I decided I was going to commit to it, I wanted the first thing people to say is: He can really rap. And then once I get them to listen, I'm not going to (immediately) start dropping albums. I'm going to slowly feed it to them. I'm going to do it like any other aspiring artists would. Instead of saying, 'Alright, I'm Dame Lillard. I'm an NBA player, y'all got to listen to me,' I took the same route as any other aspiring artist would. I'm gonna start at the bottom and work my way into it, instead of just thinking that because I'm an NBA player, I got the privilege of automatically putting my name out there.

On that note, how much work did it take to perfect your skills and rapping? Have you used a vocal coach?

I wouldn't say I had a coach, but I had a lot of people who were giving me direction and were critical of certain stuff that I did. Whether that was my cousins who do music, or me talking to Lil Wayne. I've talked to Common, I've talked to other people who work in the music industry and pretty often they would tell me the truth. Like, 'No your production needs to be better. You could do a better hook' or, 'This song needs a bridge' or, 'You need to change up your flow, change up the pattern that you rap.' I have people in my ear and I have been receptive to that information. So over time, I was still putting out stuff, but I was just taking in (the advice) and getting better and better.

What is your process of making music, and what is your level of involvement in the finished product?

It's heavy involvement, because the music represents me. But my process is, I find producers that I like and I just get a bunch of beats sent to me. And sometimes when I'm in the car going to practice or the gym, I'll plug up my phone to the Bluetooth. And in my 20-minute ride I'll just have instrumentals playing, and I'll be searching for a beat that I know I want to rap on. Once I do that, then I start to write the hook. And then I start to build the song out. That's the process for me: I find the beat, and then see what direction I want to go on it. And then I start writing.

---

3. Lillard's cousin Brookfield Deuce is an Oakland rapper who has released tracks on Lillard's Front Page Music label.

Can you compare when you're in a flow of writing and creating music to when you're in a zone on the basketball court and every shot feels like it's going in?

It's different. I think when I'm doing my music and I'm just writing and things are coming to me easily, I start to get excited about what it could become. I'll be telling my friends, 'Listen to this rhyme!' I'm more excited over it because it's like a journey.

I feel like I am going through the whole (process of) getting drafted and earning my place in the NBA all over again, but (this time) with my music. So I get excited over it in the same way that I used to get excited over my position going up in the mock NBA Draft when I was in college. I'd be telling my teammates, 'Look, I moved up the draft board! They have me going fifth instead of thirteenth!' It's almost like that. I get to relive that progression by rising up in the music world.

But as far as how it is compared to getting hot in the game, I think it's different. The more hot I get (in a game), the calmer I get. So when I'm writing, the more I flow, the more excited I get to share it with other people. Like, 'Oh that is clever' or, 'This beat slap.' But in the game, the higher I go – like if I hit a bunch of threes in a row – I get more calm. If I get too excited, that's when I lose it. That's when I do something extra instead of just letting it keep happening. So I think that's the difference.

Do you use any visualization or mental preparation before you go out on the court?

I wouldn't even call it preparation. I just get so wired up about the game when I know I'm about to play. And in my head, I'll just be playing out what I think could happen and how I might react to certain things.

Sometimes I'll just be like, 'Man, this is a big game. What if I go out there and get three fouls in the first quarter? How am I going to react to that?' I'm already starting to tell myself to be prepared for that to happen. I just play out scenarios in my head. So I guess it is kind of preparation, because I'm just going through different things that could come up. And I'm comfortable with them. Like, OK, even if it does happen, it's gonna be OK. But I don't visualize it like, 'OK, tonight, you're going to score 50 points, and it's going to come true.' I'm not doing that kind of stuff.

What is your confidence as a performing artist relative to your confidence as an NBA player? I'm guessing your confidence as a basketball player is 100 on a scale of 100, but what is it as a rapper?

Yeah, I would say the same. My confidence as an athlete is as high as is going to get; I don't question myself. And as an artist, I would say I'm very confident in what I'm saying. I'm very confident in the way I view my music. I know my music is good. I know I can put bars together. I know my songs have good meaning, and they're strong songs that are well put together.

But the one thing that I am less confident in is how well it's received. You know, you get out there and you might get on stage and sing your stuff, and people might look at you and not even listen to the music. They just like, 'Dame trying to rap,' you know what I'm saying?

So I feel like, damn, they're not gonna look at my music the way I look at it. Or they're not going to be open to listening to it and they automatically tone it out and be like, 'Man this is weak.' So I'm not confident that people are going to (positively) receive what I'm doing with my music all the time.

Do you feel like you've turned the corner on that attitude yet?

I think I've turned the corner with it as far as the music goes. Like when I release my music, it's everywhere. I get a lot of love when I put it out. But even though a lot of people will listen, that doesn't mean they will go to shows. You might get on stage, and if it's not your (headline) show and the people might be there to see somebody else and they don't know your music, they're gonna look at you like you're crazy.

You have released a number of tracks in reaction to police killings and in support of social justice, including *Blacklist* (2020) and *Bigger Than Us* (2015). Did it feel instinctive to you as an artist to take all your thoughts and put them down on paper in those emotionally charged moments?

That's all it was. I didn't even have to build the song out. I just started writing. *Blacklist* was almost like spoken word. It was like poetry more than rap. But it was just me expressing myself and giving my real thoughts, whether people liked it or didn't like it. You know, the truth hurts.

Why was it important for you to show solidarity and march with the Black Lives Matter protesters in Portland last summer?

Oh, it was important to me because I didn't want to address the situation from the position that I'm in now in my life. I think at this point in my life, I can protect myself from a lot of things that could be harmful. I live in a gated community, in a gated home with security. There are a lot of things that I can do to protect myself from things going wrong. But it's all still a possibility, because I'm a Black man, you know.

I could be driving down the street or walking out of a party or a fight could break out at a restaurant that I'm at, and it could be me. You just never know what's gonna happen. And on top of that, I grew up in a neighborhood where I've experienced these things. I've been profiled. Someone I grew up with was murdered by a cop while handcuffed.[4]

Because of all of these things, I felt like I didn't need to be another person cheering from Twitter or Instagram. Anybody can write something on the internet, but you're not putting yourself in harm's way. And you're not physically putting everything on the line like other people are. I wanted to be present with the people and show that I stand for the same thing that our people are fighting so hard for.

Have you thought about how to continue to promote social justice using your platform as an NBA player?

I haven't really thought about how I can continue to contribute towards social justice publicly. I think that's a broad question. But the thing that I have thought about is, how I can create a positive impact on Black communities – especially the ones that I've lived in and worked in, and that I'm connected to through friends or family members. How can I be more supportive of their businesses and things that are going on around them? How can I support that instead of going away from it?

---

4. The victim, Oscar Grant, went to high school with Lillard's brother and was portrayed by Michael B. Jordan in the movie *Fruitvale Station*.

You know, sometimes people look at the areas that we come from as a negative thing, when they actually have a lot of bright spots. There are a lot of things that can come out of them that are positive. But they lack resources, and they lack funding, and they lack help. And usually the people who are willing to give their time, and who are really passionate about the development and the care for the youth in these places — they've got to pay the bills. You know, they got to take care of themselves, and they've got stuff to do. They can't be a part of this when they're not being compensated for their time and care. So how much work can they actually do?

So my focus is on trying to have impact in those areas. I think that would have an impact on the youth and start the trend of helping ourselves from the start, and of creating opportunities for kids to take their education more seriously. And then go to college and see they have hope from that. I'd like to make it harder for kids to just fall into the things that they fall into now, and to put our neighborhoods and our communities in better standing.

What is your biggest thrill as a musician so far?

So far, I would say the collaborations. Like, when I'm writing a song, and I'm thinking, 'Man, Juvenile would sound good on this.' And the process of me actually getting the song to him, and him deciding to do it and then I get it back. And then we start piecing a song together with him on it — that's the biggest thrill. Like, doing something with Lil Wayne and Jadakiss and Marsha Ambrosius … just to be able to collaborate with these big, big, big artists.

'I was rapping before I knew I was going to be an NBA player,' says Lillard.

And what's your aspiration musically?

To be respected and recognized as an artist just as I am a basketball player. It's not about the money. It ain't about none of that. I just want people to be like, 'This dude is really the best. There's never been a player who played at his level and could also rap at the level that he raps at.' Like, he's a real rapper.

Could you possibly achieve the same thrills from your music career that you get in the NBA?

I don't think it's impossible, but I don't know if that'll happen. The commitment I'm willing to give my basketball career, I don't know if I'm willing to give that same commitment to my music – and I'm pretty committed to my music. But with basketball, for the last three months I've been getting up at 7 a.m. for lifting and conditioning and boxing, and then at 9 a.m. I go to the (basketball) court until 10:30 a.m.

Then I go home, take a nap and focus on my diet. And I go back at nighttime to shoot jumpers, I'm running two miles around the track, then I'm in the steam room. I'm doing a lot of stuff to be the best version of myself in basketball. That takes a huge investment and a lot of commitment.

With my music, I'll go to the studio for six hours, and I listen to beats, and I write, write and write. But I'm not about to go drive around the country to every radio station and tell them to play my music and do all that stuff. There are just certain things I'd have to be willing to do that would make my music on the level of the player that I am.

And what links the two worlds for you, basketball and hip hop?

I think they come linked together. Basketball players usually want to be rock stars or rap artists. And rap artists want to be professional athletes. So both worlds connect through the people who represent them, the LeBron Jameses and then the Jay Zs and NASes and Lil Waynes and those type of guys who are passionate about sports and passionate about music. So they have a lot in common. That's what links me to both worlds, because I'm working in both of them and I feel the same way about both of them.

Epilogue

For my tenth interview in this book, I met with Mark Butcher one morning in my west London apartment. As I was setting up the camera and microphone, Butcher picked up my Fender Stratocaster and began playing it softly. He started with gorgeous arpeggios and layered on his melodic singing to a captive audience of me and my pet labradoodle Floyd.

Once I got the equipment ready, Butcher spoke candidly for two hours. He reflected on his upbringing as a cricket prodigy and the pressures of fame and performance, as well as the joy that writing and playing music has brought him.

We later broke out a couple of my acoustic guitars and engaged in a jam of sorts. I began the first few bars of Pink Floyd's *Money* and Butcher took over as I badly muddled along. Although I've put in many hours of my own into guitar, I was out of practice and my playing was laborious and sloppy. As for Butcher, it was clear that music came naturally to him. I was playing with a pro who was entirely on another level.

It can be hard to get a sense for someone's greatness unless you've had a close brush with it, and I got to do that time and again with my subjects.

When I witnessed Damian Lillard's NBA debut in 2012, it quickly became apparent that he was a special talent. His speed and skills stood out all the way from the upper deck of the Rose Garden in Portland. "The Blazers have a future star on their hands at point guard," I wrote in my first book, *Beating the NBA*, although I had not heard of him before that day.

Listening to Bronson Arroyo belt out songs during band rehearsal astonished me. His enthusiasm for his craft is impressive, but he's also a person who knows how to turn commitment into a highly proficient skillset. It's no coincidence that Arroyo started 383 games in his 16 years in the Major Leagues.

I would feel completely intimidated standing at the plate to face him on the pitcher's mound, just as I would feel ridiculous picking up a tennis racket and attempting groundstrokes with Daniela Hantuchova or Yannick Noah. When a person reaches a certain stage of excellence, there is something sacred about their craft that should be honored.

To be that proficient at just one thing is awesome. To have the skills to do more than one thing at a world-class level is awe-inspiring. To have those two things be sports and music is, to me, as cool as it gets.

After all, sports and music are two of the great equalizers in society. As this book affirms, both are realms where ethnic minorities often thrive and where growing up poor has not been an inhibitor. Conformity, however, can be.

Society appears to be turning less judgmental of people who want to cross over into other fields. In fact, it's starting to celebrate them. Elon Musk has become one of the richest men in the world largely because he thinks outside the box and has little interest in how he is perceived.

Though Musk made his first stack of millions by co-developing online city guides, he had no reservations about branching into novel industries that have traditionally required specialist attention.

If Musk identified as an expert who should stick to one field, the world would be worse off. Instead, he has become an innovator in e-payment services, electric cars, space exploration, rapid transport and artificial intelligence.

But even Musk has not been able to resist the pull of music creation. In perhaps his most audacious move, he released the 2020 EDM single *Don't Doubt ur Vibe* in which he sang and penned all 14 lyrics. Some critics were amused, others panned his effort. It made no difference to him; he was having fun.

That brazen attitude is proving infectious.

The Australian pop star Cody Simpson is known for his singing, songwriting and dancing, and has released a book of poetry. At the time of writing, Simpson is reviving his childhood dream of becoming a pro swimmer and, incredibly, qualified for the Australian Olympic trials. He hopes to represent his country in the 100-meter butterfly in the Tokyo Olympics.

"It is my greatest ambition in life to expand the limit and perceived notion of what's possible for someone to achieve in a single lifetime," he wrote on Instagram. "I'm here to tell you (that) you can do absolutely ANYTHING if you are willing to work for it."

I've spent the better part of three years in a wide-eyed state, poring over the backstories of these great overachievers. Looking back on those moments, it dawned on me that spending many hours deconstructing their winning ways is an achievement in itself. And, like playing music to a packed house, it is one to be shared.

In reading these interviews, I hope you have experienced at least some of the joy that I did in creating this book — after all, hanging out with rock star-athletes is pretty cool — while absorbing much of the wisdom they have imparted.

More importantly, I hope they encourage you to pursue your dreams without hesitation and to never fear the unknown. In Pat Burgener's words, "Why are you waiting? Just fucking do it."

Photo Credits

Prologue
Muhammad Ali and Sam Cooke: PictureLux / The Hollywood Archive / Alamy Stock Photo
Chris Jericho: Crystal Huffman via Shutterstock
Shaquille O'Neal: Ted Alexander Somerville via Shutterstock

Elite Performance Qualities
Damian Lillard: courtesy of Damian Lillard / GSM

Pat Nevin
Top profile photo: Motez Bishara
In the stands: PA Images / Alamy Stock Photo
FA Cup: Peter Robinson, PA Images / Alamy Stock Photo
DJ photo: courtesy of Pat Nevin

Pat Burgener
Top profile photo: Motez Bishara
Snowboard: Etienne Claret
Concert photos: Laura Gilli (color) and Samuel Nugues (b&w)

Ray Barbee
Top profile photo: Motez Bishara
Skateboard photo: Steve Sherman
Guitar photo: LademannMedia / Alamy Stock Photo

Bronson Arroyo
Top profile photo: Motez Bishara
Concert photo: Chris Granger and Nikki Forte
Red Sox: Reuters / Alamy Stock Photo

Lindsay Perry
All photos by Grant Puckett

Bernie Williams
Top profile photo: Motez Bishara
World Series: Mike Segar / Reuters / Alamy Stock Photo
Guitar photo: courtesy of Bernie Williams

Rony Seikaly
Top profile photo, crowd photo and DJ photo: Motez Bishara
Syracuse: Rob Crandall via Shutterstock.

Kyle Turley
Top profile photo: Motez Bishara
NFL: Simon Bruty / Getty Images
Guitar photo: courtesy of Kyle Turley

Kevin Walker
Football photos: Stefan Holm via Shutterstock
Music photos: courtesy of Kevin Walker

Mark Butcher
Two profile photos and concert photo: Motez Bishara
Cricket photo: Ross Setford PA Images / Alamy Stock Photo

Essence Carson
Top profile photo: Jed Jacobsohn / The Players' Tribune
Tuxedo photo: Lindsay Adler
WNBA: Cory Royster / Cal Sport Media / Alamy Live News

Daniela Hantuchova
Top profile and piano photo: courtesy of Daniela Hantuchova
Trophy photo: Ben Hoskins / Getty Images

Yannick Noah
Concert photos: Frederic Legrand - COMEO
French Open photo: Professional Sport/Popperfoto via Getty Images / Getty Images
Tennis photo in Budapest: Ferenc Szelepcsenyi / Shutterstock

Chelcee Grimes
Profile photo on mixing board and guitar photo: Callum Mills
Soccer photo: John Peters / Manchester United via Getty Images

Damian Lillard
Profile photo, studio photo and concert photo courtesy Damian Lillard / GSM
NBA photo: Jaime Valdez-USA TODAY Sports / Alamy Stock Photo.

Author's page
Author with Ray Barbee: Moayad Naquib

Dedication

I know it's a little unusual to place a dedication at the end of a book, but the nature of this one serves as an extension of the acknowledgements. This is, in no small part, because of the high standards that my dedicatees set that willed me to the finish line.

In the four years that it took to complete this book, I lost six close friends — two of whom died suddenly of heart attacks, and four who succumbed to agonizing battles with cancer. All of them were very special people.

Amer Ali

Faisal Jawahery

Omar Abdelrazaq

Wahab Al-Ghanim

William Butler-Sloss

Yasmina Ykelenstam

Marking their names in a book that centers on achievement is fitting, as they are recognized and remembered as great overachievers themselves.

Acknowledgements

I must start by saying thank you to the 15 incredible people who participated in this project and allowed me to share their stories. That begins with Pat Nevin, who offered me hours of open access when this book was nothing more than a lofty idea. Pat's own book *The Accidental Footballer* was released in 2021 and is certainly a worthy read.

Thank you also to Pat Burgener, Ray Barbee, Bronson Arroyo, Lindsay Perry, Bernie Williams, Rony Seikaly, Kyle Turley, Kevin Walker, Mark Butcher, Essence Carson, Daniela Hantuchova, Yannick Noah, Chelcee Grimes and Damian Lillard.

I appreciate all of you for generously lending your time and, on occasion, inviting me into your homes — both physically and virtually. I am humbled to have interviewed each of you, and your stories have left me inspired to keep pushing for another set of goals and to go that extra mile for them.

Thanks to my literary agent Lee Constantine whose enthusiasm helped ignite the long but worthwhile writing process for this book. Thank you also to my editor Kirsty Jackson at Cranthorpe Millner for her valuable input and role in bringing this book to life.

Thank you to Shannon Bourne for her tireless effort with the layout and photo editing, and to Sian Tichar for imparting her excellent taste and priceless wisdom during the production process.

Thank you to Moayad Naquib for lending his home to interview Ray Barbee and for helping out during the Burgener interview on that windy day on Manhattan Beach. Thank you to the talented film director Jacob Migicovsky for putting together the coolest video teases of my interviews midway through this project. Thank you to Elliot Naftalin for the camera tips. Thank you to Tamara M'Bazbaz for offering her superb proofreading skills and for being a book patron.

And thank you to all the other patrons of *Athletes Who Rock!* whose support has meant a great deal to me, starting with Abdulla Bishara (thanks Dad!), Vinayak Singh, Nicole Cates, Anthony Calabro, Christian Sullivan, Michael Balluff, Noha Moukarzel, and Tim Takacs.

Finally, thank you to my furry companion Floyd for being so chilled and keeping me grounded when I thought I would never get this book done. Granted, it would have taken less time without all the long walks, but the walks were worth it.

About the Author

The author (left) with Ray Barbee after their interview.

Motez Bishara is an award-winning London-based journalist and contributing feature writer for CNN, ESPN and The Guardian. His first book, *Beating the NBA: Tales from a Frugal Fan* was published in 2013. His e-book, *When the Sheikh Met the King*, an oral history of Michael Jackson's year in Bahrain, was published in 2021.

Further works can be found on his website: motezbishara.com.